HUNGERS
AND COMPULSIONS

Hungers and Compulsions

The Psychodynamic Treatment of Eating Disorders & Addictions

Jean Petrucelli and Catherine Stuart

JASON ARONSON
Lanham • Boulder • New York • Toronto • Plymouth, UK

The editors gratefully acknowledge permission to reprint material from "Autonomy" by
Wislawa Szymborska, from Postwar Polish Poetry by Czelaw Milosz. Copyright © 1965
by Czeslaw Milosz. Used by Permission of Doubleday, a division of Random House, Inc.

This book was set in 11 pt. New Baskerville by Alabama Book Composition of
Deatsville, AL.

Published by Jason Aronson
A wholly owned subsidiary of The Rowman & Littlefield Publishing Group, Inc.
4501 Forbes Boulevard, Suite 200, Lanham, Maryland 20706
http://www.rowmanlittlefield.com

Estover Road, Plymouth PL6 7PY, United Kingdom

Copyright © 2001 by Jason Aronson
First paperback edition 2012

British Library Cataloguing in Publication Information Available

Library of Congress Cataloging-in-Publication Data
This hardback edition of this book was previously cataloged by the Library of Congress
as follows:

Hungers and compulsions : the psychodynamic treatment of eating disorders and
addictions / edited by Jean Petrucelli and Catherine Stuart.

     p. cm.
     Includes bibliographyical references and index.
      1. Eating disorders—Treatment. 2. Substance abuse—Treatment.
     3. Psychodynamic psychotherapy. 4. Psychoanalysis. I. Petrucelli, Jean. II.
     Stuart, Catherine

     RC552.E18 H86 2001
     616. 85'26—dc21

                      00-067596

ISBN: 978-0-7657-0318-7 (cloth : alk. paper)
ISBN: 978-0-7657-0884-7 (pbk.   )

Printed in the United States of America

Contents

Acknowledgments   *xi*

Contributors   *xiii*

Introduction   *xvii*

I Addictive Economies

1 The Psychic Economy of Addiction   3
    Joyce McDougall

2 Addictive Economies: Intrapsychic and Interpersonal
   Discussion of McDougall's Chapter   27
    Catherine Stuart

II Expanding the Analytic Space: Dissociation and the Eating-Disordered Patient

3 Thinking, Talking, and Feeling in Psychotherapy with
   Eating-Disordered Individuals   41
    F. Diane Barth

 4   The Instigation of Dare: Broadening
     Therapeutic Horizons   53
     Judith Brisman

 5   Out of Body, Out of Mind, Out of Danger:
     Some Reflections on Shame, Dissociation,
     and Eating Disorders   65
     Philip M. Bromberg

 6   On Preferring Not To: The Aesthetics of Defiance   81
     Adam Phillips

III   On Being Stuck: Enactments, Mutuality, and Self-Regulation with Eating-Disordered Patients

 7   Close Encounters of the Regulatory Kind:
     An Interpersonal/Relational Look at Self-Regulation   97
     Jean Petrucelli

 8   "No Matter How Hard I Try, I Can't Get through to You!":
     Dissociated Affect in a Stalled Enactment   113
     Frances Sommer Anderson

 9   The Destablizing Dyad: Psychoanalytic Affective
     Engagement and Growth   125
     Emily Kuriloff

10   Narrative, Affect, and Therapeutic Impasse:
     Discussion of Part III   135
     Lewis Aron

IV   To Eat or Not to Eat: The Psychic Meanings of the Decision

11   The Male Experience of Food as Symbol and Sustenance   147
     Margaret Crastnopol

12   The Meaning of the "Body" in the Treatment
     of Eating-Disordered Patients   161
     Ann Kearney-Cooke

13   The Armored Self: The Symbolic Significance of Obesity   171
     Stefanie Solow Glennon

14   When the Self Starves: Alliance and Outcome
     in the Treatment of Eating Disorders   183
     Kathryn J. Zerbe

V   Creativity and Addiction

15   Melancholia and Addiction?   209
     Joerg Bose

16   The Anxiety of Creativity   221
     Olga Cheselka

17   Creativity, Genius, and Divine Madness   233
     Edgar A. Levenson

18   The Muse in the Bottle   245
     Albert Rothenberg

VI   Desires and Addictions

19   Attending to Sexual Compulsivity in a Gay Man   265
     Jack Drescher

20   In the Grip of Passion: Love or Addiction?
     On a Specific Kind of Masochistic Enthrallment   281
     Darlene Bregman Ehrenberg

21   From Impulsivity to Paralysis: Thoughts
     on the Continuous Pursuit and Thwarting of Desire   293
     Jill Howard

22   A Philosophical Assessment of Happiness, Addiction,
     and Transference   305
         M. Guy Thompson

               VII   Winnicott and Masud Khan:
           A Study of Addiction and Self-Destruction

23   Masud Khan's Descent into Alcoholism   319
         Linda B. Hopkins

24   Winnicott's Complex Relationship to Hate
     and Hatefulness   347
         Marcia Rosen

25   The Outrageous Prince: The Uncure of Masud Khan   359
         Dodi Goldman

26   Further Thoughts on the Winnicott–Khan Analysis   375
         Lawrence Epstein

Index   385

Acknowledgments

As members of the William Alanson White Psychoanalytic Institute, we would like to express our heartfelt appreciation to our colleagues, who as a group create and maintain an intellectually stimulating and supportive environment. We are especially appreciative of our supervisors, teachers, and analysts.

In particular we want to thank the following at the William Alanson White Institute: Mary Lou Lionells, Ph.D., former director, for supporting the creation of the Eating Disorders and Substance Abuse Service and allowing us to do this kind of clinical work at the institute; Sondra E. Wilk, Ph.D., director of administration and development, for her tireless devotion, dedication, and creative outlook; Charles C. Harrington, Ph.D., and the entire board of trustees for their belief and openness in an innovative project in an analytic community; the conference committee members for their brainstorming and hard work—Judith Brisman, Ph.D., Olga Cheselka, Ph.D., Berry Fox, Ph.D., Diane Goldkopf, Ph.D., Elizabeth Halsted, Ph.D., Evelyn Hartman, Ph.D., Jill Howard, Ph.D., Lawrence Jacobson, Ph.D., Emily Kuriloff, Psy.D., Steven Tublin, Ph.D., Meryl

Weinman, Ph.D.; David Russek, M.D., for sponsoring us at Mount Sinai Medical Center; the staff at the institute; Diane Amato, Leila Sosa, Judith Waldman, Jose Narranjo, Marie Marcan, and a very special thanks to Elizabeth Grove for her cool-headed earthy essence that kept this project moving calmly at all times; and Fred Antonoff for his financial wizardry.

We are both grateful to our families and loved ones who tolerated our unavailability and supported our vision for the entire length of the project.

Contributors

Frances Sommer Anderson, Ph.D., clinical assistant professor of psychiatry, New York University Medical School; co-editor with Lewis Aron, *Relational Perspectives on the Body*.

Lewis Aron, Ph.D., ABPP, director New York University Postdoctoral Program in Psychotherapy and Psychoanalysis; editor, *Psychoanalytic Dialogues*; past president, Division of Psychoanalysis (39), American Psychological Association.

F. Diane Barth, C.S.W., faculty, Psychoanalytic Institute of the Postgraduate Center, National Institute for the Psychotherapies, Institute for Contemporary Psychotherapy, Center for the Study of Anorexia and Bulimia; author of *Daydreaming: Unlock the Creative Potential of Your Mind*.

Joerg Bose, M.D., director training and supervising analyst, William Alanson White Institute; clinical assistant professor of psychiatry, Cornell University Medical College; medical director, Metropolitan Center for Mental Health.

Judith Brisman, Ph.D., director and cofounder of the Eating Disorder Resource Center, New York; teaching faculty, William Alanson White Institute; co-author of *Surviving an Eating Disorder: Strategies for Family and Friends.*

Philip M. Bromberg, Ph.D., training and supervising analyst, teaching faculty, William Alanson White Institute; clinical professor of psychology, New York University Postdoctoral Program in Psychotherapy and Psychoanalysis; associate editor of *Psychoanalytic Dialogues;* assistant editor of *Contemporary Psychoanalysis;* author of *Standing in the Spaces: Essays on Clinical Process, Trauma and Dissociation.*

Olga Cheselka, Ph.D., supervisor of psychotherapy, faculty, William Alanson White Institute; consulting supervisor, Pace University Counseling Services.

Margaret Crastnopol, Ph.D., associate director of the Northwest Center for Psychoanalysis in Seattle, Washington; contributing editor to *Psychoanalytic Dialogues;* associate editor of *Contemporary Psychoanalysis;* faculty, William Alanson White Institute.

Jack Drescher, M.D., psychiatric consultant, clinical services, training and supervising analyst, faculty, William Alanson White Institute; clinical assistant professor of psychiatry, State University of New York–Brooklyn; member, American College of Psychiatrists; author of *Psychoanalytic Therapy and the Gay Man.*

Darlene Bregman Ehrenberg, Ph.D., training and supervising analyst, teaching faculty, William Alanson White Institute; editorial board of *Contemporary Psychoanalysis;* author of *The Intimate Edge: Extending The Reach of Psychoanalytic Interaction.*

Lawrence Epstein, Ph.D., training and supervising analyst, William Alanson White Institute; clinical professor for psychoanalysis, Adelphi

University; co-author with A. Feiner of *Countertransference: The Therapist's Contribution to the Therapeutic Situation.*

Stefanie Solow Glennon, Ph.D., graduate, New York University Postdoctoral Program in Psychoanalysis; faculty, supervisor, Institute for Contemporary Psychotherapy.

Dodi Goldman, Ph.D., teaching faculty, William Alanson White Institute; faculty and supervisor, Derner Graduate Institute for Advanced Psychological Studies; author of *In Search of the Real* and *In One's Bones: The Clinical Genius of Winnicott.*

Linda Hopkins, Ph.D., training and supervising analyst, Philadelphia School of Psychoanalysis; adjunct faculty, Union Institute, Cincinnati, Ohio.

Jill Howard, Ph.D., graduate, supervisor of psychotherapy, William Alanson White Institute; clinical assistant professor, Long Island University.

Ann Kearney-Cooke, Ph.D., director, Cincinnati Psychotherapy Institute; adjunct professor of psychology, University of Cincinnati; scholar for the Partnership for Women's Health at Columbia University; served on the advisory board for *Eating Disorders: The Journal of Treatment and Prevention.*

Emily Kuriloff, Psy.D., graduate, William Alanson White Institute; associate editor of *Contemporary Psychoanalysis*; clinical assistant professor at Columbia University.

Edgar A. Levenson, M.D., fellow emeritus, teaching faculty, supervising and training analyst, William Alanson White Institute; clinical professor, New York University Postdoctoral Program in Psychotherapy and Psychoanalysis; author of *The Ambiguity of Change, The Purloined Self,* and *The Fallacy of Understanding.*

Joyce McDougall, D.Ed., supervising and training analyst, Paris Psychoanalytic Society and Institute of Psychoanalysis; member of

New York Freudian Society; faculty, Object Relations Institute, New York; author of *Theaters of the Mind; Theaters of the Body; Dialogue with Sammy; The Many Faces of Eros.*

Jean Petrucelli, Ph.D., F.P.P.R., (editor), cofounder and codirector, Eating Disorders and Substance Abuse Service, supervisor of psychotherapy, teaching faculty, William Alanson White Institute.

Adam Phillips, child psychotherapist in London and the author most recently of *The Beast in the Nursery.*

Marcia Rosen, Ph.D., teaching faculty, supervising and training analyst, William Alanson White Institute.

Albert Rothenberg, M.D., clinical professor of psychiatry, Harvard Medical School; author of *Creativity and Madness: New Findings and Old Stereotypes.*

Catherine Stuart, Ph.D., (editor), cofounder and codirector, Eating Disorders and Substance Abuse Service, supervising analyst, teaching faculty, William Alanson White Institute; faculty, Postgraduate Center for Mental Health.

Michael Guy Thompson, Ph.D., founder and director, *Free Association;* adjunct faculty, California School of Professional Psychology.

Kathryn J. Zerbe, M.D., training and supervising analyst, Topeka Institute for Psychoanalysis; Jack Aron Chair in Psychiatric Education and Women's Mental Health at the Menninger Clinic; author, *The Body Betrayed: Women, Eating Disorders and Treatment* and *Women's Mental Health in Primary Care.*

Introduction

The decision to edit this anthology on eating disorders and substance abuse grew out of the overwhelming success of the Hungers and Compulsions conference created by the Eating Disorders and Substance Abuse Service of the William Alanson White Institute. From the outset, there were many considerations concerning the invitation of the speakers who are the authors of the papers included in this volume. We wanted to accomplish a number of goals. Of first and foremost importance was to be inclusive about different perspectives, not limiting our authors to those with a psychoanalytic perspective, nor to those who have a specialty in addiction, eating disorders, or compulsive behavior. We wanted to focus on clinical material rather than meta-psychology without excluding valuable contributions from that perspective. We also wanted to explore psychoanalytically informed and symptom specific treatment modalities that serve patients suffering from addictive disorders.

Part I of this book is comprised of two companion papers, one by Joyce McDougall and one by Catherine Stuart. McDougall is a psychoanalyst from the Paris Psychoanalytic Society and Institute of Psychoanalysis with a classical point of view while Catherine Stuart, co-editor of this book, and a psychoanalyst from the William Alanson White Institute, has an interpersonal perspective. Both authors enliven their chapters by providing case examples and information about the effect of their personal histories on their work. Drawing much from the object relations literature, especially Winnicott and Klein, McDougall describes the addict as being in a perpetual loop-like state of satiation/starvation fantasies that prompt and underscore his or her repetitive behaviors. She sees this as a kind of misguided journey to self-satisfaction rather than self-harm, a "child-like attempt at self-cure of a pre-existing source of psychic pain" that results in enslavement to the unsatisfiable hunger of early object loss. McDougall's thesis is that addictions are not primarily motivated by self-destructive masochism, but are ways people try to help themselves feel better. She remarks on the way addictions help people reduce or get rid of their feelings.

Stuart agrees with McDougall but shifts the focus from the intrapsychic to the interpersonal. What happens between the therapist and patient is useful and intimate. She highlights the idea that the therapist always has an impact on the patient. It is important to use that material in understanding the therapeutic relationship.

In Part II, "Expanding the Analytic Space: Dissociation and the Eating-Disordered Patient," four experts attempt to unravel the paradox inherent in the eating-disordered patient simultaneously engaging in treatment and self-destructive behavior. As anyone who has ever had the gumption to take on an eating-disordered patient in therapy, or, more mystifying, the therapist who quixotically focuses his practice on treating this most vexing clientele, will tell you if given the opportunity, it is not an experience to be entered into lightly. Coping with the seemingly irrational intransigence of the only segment of society that refuses to consume is maddening. How are we to understand or connect to individuals who seem to operate contrary to our most basic instinct to survive? These authors share the epiphanies they experienced that were central to reestablishing relatedness. Additionally, they explore how to stay alive and in contact with themselves and their patients in the therapeutic process.

In Chapter 3, "Thinking, Talking, and Feeling in Psychotherapy with Eating-Disordered Individuals," F. Diane Barth identifies and explores an important dynamic in treating eating-disordered patients that she terms "the presence not only of a client's dissociated experience but also of the therapist's." Drawing anecdotally on her work with one patient, Barth fleshes out the complications arising from this phenomenon by focusing on the mutually dissociated experience of competition in the therapeutic relationship. In the course of her paper, Barth reveals the strategies she adopts to surmount this obstacle to meaningful treatment. Specifically, Barth related a compelling clinical vignette that included an episode when a therapist "saw" a rat crawl across the wall of her office. The shadow, which appeared to be a rat, signaled her to pay attention to details of her own experience, to name and tolerate competitive feelings, and to initiate attention to her own, and her patients', desires.

Judith Brisman, in Chapter 4, "The Instigation of Dare: Broadening Therapeutic Horizons," argues that the successful treatment of eating-disordered patients demands that we transcend the conventional restrictions imposed in the analytic framework and dare to introduce and foster a spontaneity otherwise lacking in the patient's experience. Brisman questions the therapist's response to the patient's actions, asking: How do we address the disordered eating behaviors without repetition of a controlling relationship with the patient? She advocates the use of the interpersonal relationship and concludes that the crisis of the eating-disordered patient includes an experience of impasse and malaise, a struggle to speak of something hovering in the room that needs to be explored.

Philip M. Bromberg, in Chapter 5, "Out of Body, Out of Mind, Out of Danger: Some Reflections on Shame, Dissociation, and Eating Disorders," deconstructs the protean role that dissociated aspects of self play in shaping the eating-disordered patient's behavior. Deftly employing the metaphor of the holothurian, a sea creature that when attacked divides itself into unlinked parts, Bromberg theorizes that the self-destructive behavior these patients engage in may be attributed to efforts to silence the competing voices of different selves. The central issue for the eating-disordered patient, Bromberg asserts, is that because she is enslaved by her felt inability to contain desire as a regulatable affect, she is unable to hold desire long enough to make choices without experiencing the loss of the thing not chosen as close to self-annihilation. In other words, desire is anethma to the mutiple selves because the satiation of one would mean the denial of others. Thus, choice becomes impossible. Bromberg maintains that as analyst and patient slip in and out of a constantly shifting array of self-states they have the opportunity to co-construct a transitional reality within which the patient's impaired faith in the reliability of human relatedness can be restored, and eating can become linked to appetite rather than to control.

Ingeniously utilizing Melville's inscrutable Bartelby the Scrivener, Adam Phillips in "On Preferring Not To: The Aesthetics of Defiance," Chapter 6, parallels the consternation Bartleby's employer experiences in the face of Bartelby's unexplained and seemingly irrational refusal to accept more work assignments ("I prefer not to") with the therapist's dilemma when confronted with a patient who irrationally refuses to eat and prefers not to discuss it. Phillips suggests that from this vantage point, the person who refuses to eat has refined "an aesthetic of defiance" in the face of it that becomes the analyst's task to contain the struggle within himself that flares up in response to this style of living. He also addresses the symptoms of eating disorders as related to a child's "experiments in living," his efforts to make sense of a developing inner world in relation to responses from other people that invariably relate to food and eating. Phillips provides a unique perspective on what it means to have an appetite: In the context of dissociation, the challenge is to notice and to feel one's appetite much in the same way that the analyst can sometimes lose his hunger to know what the patient is sacrificing by not eating.

Part III, "On Being Stuck: Enactments, Mutuality, and Self-Regulation with Eating-Disordered Patients" involves closer looks by three different analysts involved in a powerful struggle to identify problematic aspects of their work with patients. Simultaneously, their patients were hardly oblivious to their analysts' affective responses in these areas, leading to impasses in the treatment. Resolution of the therapeutic stuckness could only occur when, in each case, the analyst reclaimed the disavowed experience of self, allowing for an analysis of the enactment.

Jean Petrucelli, in Chapter 7, entitled, "Close Encounters of the Regulatory Kind: An Interpersonal/Relational Look at Self-Regulation," illustrates some powerful moments between patient and therapist, which happen spontaneously both inside and outside the treatment room. These moments, which jolt one into a heightened state of consciousness, allowed Petrucelli and her patient an opportunity to move toward greater shared intimacy. The relational field shifted into a momentary new configuration that set the stage for therapeutic change. This was particularly powerful because the difficulty in self-regulation that is manifest in every arena within this eating-disordered patient's life forced itself unannounced into the therapeutic relationship. For Petrucelli the treatment became a process of redirecting the eating-disordered patient out of the world of food and into the arena of human interaction. These chance encounters seemed to open up the dialogue, allowing for more split-off affects to enter into the relationship even as the patient's "safety" in dissociation is threatened.

Frances Sommer Anderson, in Chapter 8, "'No Matter How Hard I Try, I Can't Get through to You!': Dissociated Affect in a Stalled Enactment," chronicles an odyssey with a binge-eating patient that had been stalemated for many years. She noted that the stuckness in the treatment took the form of an experience of "suspended animation," The self-destructive stagnant state of the patient was interrupted with intermittent nonmutative explosions. These seemed to result in an infusion of the treatment space with waste. Anderson was struck with a profound and prolonged feeling of failure when, no matter how hard she tried, she could not get through to this patient. This treatment impasse was only resolved when Anderson, recovering from bronchitis, was able, in a less guarded moment, to verbalize her frustrated experience that the patient was slowly committing suicide.

With refreshing candor, Emily Kuriloff, in Chapter 9, "The Destabilizing Dyad: Psychoanalytic Affective Engagement and Growth," demonstrates how the analyst's courage to let down the walls of the analytic self may catalyze a patient's capacity to grapple with the hard issues through an expanded relatedness and identification with the therapist. Eschewing the strict Freudian prohibition against personal involvement, Kuriloff reveals how the expressed vulnerability of the analyst can trigger a profound shift in the patient's insight. It occured when Kuriloff felt less defended against her identification with, as well as her rage and disconnection from her patient. Kuriloff's affective awakening freed the patient to struggle with her own feelings in a more alive and direct, rather than dissociated, psychosomatic fashion.

Lewis Aron, in discussing the chapters by Petrucelli, Anderson, and Kuriloff, focused on the role of affects and narrative in the psychoanalytic situation in Chapter 10. Aron ruminates on the causes of analytic stalemates and impasses. He pinpoints the problem as arising from the analysts' fear of identification with aspects of their patients' stories and characters that closely mirror their own vulnerabilities. The analysts' inability to confront their own vulnerabilities, which Aron terms "counter-resistance," inhibits their effort to keep the therapy moving fluidly. This counter-resistance may cause the analyst to over-identify with the patient muddling therapeutic progress.

Chapters 11 through 14 in Part IV, "To Eat or Not to Eat: The Psychic Meanings of the Decision," focus on the psychological significance of food and eating.

In Chapter 11, "The Male Experience of Food as Symbol and Sustenance," Margaret Crastnopol examines the roles that being fed as a child and feeding oneself and others as an adult may play in male development and psychology. Crastnopol posits that for men the act of eating may allow for the recovery of renounced maternal and feminine identifications, thereby permitting compensation for loss of mother in the resolution of the Oedipal drama by identification with father. The psychological significance of eating allows men the possibility for a type of psychic self-replenishment that encompasses both progressive and regressive elements. Crastnopol links these dynamics involving food with the capacity for empathy in men.

Ann Kearney-Cooke, in Chapter 12, "The Meaning of the 'Body' in the Treatment of Eating-Disordered Patients" focused on her utilization of group therapy and experiential exercises in working with eating-disordered women. Kearney-Cooke found through these experiential exercises that the eating-disordered women she treated have few memories of being touched or cuddled in childhood, and that these women were taught a "deprivation model" wherein they were seen as "good" if they could get by with less than they needed. In outlining a paradigm involving internalization, identification, projection, and the role of culture in the development of eating disorders in women, Kearney-Cooke postulates that the psychic distress of these women is projected onto their bodies, which are seen as imperfect, and these women then attempt to gain mastery over their distress by trying to perfect their bodies.

Chapter 13, "The Armored Self: The Symbolic Significance of Obesity," by Stefanie Solow Glennon, focuses on the unconscious meanings of fat and being fat to obese patients. She states that a "fat boundary" frequently unconsciously serves symbolically to protect the psyche from "feared penetration and annihilation," especially in patients who have been narcissistically parented. Glennon states that unconscious meanings of being fat also serve defensive functions that can lead to a "fear of being thin." In further emphasizing a "crucial distinction" between the defensive functions of compulsive eating (e.g., to anesthetize) and the unconscious need to erect an armor of fat, Glennon believes that a patient can exhibit one defense without the other even though they frequently co-exist. It becomes essential to then carefully inquire into both areas of the patient's experience and fantasies.

Kathryn Zerbe, in Chapter 14, "When the Self Starves: Alliance and Outcome in the Treatment of Eating Disorders," emphasizes the importance of "being a real object in the lives of our patients." Zerbe informs her eating-disordered patients of the unfavorable predictions of the literature at the outset of treatment as a way of "empowering them through knowledge" and as a means of dealing with her expectation of their wish for, and subsequent rejection of, an omnipotent therapist. Zerbe therefore accepts a non-omniscient, defeatist position as a counterprojective means of helping to establish a therapeutic alliance, enlisting the patient in the project of dealing with her difficulties in eating and living.

Parts V, VI, and VII move in different directions than the previous chapters. Part V "Creativity and Addiction," is a collection of essays by prominent authors on the connection between these two phenomena. The authors in Part VI, "Desires and Addictions," turn the attention to the many ways people connect with others that seem more like addiction than interpersonal attachment. The final part of this book, Part VII, "Winnicott and Masud Khan," contains four related chapters by noted experts. They apply their analytic thinking to a tragic and well-known psychoanalyst who was treated by D. W. Winnicott. These papers are connected to each other and the authors respond to the opinions of the other authors in that section.

Part V, "Creativity and Addiction," is a compilation of chapters that study the relationship between these two qualities, which seem to be incompatible, but, nevertheless, occur together frequently. The authors have interesting ideas about the connection and differences in these traits and about the humans who have these tendencies.

Joerg Bose, M.D., in Chapter 15, "Melancholia and Addiction?," starts by recognizing the attraction and desirability of a state of melancholia, especially for artists. He uses the character, Jaques from Shakespeare's comedy, As You Like It, to illustrate the artist who insists on his sadness. This quality of desirability can make melancholia similar to addiction. Bose enriches our understanding of melancholia and depression by comparing the two concepts and distinguishing between self-pity and compassion. Bose augments his discussion with examples of how melancholia and depression serve interpersonal functions and express pain. He explicates the need of the depressed person to make a certain kind of contact with others, promoting its addictive pull.

Chapter 16, "The Anxiety of Creativity," by Olga Cheselka, contains a clinical case study about a successful artist who chooses to interrupt his therapy over financial concerns, but then continues an expensive addiction. Like many artists, he thought that if he gave up his addiction he would lose his creative capacity. Cheselka links creativity to a "search for agency, meaning, and expression that is intrinsically anxiety producing." The anxiety creates a need for comfort that can be distorted into a compulsive or addictive pattern.

Edgar Levenson applies his clarity and wit to the "long, albeit equivocal, history of association" between creativity and drug use in Chapter 17, "Creativity, Genius, and Divine Madness." He observes that creativity has a strongly addictive quality. He finds similarity between recklessness and risk-taking among creative people and that practiced by addicts. He takes issue with the tendency to treat risk-taking exclusively as pathology. He finds difference between the desire for risk in addiction and the desire for safety in compulsion. Finally, he comments on the desirability of passionate risk-taking for creative people and for therapists. Therapists work best when they are free from the need to please insurance companies, their colleagues, and even patients.

Tackling a similar theme from a different perspective, Albert Rothenberg uses biographical and autobiographical material about different writers to appraise the influence of alcohol on authors. In Chapter 18, "The Muse in the Bottle," Rothenberg gives us an overview of the scope of the problem and provides details from his extensive research on the author John Cheever. Cheever suffered from alcohol abuse more than most writers. He also struggled with the theme of hostility toward his brother. He found these feelings unacceptable and overwhelming. Rothenberg understands Cheever's family dynamics as intricately linked to his problems. Cheever had complicated roles in his family as a son and as a brother. Rothenberg also looks at the possibility that Cheever's internal passions and fears may have influenced his creative choices and may have led to his becoming alcoholic. He tracks Cheever's career and the ways in which his novels reflect relationships with family members.

Part VI, "Desires and Addictions," deals with these two phenomena as compelling forces. Three of the authors in this section contemplate the relationship between romantic or sexual desire and compulsive behavior or attachment. The final chapter in this section deals with the relationship between the patient and the therapist.

Jack Drescher illustrates the traumatizing effect of homophobia in Chapter 19, "Attending to Sexual Compulsivity in a Gay Man." Drescher captures the dilemma of homosexual development in a heterosexual world that frowns upon same-sex intimacy. For some gay men, sexual activities are tinged with anxiety, and sexual desire is experienced as a troubling compelling force. Drescher emphasizes the impact of hiding and denying feelings of desire of boys who grow up to be gay. These boys are likely to have a history that includes experiences of humiliation concerning their sexual desires and behaviors. When desire is shaded with anxiety it can be experienced as dissonant. The chapter contains lively clinical examples and insightful contributions to treatment with patients who experience their sexual desire as compulsive.

Darlene Ehrenberg's section, Chapter 20, "In the Grip of Passion: Love or Addiction?" illustrates her intensely interpersonal clinical work. The patient whose case she writes about is compulsively drawn to dangerous people and behaviors. This chapter echoes some of the themes that appear in Joyce McDougall's work. Initially Ehrenberg thought the attachment was the patient's desire for pain. As she worked with this woman she came to believe that the patient was trying to escape a worse pain. In her clinical work Ehrenberg draws on the intimate connection she has with her patient, and discloses her feelings at judicious times. She does not focus on the patient's external behavior but on her internal pain. She considers the opening of the internal boundary, the emotional boundary between patient and therapist, an important factor in successful treatment.

In "From Impulsivity to Paralysis," Chapter 21, Jill Howard approaches a similar problem in her treatment of "relationship-addicted patients." She grapples with a pattern she sees in some patients—the pursuit of romantic partners who bring negative feelings to the relationship. The sought-after partner is often unavailable, remote and mysterious. To make things more complicated, these patients often enact the role of the unavailable object with others, including the therapist. Howard draws on Fairbairn's work on schizoid tendencies, and uses vivid clinical material to illustrate the many sides of a relationship with exciting–rejecting objects. She notes that patients who present with this constellation invariably bring the dynamic to their treatment in a transference–countertransference enactment that replicates their problematic pattern.

M. Guy Thompson's "A Philosophical Assessment of Happiness, Addiction, and Transference," Chapter 22, is an essay about suffering, happiness, and addiction. He emphasizes the paradox that relationships with humans are both the source of most psychological suffering and the source of great happiness. He compares addictive attachment to the transference relationship and concludes that, despite the impossibility of finding perfect happiness, it is important to enjoy the measures of "happiness we are capable of procuring."

The final section of this book is a collection of four interconnected papers that focus on Winnicott's treatment of a brilliant and talented psychoanalyst, Masud Khan. The authors are familiar with each other's work and, as a result, their thoughts are well formulated. While the authors do not necessarily agree with one another, they are respectful of the differences in their thinking.

In Chapter 23, "Masud Khan's Descent into Alcoholism," Linda Hopkins presents Khan's life as a compelling mystery. Khan destroyed his career, relationships, and health through his addiction. Using his personal and professional history, Hopkins wonders whether Khan might have been helped had his addiction been understood by him and by the important people in his life, including Winnicott. She notes that Khan himself refused to see a patient until the patient was able to control his drinking. He felt that treatment was useless when a patient was actively drinking.

Marcia Rosen's Chapter 24, "Winnicott's Complex Relationship to Hate and Hatefulness," focuses on Winnicott's work about the usefulness of hate in clinical work. She weaves a detailed understanding of his theoretical position, his actual work with hateful patients, and her understanding of his personal life and complicated relationship with Khan. She points out the paradox that Winnicott was not able to use his hate even though he wrote about its usefulness in clinical work

Dodi Goldman is an author of two books about Winnicott. In Chapter 25, "The Outrageous Prince: The Uncure of Masud Khan," Goldman thinks of Khan's outrageousness as evidence of a profound need to be able to observe one's impact on others, and his self-destructiveness as a paradoxical salve to feelings of helplessness and threats to the sense of self. When he attends to Winnicott's treatment of Khan he reminds us of the unfairness of this kind of critique. He suggests three possibilities about the treatment—it worked, it failed, and Khan could not be helped. He gives us well-informed speculations concerning Winnicott's thoughts regarding Khan and the dynamics between them. His contribution is to elaborate the possibilities, and remind us about the impossibility of knowing answers in our work for our work is not a cure for all patients.

The final chapter, by Lawrence Epstein, "Further Thoughts on the Winnicott–Khan Analysis," presents another enriching discussion about the relationship between these two prominent men. Epstein addresses aspects of analysis with extremely hateful and destructive patients and the particular demands these patients place on their therapists. He addresses the transference–countertransference matrix that we now understand to be necessary, especially with patients who are filled with negative feelings. He has written extensively about patients who make analysts feel badly and shares the depth of his understanding about these complex treatments. Notably, he addresses the need for an analyst who is interested and capable of hearing everything on the patient's mind.

This anthology on eating disorders and substance abuse represents the concerted effort of many clinicans who are dedicated and devoted to their work and their patients. If there is a single thread that dominates the analytic experience, as evidenced by the thought-provoking papers that constitute this anthology, it may be each therapist's recognition that successful therapy is a mutual process. It is not simply the patient who must struggle toward self-knowledge and growth in the course of a treatment, but the therapist was well.

Jean Petrucelli and Catherine Stuart

I

Addictive Economies

1

The Psychic Economy of Addiction

Joyce McDougall

relating to soul (ex) mind

TERMINOLOGY

I begin my conceptualization of the psychic economy of addictive pursuits by considering the word *addiction*, since it played a significant role in my early interest in the psychic economy underlying addictive behavior. The word *addiction* is derived from the Latin *addictus*, which refers to a transaction by which an individual is given into slavery. In my earliest writings on the subject of addictive problems I consulted my English-French dictionary to find an equivalent French word for *addiction* and discovered only *toxicomanie*. The point of this etymological digression is that, from the perspective of the psychic economy involved, the French terminology suggested an economy based on a desire to harm oneself, whereas the Anglo-Saxon term implies an entirely different notion, namely that the afflicted subject is enslaved to one unique solution for dealing with mental pain.

These considerations led to a central dimension in my attempts over the years to conceptualize the conscious and unconscious goals that lie behind all forms of addictive behavior. My interest began in the 1950s. I had just moved to Paris, and one of my first patients was a highly disturbed American boy named Sammy. Although I was only a student in training, Sammy had been sent to me for treatment because at that time there were few English-speaking therapists in Paris. When Sammy returned to the United States to attend the Orthogenic School in Chicago, his mother asked if she might come to see me, in particular because of an alcohol problem. Two years later when the parents moved back to the States, I wrote a book on Sammy's treatment as well as that of his mother, since at that time there had not been a day-to-day account of a child therapy in France, nor any substantial literature on child psychosis. When I sought to describe in French the troubles that assailed Sammy's mother and discovered there was no word for *addiction*, I was shocked by the notion that addicts of any kind should be motivated by a manic desire to poison themselves. This appeared strange and indeed discordant with my understanding of the major psychic tensions underlying addictive behavior. Although I had already discovered, among the conscious and unconscious elements behind hungers and compulsions, that there was frequently a masochistic wish to harm oneself, this was far from being the *dominant* dimension insofar as my own clinical observations were concerned.

I therefore took issue, publicly, with the term *toxicomanie*, and proclaimed in a lecture that an addictive pursuit, even in the case of drug abuse, was not a determination to poison or to harm oneself; on the contrary, it was an act that carried the illusion of doing something to *help oneself* through the difficulties of everyday life. I then offered the English equivalent, backing up my statement with the etymological argument. Because of my published protest against this terminology, the word *addiction* has today become standard in the psychoanalytic writings in France, although *toxicomania* is still retained as a psychiatric diagnostic category when alluding to drug abuse. I ended my lecture by noting important questions that remained unanswered: What are the sources of the addictive solution to mental pain? Why do we choose such deleterious means of dealing with emotional experience?

Shortly after the departure of Sammy's mother, I furthered my personal understanding of the psychic economy of addiction when I decided to stop smoking, since much publicity was given at the time to the serious health hazards connected with tobacco addictions. I confronted the pressures that had prompted my own addictive behavior and I discovered that I reached for a cigarette whenever I had to accomplish a disagreeable task, when I was happy or excited, and whenever I was sad or anxious. I realized that I had been creating a smoke screen over most of my affective experience, thus neutralizing or dispersing a vital part of my internal world. Stunned by this discovery I promised myself that I would apply my insight in an attempt to conceptualize the psychic structure of addictive behavior.

In fact it was a remark made by Sammy's mother that first alerted me to a curious element of an economic order in her alcoholic addiction. At one session, in trying to understand the reasons for her irresistible urge to drink whiskey at all times of the day, she said, "Sometimes I don't know whether I'm sad, or angry, or hungry, or wanting to have sex—and that's when I begin to drink." Although it may seem self-evident, this was my first inkling of the notion that *one of the goals of addictive behavior was to get rid of one's feelings!*

THE CHILDHOOD SOURCES OF ADDICTION

I come, therefore, to an important dimension in my understanding of addictions, namely that, consciously, the major quest of the addict, whether it is expressed in bulimia, alcoholism, tobacco addiction, addictive sexuality, or drug abuse, is the search for pleasure (and not a crazy wish to poison or harm oneself).

In short, although addicted individuals may feel enslaved to tobacco, alcohol, food, narcotics, psychiatric drugs, or addictive sexuality, the fundamental goal of the addictive pursuit or object is experienced as essentially "good" because they rapidly procure a sense of well-being. In extreme cases the addiction may even come to be considered the major pursuit that is felt to give meaning to the individual's life.

Thus one important dimension in the psychic economy of underlying addictive acts is the goal of dispelling, as rapidly as possible, all feeling of anxiety, anger, guilt, depression, or any other affective state that is liable to give rise to psychic pain and tension. Indeed such tension may even be mobilized by affects that would appear to be pleasurable but that release feelings of excitement or liveliness that are experienced as forbidden or dangerous. So, once discovered, the addictive solution to psychic tension is inevitably sought to attenuate the greater part of the individual's anxiety-arousing experiences. In other words, addictive dependency always involves *an intricate mixture of pleasure and pain*.

Regarding the role of addictive behavior as an analgesic or pain-dispelling mechanism, I would add an important factor, namely that the addictive solution gains considerable power in that it is almost invariably a response to a preexisting source of psychic pain, usually originating in infancy, and therefore, like all psychological symptoms, may be considered as a childlike attempt at self-cure. In essence, then, addiction is a *psychosomatic* solution, rather than a *psychological* one, to conscious or unconscious psychic pain and stress.

In listening to our addicted patients (particularly bulimic and tobacco-addicted patients), we readily perceive both their need to take flight from a feeling of malaise or mental pain and their euphoric anticipation of bringing the unpleasurable experience to a rapid halt.

One of my bulimic patients, a young French woman in her early thirties, came to therapy for bouts of severe depression and because she suffered from an irrepressible need to binge, sometimes followed by vomiting. It took two years of therapy before Bernadette could admit that at the end of every session she headed straight for the nearest patisserie to devour a quantity of delicacies that, it turned out, served to dispel feelings of abandonment and of emptiness aroused at the end of each session, but of which she had been totally unconscious until then. Consequently, I then wanted to know which delicacies she devoured most frequently to see what their unconscious dynamic significance might include. Among them were *pets de nonne* (literally "nun's farts"), *mille-feuilles* ("a thousand leaves"), *marrons caramelises* (carmelized chestnuts), and especially *bouchees de la reine* ("mouthfuls for/of the queen"). Thus, interesting signifiers were involved in this list of devourable objects that undoubtedly added zest to the pleasurable addiction of my bingeing analysand. In fact we discovered that, in many hidden ways, she was devouring *me*—my body and its various contents—and with distinct anal overtones. From there we were able to reconstruct that her devouring need was closely allied to her terror in the past of being devoured by her own mother and her need to incorporate a substitute for this ambivalently loved and feared mother figure of the past. On the occasions when her bingeing was followed by vomiting, we also learned that the unconscious devouring of the mother-therapist rendered the substitute incorporation dangerous and then had to be expelled.

Another patient, Nancy, is quoted elsewhere (McDougall 1995) to illustrate aspects of her psychosomatic suffering. What was not included in that publication was that, in addition to her psychosomatic symptoms, Nancy was severely bulimic as a little girl. In attempting to reconstruct different aspects of her compulsive eating throughout childhood, she painted a portrait of her mother as an engulfing force who sought total mastery over her child's physical and psychic self. When children experience themselves as nothing more than a libidinal or narcissistic extension of their mothers, this apprehension tends to arouse terror of the psychic death implicit in such a "devouring" relationship. However, the flip side of all such mother–child relationships is that, behind the rage at the devouring mother, there is also a megalomaniacal satisfaction in recognizing the mother's desperate need: "Without me, she would fall apart." Thus, the bond between mother and child, impregnated with primitive pregenital strivings, tends to perpetuate itself despite every appearance of external rebellion against it.

Nancy was constantly ill as a child and a severe asthmatic, but in addition, as a result of her compulsive eating, she was very fat and was teased about it constantly by her schoolmates. Her father was a prisoner of war when she was 18 months old, and during the five years that he was absent Nancy slept with her mother and, as she put it, "inundated Mother every night with streams of urine." Her mother appeared to accept this urinary connection with kind complicity, and, as we were able to reconstruct it during our analytic voyage, this was experienced by Nancy as a primitive erotic sharing with her mother. A dimension that was not dealt with in the original publication was that Nancy ate excessively to please her mother, but this was also experienced as a way of making pregenital oral love with her mother (and included the fantasy that by devouring her she would *become* the mother).

When Nancy was 6½ years old, her father returned from the war, and although her asthma ceased rather miraculously upon his return, both her enuresis and her bulimia continued until the birth of her baby brother when she was 9 years old. This latter event shattered Nancy's illusion about being mother's chosen sexual partner and brought to an end the pregenitally expressed love affair with her—in both its urethral and its oral versions. Nancy at last had a room of her own, and from then on not only was her bed dry but her childhood bulimia ceased.

In summarizing the maternal representations revealed by my patients with eating disorders (and I find the same to be true of many psychosomatic sufferers), I learned that two opposing characteristics are frequently attributed to the internal mother. On the one hand she is often described as refusing close bodily contact, which usually communicates as the mother's terror of being devoured, absorbed, and emptied out by her baby. But on the other hand, she is just as frequently remembered as being overly close and dependent in her psychological demands upon her infant. In these instances the mothers are frequently depicted as being highly interested in their children's physical pain but unable to hear or deal with their psychic suffering.

Feelings of confusion or depersonalization surge forth at precise moments in the therapy of bulimic patients when pregenital cravings, such as those manifested by Bernadette and Nancy, are aroused. Such feelings reveal contradictory wishes toward the maternal body and self: On the one hand, there are violently destructive wishes toward the mother, and on the other, a desire to exchange bodily substances or even merge totally with her. As a result, the therapy of severely addicted patients will often reveal both neurotic and psychotic anxieties. As we know, neurotic anxieties attack the patient's adult rights to sexual and narcissistic enjoyments, whereas psychotic anxieties threaten the patient's very sense of identity, of bodily integrity, and of life itself. Therefore, beyond the realm of pregenital libidinal aims, with their attendant anxieties, we come to that of archaic and mortally dangerous eroticism, frequently expressed in phobias such as a terror of water or empty spaces or (in relationships with others) fears of dissolving or exploding, or of being invaded and imploded. Additional anxieties in the course of the psychoanalytic adventure are attached to anguishing expectations of being emptied out, vampirized, falling into nothingness, or being crushed by overwhelming forces. The projective dimension of these different anxieties are represented in the unconscious as a wish to implode, vampirize, empty out, or crush the other (the mother, the father inside the mother, future siblings), and these fantasies eventually come to light and achieve verbal expression.

Some time ago Nancy was able to tell me for the first time why she has always hesitated before entering my consulting room, a tiny stumbling movement that I have observed throughout the last five years. Although Nancy often used metaphors of vampirization, during one session she mentioned for the first time a fantasy of being possessed by strange forces. This provided me with the opportunity to point out to her that I had noticed that she seemed afraid to walk into the consulting room without a ritual hesitation, and I asked her whether this stumbling movement might reveal a secret wish on her part to "take possession" of my room, in other words, my body and my self. The projective identification was immediately evident to her and she was able to acknowledge a sudden awareness of such a wish, as well as her fear that I could take psychic possession of her, as she felt her mother had done.

From the child's point of view there is a paradoxical demand in the type of mother–child relationship I am describing. There is a longing to continue the blissful pregenital love affair with the mother (usually expressed through symptoms of bodily dysfunction such as allergies, insomnia, encopresis and enuresis, bulimic or anorexic tendencies, and so on), but also an inarticulate stifled rage against this archaic libidinal tie that is interpreted by the child as an omnipotent demand on the mother's part. It is the mother's unconscious needs and fears that form the most powerful and dynamic elements affecting the somatopsychic couple formed by the mother and her nursling and that, most importantly, includes the place of the father in the mother's inner world.

Children bring their own solution to the problem of separating from the mother as well as coping with the bi-parental unconscious, and the end result is not necessarily an addictive psychic economy.

How, then, may we postulate regarding the origins of the addictive solution? It is to Winnicott that we owe the most creative theories and detailed observations of what he conceptualized as a "mother baby constellation" stressing the psychic unity composed of mother and nursling. He frequently proclaimed that "there is no such thing as a baby," signifying that a baby is in a symbiotic relationship and that the couple cannot be understood separately. He also introduced the remarkable concept of transitional space and transitional objects in order to study the delicate psychic economy underlying the infant's capacity to emerge from this state of absolute dependency to that of independency.

Thus it is possible to propose that the mother–infant relationship may be decisive in laying the foundations of certain patterns of psychic functioning. A "good-enough" mother, in the Winnicottian sense, experiences a feeling of merging with her baby in the earliest weeks of its life. However, as Winnicott points out, if the fusional attitude persists beyond this time, the interaction becomes persecutory and pathological for the infant. In the state of total dependency on their mothers, infants tend to conform to whatever is projected upon them. A baby's motility, emotional liveliness, intelligence, sensuality, and bodily erogenicity can only develop to the extent that the mother herself invests these aspects positively. But she may just as readily inhibit their narcissistic enhancement in her infant's somatopsychic structure, particularly if her baby is serving to palliate an unfulfilled need in her own internal world.

This mother–baby pattern then affects the development of transitional phenomena (transitional activities and/or objects) and tends to create a fear in the infant of developing its own psychic resources for dealing with tension. What Winnicott termed "the capacity to be alone" (that is, "alone" in the mother's presence) may be endangered, so that the infant constantly seeks her presence in order to deal with any affective experience, whether arising from inner psychological or outer environmental impingements. These considerations led me, in earlier research, to formulate the following hypothesis: because of her own anxieties or unconscious fears and wishes, a mother is potentially capable of instilling in her nursling what may be conceptualized as *an addictive relationship to her presence* and her caregiving functions. In this case, it is the mother who is in a state of dependency with regard to her infant.

Consequently, there is a potential wish that the small child will fail to establish an inner representation of a caregiving maternal (and later paternal) figure that would normally include the capacity for containing and dealing with psychological pain or states of overexcitement. The child who is unable to identify with such an inner representation remains incapable of self-soothing and self-care in times of inner or outer tension, so that an attempted solution to the lack of the self-caring introjects is inevitably sought in the external world, as it was in early infancy. (In this context the work of Henry Krystal has been a notable contribution.) Thus in adolescence or adulthood food, drugs, alcohol, and tobacco are discovered as objects that may temporarily palliate psychic stress and thereby fulfill a maternal function that individuals are unable to provide for themselves. Consequently these addictive objects take the place of the transitional objects of childhood, which embodied the maternal environment and at the same time liberated the child from total dependency on the mother's presence.

However, unlike transitional objects, addictive acts and substances, although they are unconsciously seen by the individual as attempting to do the work of transitional objects, necessarily fail in that they are somatic rather than psychological attempts to deal with absence or any other cause of psychic pain and therefore provide only temporary relief. For this reason, in my earlier writings I referred to addictive substances as "transitory" rather than "transitional" objects, and coined the term "neoneeds" to categorize addictive craving.

In searching to conceptualize the origins of the addictive solution to separation and individuation, it seems probable, therefore, in light of clinical experience, that the early mother–child relationship may be decisive in laying the foundations of an enduring pattern of psychic functioning. To come back to Winnicott's concept of potential space, it must be admitted that, in his concern with the maternal environment, he paid little attention to the role of the father or to that of the oedipal constellation. In much of the clinical research concerning addictions, the father is frequently represented as absent, if not dead—or if present, as inconsistent, delinquent, incestuous, and, in certain cases, himself dependent (and not infrequently alcoholic). In my own clinical experience, the father has more often been presented as absorbed in his professional activities and thus relatively absent. But the important dimension is the role of the father concealed within the addictive act itself and in which the addictive object is frequently revealed, among its other unconscious meanings, as a protection against the dangerous aspects of the maternal imago. Here is a striking example:

Delphine asked for a consultation for reasons concerning her career. Among other details, she told me that nine years ago she had terminated a lengthy analysis during which time she was able to overcome a serious cigarette addiction, in view of alarming cardiac symptoms. But she went on to say that after eight years of abstinence, she turned to cigarettes again and for over a year now has been back to smoking a pack a day. Perhaps sensing my countertransference reaction of concern, she added that she had no intention of stopping smoking, even if her cardiac fragilities were still in evidence. Leaving aside the somewhat suicidal aspects of her decision to continue smoking, I invited her to tell me what had caused her to start again.

Delphine: Well, a year ago I received a letter from my mother making many of her habitual, infantile demands and I think this is what set off an unusually bad attack of tachycardia, to such an extent that I really felt I was in danger of dying. Without thinking, I rushed to a nearby tobacco stand and bought a pack of Gauloises [a very strong brand of cigarettes]; I smoked one right away for the first time in eight years and found that it calmed me immediately.

Therapist: What do you think the cigarette represents for you, apart from its calming aspects?

D: Oh, I know what it is; my father, who's no longer alive, was a heavy smoker and I admired and loved him immensely. He refused to stop smoking in spite of my mother's nagging.

T: So the cigarette is like a symbol of your father?

D: Yes, that's true—smoking helped him to stand my mother's endless demands and attacks on him.

T: And if I understand rightly, when you started

	again, it was connected with a feeling that you were being attacked by your mother?

D: Yes! She was tearing at my heart, destroying me the way she always did.

T: So, in a sense you put a cigarette-father in between you and a dangerous, life-threatening mother?

D: Exactly!

Many bulimic patients, after having successfully overcome their eating compulsion, recount a similar internal drama when, as so often happens, they rapidly regain all the lost weight. This terror of the dangerous introject is only one contributing factor in the difficulty of renouncing the addictive solution.

The following vignette illustrates a further aspect of the dynamic significance of the father in addictive behavior. It concerns a patient whom I quoted at length in a recent publication.

CASE VIGNETTE

Benedicte, a writer, came to therapy because of serious blockage in her creativity. When she was only 15 months old, Benedicte's father died of rectal cancer and her mother, who never remarried, came onto the analytic stage in much the same way as the mother described by Delphine.

At one session in which Benedicte referred constantly to her smoking and her inability to stop in spite of increasing bronchial problems, I asked her what she thought the act of smoking meant to her.

B: I can't imagine wanting to smoke when I'm with friends. It's such a hostile act. I'm amazed at the couples I see dining together who smoke. Why do they bother to see each other if they dislike each other that much? I only smoke when I'm alone in my apartment, where I often feel anxious and abandoned, or when I'm in the street. In the street it's not anxiety but hatred of everyone else. I do this aggressive and disgusting thing with a cigarette stub in the corner of my mouth or puffing out smoke. I show my hostility this way. At home I only smoke cigars but I never smoke them when I'm out for fear of disgusting people. The thought of my father comes up there (long pause) and I'm trying to avoid figuring out why cigars are disgusting.

T: Another anal secret that you shared with your father?

B: I'm trembling with fear of what you're going to say. I can't talk about my body.

T: Are you afraid I'll be disgusted by your body, as you felt your mother was?

B: Yes. I can't forget my mother's terrible disgust at my body products. I wonder if smoking is a way of keeping her at bay?

T: And conserving the loving diaper-tie with your father?

B: Of course! It's a way of keeping close to my father. Also I think of cigars as particularly masculine . . . and naturally . . . er . . . anal. Even my cigarettes must be heavy tobacco without filters, like Gauloises. (Long pause) My mother took everything away from me. The cigars protect me from her destructive attacks. (Another long pause) You know, I can't write if I don't smoke. She would take that away too. She effaced the positive image of my father with the negative one of the man who disappeared. Now that I come to think of it, when I'm alone my hostility is mainly against her.

T: So the people in the street are all bad mothers?

B: Yeah, even though they aren't doing anything. Just being there is enough.

T: Breathing up your air?

B: Exactly! My mother didn't want me, but she wanted to get rid of anyone who interested me or was interested in me. A violently jealous woman.

Benedicte depicts here the classic portrait of a mother felt to regard her child as a mere narcissistic extension of herself—a mother image that is so often revealed with severely addicted patients of both sexes.

There have been many contributory elements to the force of Benedicte's tobacco addiction. She had also explored suicidal wishes that might be hidden behind her excessive smoking. But here she adds further insight into the underlying significance of her smoking by presenting it as a murderous act of revenge against her mother, as well as its opposite—paternal protection from the hated mother image.

At the following session Benedicte's throat is closed up. She chokes and coughs throughout the hour and her thoughts turn once more to her hatred of her mother—"that vampirizing demon!" Then suddenly, in one of the folds in the wooden beams in my consulting room, she sees what she perceives of as a man's face.

B: In my new apartment I saw a similar face—it was my father's—as though there were a paternal presence in my new dwelling place. (Pause) A song keeps coming into my mind: Stevie Wonder's "Isn't She Lovely."
T: What do you associate with this song?
B: I once read that he wrote that song for his baby daughter.

Her associations turn once again to her hatred for her mother and how she would refuse to answer her mother's eternal questions about what she was thinking.

B: I used to feel inwardly so angry with her that my throat hurt. Her constant song is that I'm the only person who can bring her life, but the rest of the message reads, "Your body, your mind, your whole being, is part of me—it's all mine."
T: Perhaps you needed to see a man's face here to protect you from a vampirizing mother-analyst who's always seeking to know what you are thinking.

Benedicte hotly denies this intervention and its implications. I noted, but did not express, that she might well fear that the hated mother image will wipe out the idealized one that she projects onto her lovers and onto me; she herself has observed that in her love relationships she seeks to bring life to her partners, and we were able to reconstruct the hitherto unconscious part of the fantasy that her lovers are expected in return to "give life" back to her.

The following day she said, "After yesterday's session I asked myself why I could not tolerate the fantasy of you as a vampirizing mother. Then I began to think about everything I refused to accept from my mother, especially her body. This female body of mine has always hampered me somewhere inside. I could never have a child. Although I can imagine having a born child, there's no space inside me for one to grow. Unimaginable! I always knew that females had babies and males didn't and that therefore I wouldn't, as though I were confused about my basic identity. Didn't know what I had to struggle to keep and what I should get rid of. (Long pause) I felt this distinctly about my body for many years but I never had words for the feeling before. It was also connected with the animals I loved. They were all male."

Later in the session:

B: You know, during the vacation our work went on all the time we were apart. Maybe I shouldn't feel so dependent but life would seem shallow if I didn't have this experience. I even began the session on the way here, telling myself that up until the present nothing could ever make me cry. Nothing was ever to hurt me again. Friends disappear—I never make any contact, never write, never reply to letters. Yet I care very much about them inside me.

T: Would this be connected with you father? It seems these friends are treated as though they were dead but are kept alive inside you. So there's no need to write to them; it's sufficient to keep inside contact.

B: Yes, that's for certain—and it's particularly strong when I feel they have abandoned me in some way. It's as though I have to punish them for having gone . . . even a change in their lives, or their relationship with others, awakens in me the same sense of injustice. They have no right to change. That's when I have to smoke.

Toward the end of the session she said, "I thought I was immune, for the rest of my life, to ever feeling hurt again. Yet here I am, learning to cry once more."

Benedicte continues to cough and splutter throughout the following session and announces in a defiant tone of voice that she has been smoking "crazily," even though she can't breathe at the present time.

T: Who is stopping you from breathing?
B: My mother—she never could let me breathe freely.
T: Is the cigarette a way of replacing your mother? Recapturing a certain way of relating to her?
B: Huh! I'll have to think about that.

Later in the session her associations made me add that smoking seemed also to be a way of stifling her mother inside her—stifling the anguish her mother still causes her.

B: I have to fight her off just like I always have to struggle against doing what I ought to do.
T: Like stopping smoking as your doctor has advised? (Here my countertransference got the better of me!)
B: Yes! But I must smoke even if it kills me.

This led Benedicte to reflect on her other forms of protest—refusal to write to friends on their birthdays, for births and deaths, send Christmas cards, etc. Although these refusals upset her friends, they are a legacy of her reaction to what she calls her mother's "false relationship to the world."

She continues to cough frantically and tells me she has coughed so hard that at home she nearly fainted for lack of breath. "There is absolutely no trace of pleasure left; it has become a deadly compulsion," she says.

We reconstruct the internal drama—that she is invading, attacking, stifling her inner self through her body just as she felt her mother did to her mind.

T: This sounds like you're identifying with a dangerous image of your mother.

B: Yes, I'm sure that's so, but what I don't understand is, Where does the pleasure come from?

T: Perhaps a way of looking for that ideal, soothing fusional mother that you don't believe you ever had.

It seemed to me that for Benedicte the cigarette was both a good and a bad mother—one on the inside and one on the outside—just like the transitional object that also requires two objects: an outer concrete one and an inner psychic one. She says, "I also smoke to ruin good experiences. And if I had no cigarette? Well, I would probably cut myself or seek out a painful sight, like that of a dead bird or a blind cat."

Benedicte suddenly asked, as she often does toward the end of a session, or even well in advance of the end, "Is our time up?"

T: Why do you think of that at this particular moment?

B: I guess it's because here too separating has to be a half-killing, suffocating experience. It needs time. If I still have thirty minutes left, I can do a magic thing, but if the work is unexpectedly interrupted, I'm thrown into panic. That's why I always control your movements so as to know when the end of the session is approaching.

T: Could your sudden interest in the approach of the end of the session also be a way of avoiding talking about something?

B: Strange you should say that. Well, as a matter of fact, I was thinking about my recent refusal to have sex just because of sexual need. (Long pause) Masturbation is a very rare event for me. In fact I've never thought of it as an alternative to sex. I usually reach for a cigarette when I have such an urge. [I thought here of Freud's statement that he considered masturbation as the earliest addiction.] I have difficulty in talking to you about this and I can't say anything about my fantasies.

T: Afraid that I might not approve? Or that your fantasies might get taken away if you reveal them here?

B: I guess I lend you those thoughts. But, truly, does *anyone* ever admit that masturbation is acceptable?

T: Woody Allen said, "Masturbation is a way of making love to someone you really care about."

B: Huh! Well, do I really care about myself? (Pause) I have difficulty in being in contact with my own body . . . could never use my hand in any way to touch my sex. It has to be another person, or an object.

T: Your body, your sex, are not yours? Who owns these parts of yourself?

This autoerotic breakdown is frequently linked with an inhibition in transitional object development especially if the internal mother is felt to cast the child out if the child dares possess his or her own genitals and body, or shows any independence in thought, word, or deed. This fragment of Benedicte's analysis is exemplary of the struggle against libidinal impulses that are revealed in many addicted patients.

This clinical vignette also demonstrates that the addicted state may be sought after not only to deal with violent emotions or rage, anger, terror, abandonment, and so on associated with a breakdown in the mother–child relationship, but also, perhaps, with the hope that the addicted state may momentarily re-create the nostalgic illusion of childlike bliss.

ADOLESCENCE AND ADDICTIVE BEHAVIOR

Having stressed the importance of the early mother–baby relationship, we should not overlook the fact that adolescence is also an important phase in the onset of addictive behavior. Adolescents are not only exposed to the vicissitudes of identity consolidation in connection with their social group, but also confronted with social exigencies that are highly contradictory. On the one hand, there is much verbal encouragement to "liberate oneself" including so-called sexual liberation, this being frequently promoted by parents who, in certain cases, not having experienced this liberty, secretly covet it for themselves. On the other hand, adolescents are also in a situation of prolonged financial dependency on their parents. Over the last few years, in supervision work with younger colleagues, I have followed a surprisingly large number of bulimic adolescents (particularly girls) in which an unconscious aim associated with their excessive weight was that it would serve to ward off the danger of being sexually attractive. Anorexia, which must also be considered as an addiction (a craving for the sensation of emptiness or nothingness), frequently serves similar unconscious defensive aims. In addition, bulimic and anorectic adolescents experience a further common secondary gain—that of provoking anxiety in the parents.

Caroline, 14 years old, is an only child. Her parents, both psychiatrists, consulted with me because she is so overweight that the family doctor fears for her high blood pressure and potential cardiac pathology. I referred Caroline to a child therapist and continued, at their request, to see the parents.

The father, who adores Caroline, nevertheless constantly criticizes her at the table for overeating, and according to the mother, "He drives her crazy. This is not the way to help her overcome her constant overeating." The father, on the other hand, accuses his wife of being in complicity with Caroline's bulimia. She objects that this is not the case, but she has to protect their daughter from the father's attacks. While she was pregnant with Caroline, the family was forced to flee from a war-infested country, and, looking back on it, she feels that she may have communicated to the fetus her terror along with her need to search for security. Her husband feels that the mother has a compulsive need to overprotect Caroline, thus rendering normal separation highly problematic.

Both parents agree that Caroline adores her father and it seems probable that her enormous weight, which so displeases and disgusts him, is at the same time a protection against Caroline's oedipal longings.

WHAT DO "NEONEEDS" ACCOMPLISH?

The addictive solution is an attempt at self-cure in the face of threatening psychic stress. In *The Many Faces of Eros* (McDougall 1995) I proposed that the psychic states leading to addictive solutions fall into three main categories that determine the amount of "work" the addiction must accomplish and give some indication of the severity of the addictive proclivity:

1. an attempt to ward off neurotic anxieties;
2. an attempt to combat states of either severe anxiety, sometimes with a paranoid slant, or depression, frequently accompanied by feelings of inner death;
3. an attempt, through addictive pursuit, to take flight from psychotic anxieties, such as fear of bodily or psychic fragmentation or even a global terror of facing a void in which the sense of subjective identity is felt to be endangered.

Since deprivation in the internal psychic universe cannot be repaired by substances or objects encountered in the external world, addictive behavior will inevitably suffer a compulsive dimension.

In addition to the desperate need to discharge insupportable affective pressures, all forms of severe addiction seek to repair a damaged self-image that invariably includes an attempt to settle accounts with the parental figures of the past:

1. *Defiance of the inner maternal object,* who is experienced as absent or lacking in the capacity to soothe the troubled child hidden within. The addictive substitute from now on will

always be available as a stand-in for the missing maternal functions. In essence, the message is, "You can never again abandon me; from now on, I control *you!*"

2. *Defiance of the inner father*, who is believed to have failed in his paternal functions and therefore is dismissed.

3. *Defiance of death itself*, which takes two forms. First, there is an omnipotent stance that boasts, "Nothing can touch me—death is for the others." But when this grandiose form of defense breaks down and the sense of inner deadness can no longer be denied, there is, second, a yielding to the death impulses: "Perhaps the next fix, bout, or encounter will be the overdose—so what—who cares?"

One of my bulimic patients recently admitted that she would never be able to control her constant need to eat: "Perhaps my overeating will result in a myocardial infarct if I don't manage to reduce my excessive overweight. But so what?" This statement had the effect of mobilizing uncomfortable countertransference feelings, which were also part of my analysand's intention, as I was able to elaborate with her—an attempt to see if I cared more than her internal mother did about her long periods of childhood hunger for affection.

CONCLUSION

Dependency is an intrinsic part of the human condition. Beginning with the nursling in symbiotic dependence on the breast-mother universe, we continue to be shackled to a series of dependencies, even though we may remain relatively unaware of this, since humankind tends to live in conformity with the normal standards of each individual's sociocultural environment. In this way we are all highly dependent and submitted to a series of collective ideals that form the basis of any social contract. We did not sign this agreement that was decided long before our existence, but it nevertheless imposes upon us a major form of incontrovertible dependency. We are also submitted to the ravages of time and our incapacity to control it. And we must not forget our dependency on language and its incisive imprint on our psychosexual construction and psychosocial structure. In other words, dependency is our destiny—along with our unceasing struggles against it. To try to avoid these different dependencies is, in a sense, inhuman.

Victims of addiction are engaged in an immense defiance of universal human dependencies, including the illusion of rediscovering the lost paradise of infancy where one is free of all responsibility and time does not exist. Yet some are prepared to join us in the task of slowly bringing to consciousness the as-yet-unverbalized primitive terrors that are struggling for expression. These affective experiences have been firmly excluded from consciousness, in large part because of the violent pregenital fantasies of what comprises human relationships; in particular, love relations are frequently fantasized as a mutually disintegrating experience, in which love is equated with death. The struggle to find words to communicate and elaborate these early events is an inaugural experience in any individual's life.

I applaud all of those patients, victims of hungers and compulsions of every kind, who have nevertheless had the courage to undertake the psychotherapeutic adventure with its multiple risks, and who have chosen to eat from the tree of knowledge, knowing the price to pay may well be definitive exclusion from the illusion of paradise.

REFERENCE

McDougall, J. (1995). *The Many Faces of Eros: A Psychoanalytic Exploration of Human Sexuality.* New York: Norton.

2

Addictive Economies: Intrapsychic and Interpersonal

Discussion of McDougall's Chapter

Catherine Stuart

Throughout her career, Joyce McDougall has been addressing the thoughts, fears, needs, and anxieties of her clients who have addictive concerns. This is no small achievement, as addictions encompass a wide range of problems, and there is controversy about the appropriate treatment. McDougall is one of a handful of analysts who have made significant contributions to this field and in doing so has enhanced the treatment of these patients. Her perception of addictions as efforts at self-care and her attention to transitional and transitory phenomena are especially notable.

Her chapter exemplifies the richness of her contributions to the clinical and theoretical work on addictive behavior. In her work with patients she embodies an analytic stance that is simultaneously empathic with the patient's emotional life and skeptical about the patient's psychological symptoms (Bassin 1998). Her clinical vignettes depict the complexity of the experience between patient and therapist. Her detailed case examples give us both dialogue and emotional tone. She is emotionally present, aware of the currents between patient and therapist; of the historical, present, and future experience; and of the expressed and unexpressed aspects of consciousness, the verbalized and unverbalized fears and desires, and the conflicts and needs.

McDougall understands the importance of treating the whole person and looking for the deepest level of his experience. For patients with addictive patterns, action and physical sensation may stand in for other kinds of symptoms, defenses, and modes of communication. Her approach reminds us that actions can be used as material for fruitful inquiry as readily as any other symptom, particularly when the therapist's detailed inquiry focuses on context of the action.

I view McDougall's intrapsychic perspective on addiction from an interpersonal psychoanalytic perspective. Both perspectives are valid. Mine emphasizes the therapist's contribution to the relationship with the patient, and the ways in which one person's addictive patterns embroil many other people, including the therapist. McDougall's perspective offers theoretical constructs in which addictions are seen as attempts to discharge painful psychic states, such as problems of inner emptiness, deadness, or internal fragmentation.

Patients with addictions often have problems identifying their feelings. These patients express contradictory wishes suffused with love and hate. Addictive patterns and eating disorders can be attempts to defy either parent, or to defy death itself. In hypothesizing the origins of an addictive economy, McDougall places emphasis on the mother–infant dyad, particularly the difficulties in negotiating fusion and separation. These preoedipal difficulties affect the child's ability to develop transitional objects and the ability to self-soothe. As adults, these individuals experience problems in obtaining sexual and narcissistic gratification.

McDougall's perspective draws on both object relations and Freudian theory. In my view, there is no single cause of addictive behavior. Many factors, such as genetics, culture, physiological responses, and developmental issues, contribute to substance abuse, eating disorders, and compulsive sexuality. However, none of these factors explains why one person develops addictions while another does not. Addiction can begin at any life stage and does not necessarily signify the existence of problems that began in early infancy. It is also important to keep in mind the ways in which addictions become deeply entrenched, although they lose their power to provide pleasure or relief from pain. Addiction becomes part of a person's identity. One becomes a smoker, a drinker, an addict. The identity reinforces the action and the repeated action reinforces the identity, which influences one's self-perception (Wheelis 1973).

Different pathways lead to these problems, and while addictive quests serve some similar functions, such as escape from psychic pain, they frequently have different objectives. Even within a subcategory such as bulimia, there are different aims. Addictive patterns can reflect identification with parents or peers, or a way to define oneself. Addictions can be thought of as syndromes that generate interpersonal and intrapsychic problems.

From an interpersonal perspective, an individual's addictive pattern is not only a search for pleasure and relief from psychic pain but also an attempt to find a way around the thorny problems of being in relationships. The addict has a contradictory stance toward people, turning toward and away from them simultaneously (Brisman 1995). Understanding the complex interpersonal patterns that occur in the life of an addict is the most important factor in the treatment of addiction, because addictive behaviors entrap others in the addict's deleterious dynamics.

Therapists must recognize their countertransference responses to addicted patients. Some of these responses occur before we meet the patient, and others during the first session. The patient can present as a helpless victim in desperate need or as hyperindependent, not needing or wanting help from anyone. Some feel responsible for everything that happens to them; others take no responsibility. Some patients are gifted at knowing what they think we expect and hide their real needs.

My psychoanalytic approach views addictive patterns as a way of being in the world and a way of being with people. Careful attention to transference–countertransference patterns is essential in understanding the patient.

Contemporary psychoanalytic practice has incorporated many ideas that were once considered radically Interpersonal. These changes have made psychoanalysis and psychoanalytic psychotherapy more effective with addicted patients. One important change has been the ways in which therapists use their personal experience and the transference–countertransference patterns to inform their work. We can talk to our patients about the impact they are having on us and our impact upon them. We allow ourselves to draw upon ways in which we are similar to our patients.

Our observations, personal experience, and early clinical work affect how we view addiction. McDougall's personal history and early work with patients led her to understand the aims of the addiction as helping patients rid themselves of unwanted affects. My recollections of my experience in the early phases of giving up smoking led me to understand addiction in terms of interpersonal patterns. My feelings were intensified, especially my negative affective states, but my anxieties were interpersonal. I felt my responses were disproportionate to events, and I did not want to inflict my emotional states on others.

Soon after I stopped smoking, and during my psychology internship, I had the opportunity to work with a patient who had given up drinking eleven years earlier, but who continued to smoke despite health problems. He sought therapy because of a deep depression that he attributed to a recent trauma. He had sustained the loss of part of his lower leg eighteen months before starting therapy. After the surgery he initially seemed psychologically adjusted, so much so that his doctors considered him a role model for people undergoing rehabilitation. But after he learned how to walk with his prosthesis and had settled back into his routine life, his depression began.

In therapy, as he worked through his grief about losing his leg, he talked about the losses in his early life, and his feelings of inadequacy. The most painful issue from his childhood was the accidental death of his parents when he was 8 years old. He subsequently lived with an uncle and his family who were kind to him, but he never felt he was completely wanted by them.

Now as an adult, he was experiencing deep disappointment because he and his wife had not had sex in years. Despite his strong wish to rekindle the intimacy between them, he could not bring himself to approach her about this subject. He felt especially vulnerable to feelings of inadequacy and did not want to risk being rejected or making his wife uncomfortable. He explained that she never gave him an indication that she had a desire for sex, and he was sure that she was not interested. He considered their relationship to be emotionally sustaining and essentially a good one. He also felt guilt and shame about his history of problems with alcohol. He felt exposed in relation to his wife, and these painful affects were intensified by his feelings about his disfigurement. He was afraid to ask her to respond to his needs and desires. At the time, as a new ex-smoker myself, I was sympathetic to his use of cigarettes to relieve interpersonal distress.

During the year he was in therapy with me, he never expressed a desire to drink but had difficulty giving up smoking. The cigarettes helped rid him of unwanted feelings, including longings based on his early experience. He felt that he deserved the gratification since he did not feel gratified in other areas, especially in his marriage. The smoking also expressed an aspect of his self-representation as being guilty.

As the treatment progressed, he developed a romantic transference toward me. I became uncomfortable, but my supervisor was helpful in pointing out that the patient's problem with his wife, which was a repetition of his problems in living with his uncle's family, also echoed in our therapy relationship. I was not only sexually unavailable, I was also uncomfortable with his sexual desire and even more uncomfortable with the idea that he might feel shame about being in a position in which his desires were unacceptable. My vulnerabilities complicated the situation. As I became more open, and able to tolerate his feelings in our relationship, he became more expressive with me and finally with his wife.

Interpretations that stressed the early childhood origins of his difficulties were necessary, but they did not help him gain a sense of himself as a mature adult. At first, it was easier for me to talk about his needs in terms of his early issues rather than talk about the way his adult issues echoed in our work. Working through the enactment facilitated a deep shift for both of us. The technical advance of recognizing the role of the therapist's involvement in analytic treatment (Ehrenberg 1984, Levenson 1983, Mitchell 1988) has been especially effective with patients who prefer action to insight. Viewing the relationship as interactive and as a cocreation is an opportunity for promoting deeper exploration.

The main points of divergence between McDougall and myself is that while she acknowledges the two-person principle, she does not go sufficiently far in recognizing the contribution of the therapist to the therapeutic relationship. This contribution is always present, but a more complete acknowledgment of the therapist's participation reveals many potential avenues for therapeutic exploration that cannot be ignored if the goal is to work at the deepest level of experience. This has to include a listening stance that puts interpersonal patterns in the central role and pays careful attention to the aspects of the treatment situation that highlight the ways each person is affecting the other. I will use McDougall's own clinical examples to illustrate some of our differences.

McDougall's patient Bernadette leaves her sessions and goes out to get pastries. From the perspective of an interpersonal economy, it is clear that the urge to eat has something to do with their relationship. While Bernadette may not be able to name her feeling, she is conscious of an inner state of psychic discomfort. Her trip to the pastry shop is a complex action that will result in her trading one unpleasant inner state for another.

What is out of awareness is interpersonal in that she is keeping this pattern a secret from her therapist. It has been going on for two years but she never tells McDougall. She may be protecting her from something or protecting herself from McDougall's reaction to her. In either case it is not an example of repression, or any defense of that nature. It is something Bernadette knows but decides not to tell her therapist—what Sullivan called selective inattention.

An inquiry into the exact moment-to-moment shifts in the patient's experience might lead to an understanding of what is going on between them that triggers the patient's state of wanting pastries. But the hiding is out in the open for the moment. Interestingly, McDougall focuses on an interpersonal aspect of the relationship but does not focus on the secrecy. My own association was that this lack of attention could be a manifestation of the therapist's wish to avoid acknowledging something that was going on between them. Perhaps the patient feels shame over being needy, dependent, and out of control, and perhaps she imagines her therapist to be in a state of perfection concerning eating issues. Perhaps McDougall's positive view of the patient prevents her from inquiring into the possibility that the patient's expectation of reflected appraisal is tinged with negativity.

It may be equally important to examine the use of the word "devouring" to describe Bernadette's hunger. Our feminist colleagues (Gutwill 1994) have highlighted the disparaging attitudes in our culture toward a woman's appetites. If McDougall introduced the word, Bernadette might have had some feelings about her therapist seeing her as devouring. After all, therapists, like mothers, give their charges words to describe their internal states. The words then shape and color the sense of self. The interpretation, "She is devouring me," addresses the wish to have more of her therapist-mother, and hints at a destructive element in the wanting, but not the guilt or shame that leads to the need to keep this a secret. Her fear of devouring or her shame about being seen as devouring is not mentioned directly.

I can also imagine a fruitful inquiry into the origins of the patient's view that her own needs, even if they are preoedipal, are unreasonable within the context of human relationships. I would also want to find out if and when something similar happens with others and when she started hiding her eating. As an interpersonal economy, the problems with eating are a reflection of her fear of being seen and known by her therapist. Levenson (1991) has highlighted the "remarkably consistent recurrence of patterning in the material, in dreams, fantasies, associations, random thoughts, memories or accounts of present experience" (p. 202).

In fairness to McDougall and to the idea that different theories overlap in their application, it seems that implicitly McDougall treats Bernadette's needs as reasonable and understandable outcomes based on the patient's history and relationship with her mother. This allows the patient freedom to put her longings into words in the presence of someone who understands them. In fact, McDougall's interpretation did facilitate the process and bring the problematic feelings into their relationship and into symbolic language.

The case of Benedicte is challenging and brings up some of the most troublesome controversies in the treatment of addictive patterns. Benedicte's addiction is threatening her life. She talks about her smoking and her related illnesses, and she demonstrates her illness in sessions. Surely she is aware that she is having a strong impact on her therapist, who is concerned about her smoking. This is an example of how an intense enactment can begin, even before there is a solid relationship between the patient and the therapist. An inquiry into the patient's fantasies, fears, and/or desires about her therapist's reactions might reveal important themes of the treatment.

These issues also give rise to questions about setting limits, which is another controversial area. Having to set limits places the therapist in a parental position, and not doing so can be colluding with the patient's self-destructive tendencies. There are also questions about when and if setting limits is effective, and questions about how much this degree of addiction interferes with therapy.

Benedicte's addiction has such a hold over her life (and is omnipresent in her treatment) that it may be worthwhile to place the addiction at the center of the therapeutic inquiry. Is she unconsciously asking for help, or trying to suffocate or punish her therapist-mother by continuing to engage in this suicidal pattern?

What are her fantasies of McDougall's feelings and thoughts about her smoking? Each time she mentions it I would wonder why she is bringing it up at that particular moment. I would also consider talking to her about her effect on me if I felt she was ready to hear it and use it productively. Another conjecture is that Benedicte is very disappointed in her return to cigarette smoking after having achieved abstinence. She may want to protect herself or McDougall from intense feelings of failure.

In this case, if Benedicte is as physically ill as she sounds, I might feel inclined to look at exploring the deeper meaning of her addiction as a resistance to the critical issue of looking at what it would take to help her give up her destructive patterns. There are dangers in this vigorous approach. One is that the patient may not be able to grapple with these issues and needs a safe space to contemplate these and other life choices without pressure from an authority figure. Treatments for addiction can fail if the therapist favors one side of the conflict while the patient protects the other side. Another danger is that the therapist may be entering into a relationship with the patient that echoes the relationship between the patient and her parents. This position may foster dependency on the therapist, allowing the patient to give control over to her.

Lastly, I would inquire into the details of her smoking. What state is she in when she makes the decision to smoke; exactly what is it like? Is it enjoyable? How does the smoke feel in her mouth and throat? Does she inhale? These details help break through the patient's defenses and promote an atmosphere in which the patient can pay attention to and name different internal states, and their context. Hopenwasser (1998) has noted that physical sensations are sources of information that can be clinically useful.

Addictive patterns are problems that affect large numbers of patients, and there have been many attempts to understand their origins and the components of effective treatment. These disorders, especially when they are severe, are notoriously difficult to treat and evoke strong reactions in their therapies. Psychoanalysts have a lot to offer in improving the outcome of treatment for these syndromes. McDougall's work reveals her continued commitment to exploring the internal experience of the addict. In her vignettes we hear her productive interactions with patients. She emphasizes the intrapsychic aspects of addiction and shows us how she uses this model with her patients. I believe it is essential to emphasize the transference and countertransference, as the interactions that occur between the patient and therapist are often more accessible, contain the early history, and reveal the deepest dimension of the therapeutic adventure.

REFERENCES

Bassin, D. (1998). Book review: McDougall, J., *The Many Faces of Eros: A Psychoanalytic Exploration of Human Sexuality. Psychoanalytic Psychology* 15:3.

Brisman, J. (1995). Addiction. In *Handbook of Interpersonal Psychoanalysis*, ed. M. Lionells, J. Fiscallini, C. Mann, and D. Stern, pp. 537–552. Hillsdale: Analytic Press.

Ehrenberg, D. B. (1984). Psychoanalytic engagement II. *Contemporary Psychoanalysis* 18(4):535–555.

Gutwill, S. (1994). Women's eating problems: social contest and the internalization of culture. In *Eating Problems: A Feminist Psychoanalytic Treatment Model*, ed. C. Bloom, A. Gitter, S. Gutwill, L. Kogel, and L. Zaphiropoulos, pp. 1–27. New York: Basic Books.

Hopenwasser, K. (1998). Listening to the body: somatic representations of dissociated memory. In *Relational Perspectives on the Body*, ed. L. Aron and F. Anderson. Hillsdale, NJ: Analytic Press.

Levenson, E. A. (1983). *The Ambiguity of Change.* New York: Basic Books.

——— (1991). *The Purloined Self: Interpersonal perspectives in Psychoanalysis.* New York: Contemporary Psychoanalysis Books.

Mitchell, S. A. (1988). *Relational Concepts in Psychoanalysis: An Integration.* Cambridge: Harvard University Press.

Wheelis, A. (1973). *How People Change.* New York: Harper & Row.

II

Expanding the Analytic Space: Dissociation and the Eating-Disordered Patient

3

Thinking, Talking, and Feeling in Psychotherapy with Eating-Disordered Individuals

F. Diane Barth

Many years ago I began working with Mathilde, a talented young actress who was appearing at the time in her second Broadway show. Although disappointed that she had not yet been cast in a starring role, Mathilde knew that her career was moving in precisely the direction she wanted. She had numerous friends and a steady, if not particularly supportive, boyfriend, so, as she told me repeatedly, she could not understand why she was so terribly unhappy. Bubbly, cheerful, and fun-loving, she frequently felt acutely unattractive, inadequate, and terribly lonely. She came into therapy because she was miserable and felt ashamed and critical of herself—and because she binged and threw up several times every day. Despite her pain about this symptom, it was sometimes hard for me to sympathize with Mathilde. Besides being successful in a field in which success is hard to come by, she was incredibly beautiful, intelligent, and funny. As she put it, she could "sparkle" when she needed to and she was able to charm almost anyone—including me, despite my occasional lapses of sympathy. She loved being loved, and while I never had a sense that her delightful personality was false or artificial, over time it became clear that a great fear of being disliked severely restricted her range of affects and had a direct connection to her bingeing and purging behavior.

For the most part, I genuinely enjoyed working with Mathilde, who was relatively insightful, very hard working, and clearly found therapy helpful. Her bingeing and purging diminished, her sense of self improved, and, after a brief stormy period with her boyfriend, she ended that relationship and moved into one that seemed to promise much greater satisfaction and fulfillment. However, despite these positive signs, I was puzzled by a peculiar phenomenon that appeared shortly after we started working together, and continued throughout the early years of our long relationship: after every session, even if it was apparently productive and useful, I inevitably felt unhappy about and/or critical of something I had said or done. Furthermore, no matter how I was feeling about myself before Mathilde entered my office, when she left I almost always felt inept, unattractive, stupid—and twenty pounds heavier than I had at the beginning of that session.

There were, as I gradually learned, many different meanings to these disturbing feelings. In this chapter I focus on only one of those meanings, not because I believe it was necessarily the most important, but because it is reflective of a difficult, seldom discussed, but, in my experience as therapist, supervisor, and teacher, very common dynamic in the therapeutic process with individuals with eating disorders: the presence not only of a client's dissociated experience, but also of the therapist's. I offer as food for thought the question of how we, as therapists, can translate what we might call mutually dissociated affects into a language that we can use within and as part of the therapeutic process.

Hoffman (1983) was, in many ways, an early spokesperson for what has become a new wave of analytic thought about the impact of the analyst's dynamics on the analytic work. As Aron (1991) put it, the analyst's "unconscious psychology" can play a significant role in the analytic work, and patients' fantasies about this psychology are, at least in part, "attempts to grapple with and grasp, in their own unique way, the complex and ambiguous reality of their individual analyst" (p. 35). At the same time as we have become far more cognizant of these important factors, psychotherapist have also become more concerned with and aware of the phenomenon of dissociation, a concept that is also undergoing significant and fascinating exploration in current psychoanalytic thinking. Bromberg (1998), Davies (1998), Harris (1998), Phillips (1993), and Stern (1997) have presented reformulations of dissociation in which the therapist's actions play a significant role in the process. Yet, because a therapist's dissociated material is unavailable to her, it is frequently extremely difficult to tease out just what role it is playing either in the therapy in general or in a particular set of interactions with a specific client at a given moment in the work.

In many instances, there is no urgent reason to attempt to push this unavailable material into the analytic process, since it will inevitably make its way into the work and eventually become grist for the analytic mill in some way or another. There are, however, certain experiences and affects that both therapist and client have difficulties with, which they may both resist opening up, and which, if some way is not found to bring them into the realm of the articulable, can gradually lead to analytic stalemate at best, and failure at worst. One version of this experience was both captured and disguised by my self-criticism and my physical feelings after a session with Mathilde: the cluster of emotions that are represented by the term *competition*. These were feelings that, to say the least, I was uncomfortable with, and that Mathilde, as I will describe shortly, simply could not process.

Dissociation is a key aspect of the difficulties many of us have with issues of competition. I do not view dissociation as arising from a specific developmental stage, nor do I find it particularly useful as a diagnostic tool, since I have found dissociative activity in individuals at all levels of functioning. In fact, I believe that this apparently pathological activity is sometimes a highly adaptive defense, although it can also be an extremely destructive one. For the sake of clarity, I use the term *dissociation* to refer to those aspects of an individual's self that she or he cannot, for whatever reasons, recognize, own, process, or locate affectively.

Eating disorders are in part influenced by unrecognized or unprocessed competitive feelings, but traditional formulations of this material tend to utilize a severely constricted blueprint that excludes much of the multifaceted experience of envy, jealousy, self-esteem, self-definition, admiration, and pleasurable contact that are only part of competition. Classical, contemporary, and even some feminist analytic theories both reflect and reinforce many of the narrowly defined, ambiguous, and conflictual intrapsychic and cultural beliefs and feelings about competition in and between women that contribute to the development of eating disorders. As a result, when this material arises in the therapeutic relationship, the therapist—male or female—and client may both suffer from an inability to find words with which to manage or process their experience.

Adrienne Harris (1998) begins an article with a statement that, coming from a woman, seems both courageous and amazing: "I think of myself as aggressive and must confess to a lifelong, highly competitive streak" (p. 31). But it is telling that she feels that she "must confess" to this characteristic. As Joan Lang (1984) put it, even with all of the changes in women's roles today, competitive feelings simply are not viewed as part of a "feminine" self. Although women are encouraged to compete aggressively and are often criticized when we drop out of competition, openly competitive feelings are often viewed as somewhat distasteful, off-putting, or unfeminine. Harris writes, "Competitiveness is often experienced by a woman as a damning character flaw" (p. 40). Ruth Moulton (1986) states, "To win approval, the woman must not threaten others; it is dangerous to surpass them; the woman will be hated, excluded, punished for it" (p. 161). While men as well as women have difficulties with competition, competitive rivalry in men is socially condoned and recognized as a way of connecting. For women it is often kept out of awareness, as Brisman (see Chapter 4) describes so eloquently because it feels "too nasty, too dirty, too unprofessional."

It is, therefore, not surprising that women, whether therapists or clients, have difficulty sitting with or even knowing about our competitive feelings toward one another. Yet the derivatives are there, for example when a therapist, listening to a client obsess about her weight and her food intake, finds herself silently considering her suddenly too tight waistband and vowing to finally begin that long-delayed diet. The derivatives are there as well when a therapist declares to herself that she will never monitor her food intake again, and will never ever set foot on another exercise mat. I am not suggesting that these thoughts and actions always represent unrecognized or unacceptable competitive strivings between ourselves and our clients, nor am I saying that competitive issues are the basis for all eating disorders. But when thoughts and feelings are dissociated not just by clients but also by therapists, the question of exploration becomes significantly more complicated.

One concept to which many of us turn when we cannot explain our feelings with a specific client is the idea of projective identification. It will take us too far afield for me to summarize the contemporary lively and useful dispute over this concept, so I refer the interested reader elsewhere (e.g., Bromberg 1998, Davies 1998, Harris 1998, Schafer 1997, Stern 1997) for interesting and thought-provoking discussions of the idea. The term *projective identification* performs a crucial function by providing therapists with words with which to think about and process otherwise unverbalizable and unthinkable interactions between our clients and ourselves. It is my belief, however, that therapists sometimes invoke this concept in an unconscious attempt to alleviate our discomfort with intense and uncomfortable nonverbal experiences. In my work with Mathilde, for example, the idea of projective identification helped me manage my unease, but it did not help me understand the complex interplay of dynamics that were represented by my self-critical thoughts and feelings. Nor did it help me find words with which to talk with Mathilde, or to help her talk to me about the split-off feelings that I might have been processing for both of us.

Essentially, if you're unaware of some of your processing it can be hard to bring it in or help the client with it.

One valuable tool within the expanded toolbox available to therapists today is a focus on the apparently insignificant details that make each life unique, that make each individual who she or he is. Stern (1997) quotes the philosopher Herbert Fingarette who comments that "the skill of saying what we are doing or experiencing [is] a model for becoming explicitly conscious of something" (p. 86). I believe it is more than a model. Sometimes chatting with clients about movies, television programs, diets, clothing, the World Series, the danger of pesticides versus being bitten by an encephalitis-infected mosquito, and anything else that is important to them, no matter how concrete or trivial it may seem, can—in conjunction with all of the other analytic tools we use—be very useful in building the skills that both client and therapist need to observe and talk with one another about the painful affects and experiences to be found in the far reaches of our dissociated processes.

George Klein (1976) emphasized that symptoms exist for a reason and that they are in fact often adaptive, even when they are also painfully maladaptive. Dissociation, as Stern (1997) has put it, "drain(s) experience of the feeling(s)" (p. 126) that make it real or meaningful, but it also provides an important self-protective function. Failure to find symbolic representation can, as Bromberg (1998) writes, shield against emotions that are felt to be capable of "doing violence to one's experience of selfhood and sometimes to sanity itself" (p. 184). Mathilde often brought in dreams that, in the context of my visceral reactions as well as her associations, seemed to reflect, among other things, her fears of my competitive impulses. In one, for example, she dreamt that I cut off all of her beautiful hair. When I asked what my motivation might have been, she shrugged. Pushing a little harder, I wondered out loud if she imagined I might sometimes be competitive with her. In horror, she denied not only the possibility, but also the potential space (Bromberg 1998, Ogden 1986) in which we might explore further. "I saw a movie last night right before I fell asleep. It was an image in the movie." Period. The end.

We therapists sometimes attempt to get to what we consider to be the real emotions in order to stay connected and alive in the room with a client who feels disconnected and even sometimes dead. We want them to get to their feelings so that we can get away from ours. I find it useful to remind myself that eating-disordered behavior and dissociation are often, paradoxically, the only ways that a client can stay alive with me, and that I have to find a way to tolerate the fluctuations of not only her dissociative activity but also my own in order to be with her. Sometimes this means sitting in confusion, doubt, or boredom, with my own uncomfortable physical sensations, and even with a return of a client's eating-disordered behavior itself. Phillips (1993) writes that worrisome symptoms are sometimes a way that adolescents "get out of their parents' orbit even while maintaining sufficient contact with it" (p. 49), and I believe that this is powerfully true for many eating-disordered clients, not only with their parents, but also with their therapists. Eating disorders can be ways of negotiating what Benjamin has described as the ongoing tensions between connection and separation, identification and recognition of difference that are so often so terribly difficult, but so important to being fully alive.

A colleague told me the following story: It had been a long day early in the fall. Her children were having some difficulty settling into the new school year, and she was worried about not being home to supervise their homework. Her last client of the evening was a compulsive overeater, a woman of whom she was quite fond, but who was sometimes so unrelated it was difficult to stay awake in the room with her. That evening, although she tried hard to pay attention, the therapist just could not focus carefully on yet another recitation of the client's unhappiness and dissatisfaction with her life, her job, her family, and her future. The therapist began to drift off into her own worries about her children. Suddenly, out of the corner of her eye, the therapist saw a rat on the wall of her office. Jolting to attention, she cautiously looked at the section of her wall where the rat had appeared and saw that the image had been triggered visually by a hinge on her office door. By now she was wide awake and very curious about what had stimulated this "off the wall" (Bollas 1989) image. What could it tell her about her client? about herself? about something that was, or was not, happening at the moment in the relationship? Why had this incident occurred just now? And why a rat?

This therapist, a talented, experienced psychoanalyst, realized that, among a number of other dynamics, the rat represented her own discomfort with some surprising competitive material that was just beginning to tentatively move into the analytic space. However, and this is the rub, she could not find a way to bring this sudden awakening into the room. Instead of leading to fruitful dialogue or exploration with the client, the image and all it meant seemed to die on the vine. But did it really? Phillips (1994) writes that "the capacity to be bored can be a developmental achievement" (p. 69), because it is a necessary precedent to finding out what one desires. For many women, eating- and non–eating-disordered alike, the capacity to tolerate competitive feelings is also a developmental achievement, one that allows both desire and difference to be acknowledged. Eating-disordered clients often have little ability to process these experiences, except within the concrete realms of food and their bodies. It is my belief that by casually, gently paying attention to the small, apparently meaningless details of a client's life, we build the relationship, the structure, the capacity to observe and think about oneself, and the mutual trust that makes the rest of the analytic process possible.

Davies (1998) writes, "The very creation of [a] relatively 'safe place' in which the patient can first experience and then explore becomes clearly predicated upon the analyst's capacity to sustain and tolerate the . . . countertransferential responses specific to passionate desire in the analytic relationship" (p. 748). I believe the same is true for competitive feelings. Recognizing the importance of the literal details of a client's life also contributes significantly to our ability to sit with the painful, disturbing, off-putting, or even simply irritating affects that often emerge in the nonverbal arena in our work; and our ability to sit with these feelings is a prerequisite to our clients' ability to sit with them with us, and gradually, even without us.

I sit and I listen, and ask questions and articulate emotions when and where I can. I gently ask for available details about any experience, whether it is the order in which a client eats the food she knows she is going to throw up, the pleasure with which she selected a new sweater set, or the way that she understands her rage at her sister, who has suddenly found a wonderful new boyfriend. Eventually we begin to "stand in the spaces," as Bromberg (1998) puts it, making room for "not me" parts of ourselves and finding language for affects that we've been feeling but not seeing. While Mathilde, for example, has not yet begun to talk about our competition, as we've talked about her weight and work, shopping and dieting, bingeing and vomiting, exercise and lack thereof, favorite and least favorite television shows, lives of her friends, and so on, we have also begun very tentatively to look at some of the times that friends seem to be competitive with her. These days I sometimes name the feeling, gently and questioningly, and sometimes she names it herself. She has begun to recognize the highly competitive nature of her work, and to be curious about her reasons for choosing such a career, given her avowed terror of competition.

She has not quite reached, and maybe never will, the place that another client recently suddenly took herself and me, as well. In an extremely poignant moment, this young woman, an avid cyclist, began to ask me about my bike-riding experience. We had been talking for a while about some of her issues with competition, and her fear of competing with me; so in answer to her question, I grinned and said, "You win. I have an old beat-up bike and only ride on flat trails." To my surprise, she responded by calling me on dropping out of the competition with her. She said, "I need you to stay in there. There's something very connected about being in competition with you. It makes me feel very close to you."

Benjamin (1999) writes, "The structure of complementarity, the see-saw in which we can incessantly reverse positions through identification, is fundamental to our intrapsychic understanding of mind" (p. xiv). Competition is only one of any number of mutually, or perhaps we might say conjointly, dissociated experiences that make not only the seesaw difficult to balance, but also its two ends almost impossible to see. In these situations, as we gradually bring into the therapy some of the most mundane and visible details of an individual's life, therapist and client together can slowly close the gap between spoken words and lived experience.

REFERENCES

Aron, L. (1991). The patient's experience of the analyst's subjectivity. *Psychoanalytic Dialogues* 1:29–51.

Benjamin, J. (1999). *The Shadow of the Other.* New York: Routledge.

Bollas, C. (1989). *Forces of Destiny: Psychoanalysis and Human Idiom.* London: Free Association.

Bromberg, P. (1998). *Standing in the Spaces: Essays on Clinical Process, Trauma and Dissociation.* Hillsdale, NJ, and London: Analytic Press.

Davies, J. M. (1998). Between the disclosure and foreclosure of erotic transference-countertransference: can psychoanalysis find a place for adult sexuality? *Psychoanalytic Dialogues* 8:747–766.

Harris, A. (1998). Aggression: pleasures and dangers. *Psychoanalytic Inquiry* 8:31–44.

Hoffman, I. Z. (1983). The patient as interpreter of the analyst's experience. *Contemporary Psychoanalysis* 19:389–422.

Klein, G. (1976). *Psychoanalytic Theory.* New York: International Universities Press.

Lang, J. A. (1984). Notes toward a psychology of the feminine self. In *Kohut's Legacy: Contributions to Self Psychology,* ed. A. Goldberg and P. Stepansky, pp. 51–70. Hillsdale, NJ, and London: Analytic Press.

Moulton, R. (1986). Professional success: a conflict for women. In *Psychoanalysis and Women: Contemporary Reappraisals,* ed. J. Alpert, pp. 161–182. Hillsdale, NJ, and London: Analytic Press.

Ogden, T. (1986). *The Matrix of the Mind: Object Relations and the Psychoanalytic Dialogue.* Northvale, NJ: Jason Aronson.

Phillips, A. (1993). *On Kissing, Tickling and Being Bored: Psychoanalytic Essays on the Unexamined Life.* Cambridge, MA: Harvard University Press.

Schafer, R., ed. (1997). *The Contemporary Kleinians of London.* Madison, CT: International Universities Press.

Stern, D. (1997). *Unformulated Experience: From Dissociation to Imagination in Psychoanalysis.* Hillsdale, NJ, and London: Analytic Press.

4

The Instigation of Dare: Broadening Therapeutic Horizons

Judith Brisman

The emergence of threat, the embrace of dare are often at once unspoken, yet palpable goals of the treatment of any therapy patient. Indeed, how to allow patients to voice threatening aspects of self, often not encoded in words, is a theme permeating postmodern analytic thinking (Bromberg 1998, Davies 1996, Mitchell 1993, Slavin 1996).

The eating-disordered patient offers a unique opportunity to consider this question. These patients' lives are indeed exquisitely measured, with dare and creativity shunted, often expressed in the darker recesses of disordered eating. The realm of play, in which emotions, experiences, and identities can be tried on and reworked, is thwarted. Spontaneity, necessary for moments of intimacy between any two people, is silently abated.

The lives of eating-disordered patients are measured, protected, shrouded by words. In many ways, words are not informational. They are not vehicles for self-expression or connection to others (Brisman 1998). Instead, they are part of a measured armor, used to keep the world at bay.

Barth (1998) notes that parts of the self not discussed by these patients may not even be associated with words. Actions, such as bingeing, purging, or starving, are the vehicles both for the expression and the containment of unmeasured, unmastered experience and emotion. In that regard, the symptom concretizes and embodies the danger inherent in any intimate exchange.

The normal course of action in any therapy is to allow the danger to emerge in the verbally loaded therapy setting, and provide a frame within which that very danger can be discussed and understood in such a way that leads to an expansion of the self.

The problem with the eating-disordered patient is that traditional means of providing this safe-enough arena are thwarted.

For example, the ever-present threat of symptom exacerbation may unintentionally thwart the therapist's maintenance of an atmosphere of safety. The patient's preference for action versus reflective discussion interrupts the therapeutic ambiance. The therapist may hover over the patient, attempting to control the outside dangers (e.g., that of starvation or the physical debilitation of vomiting or laxative abuse). The therapist's response can unintentionally exacerbate interpersonal dangers of intrusion and coercion. This may appear to be a significant transferential–countertransferential development. However, the patient who responds to experiences with action is not interested in understanding. In the face of such interpersonal tensions, she will likely retreat to food or leave treatment altogether.

Traditionally, an established frame, imposing the boundaries of patient–therapist interactions and structuring the work of the therapy allows for a unique sense of safety, peculiar to the therapy relationship. Mitchell (1993) emphasizes how much *cannot* happen in this dyad. It is the very constraints of the analytic relationship that show for an unfolding of a kind of intimacy and self-reflection that is not available in any other way. The eating-disordered patient, however, demands a reconstruction of what safety really is. Here, actions, as Davis (1991) has emphasized, may well be considered as thoughtful, and certainly as meaningful, as words.

Exacerbation of disordered eating can be an opportunity, a red flag that darker aspects of self are hovering in the room. It is a time, as Bromberg (1996) would caution, that the therapist needs to be attuned to shifting relational states and one's subjective experience of the relationship with the patient. And it may well be a time to act, or more to the point, not to censure actions that originate from the interplay of disassociated aspects of self—both that of the patient and that of the therapist.

By "actions," I am referring to actual behaviors, gestures, and interactions initiated by patient and therapist that are commonly appreciated as "acting out" in therapeutic parlance. These are movements, gestures, or behaviors that are either consciously imparted or more spontaneously derived that position the therapist more actively in the patient's world. What I am referring to is *not* foremost the construction or instruction of a new way of relating, but as Levenson (1983) would emphasize, a deconstruction of the familiar, yet narrowing means of interacting with the patient. I am talking about a loosening of the boundaries from within which we operate. As Hoffman (1998) emphasizes, a strict adherence to the analytic rules can be as provocative as deviating from them. The more artful and courageous analytic work entails knowning when other ways of interacting should be considered.

In earlier papers (Brisman 1992, 1995, 1998), I have described a treatment approach in which a psychodynamic model is integrated with behavioral interventions that actively address disordered eating. Here the emphasis is on the need to jump into the patient's world as a means of meeting and engaging her, broadening the restriction on actions commonly defining analytic work.

One aspect of this early work is the use of contracts in which the therapist is positioned to be more present in the patient's day-to-day life. The contract is a verbal agreement made between patient and therapist in which the patient agrees to take one step that could lead toward symptomatic abatement. This could be, for example, not vomiting one night before the next session, or putting feelings into words in a journal before one binge. Often the patient is encouraged to initiate contact with the therapist during moments of difficulty. This may mean a message on the answering machine, a note, e-mail, or, infrequently, a phone conversation. The point is not moment-to-moment support, but a means of keeping the therapist alive during the patient's most inchoate experiences outside of the treatment room.

While symptomatic change is a significant goal of therapy, just as important is the therapist's attempt to enter the dissociated world of the alienated self and to allow it entry into the world of the therapeutic relationship. Who was the patient when the contract was kept or forgotten? What actually happened between the therapist and patient? The ways in which food and bodily obsessions are used to strangulate the relational exchange with the therapist are now alive in the room, available to be more directly experienced by both therapist and patient, available for the introduction of words.

Bromberg (1998, p. 258) emphasizes the use of the interpersonal experience between patient and therapist to symbolize and contain previously unattainable aspects of self. "It is in the process of 'knowing' one's patient through a direct relatedness . . . that those aspects of self which cannot 'speak' will ever find a voice." His work focuses on the experience within the treatment arena, but I am talking about what happens both inside and outside.

ANNA

Anna, 29, sat on my couch pouting. There were times she could have been mistaken for a teenager.

"I'm sick of shaving my legs" she told me. "I've never gone without shaving before—part of that pleasing thing. But I just decided not to bother a couple of weeks ago. It's sort of disgusting to look at but I was just so sick of always trying so hard. It's funny—I sort of like it. When I'm running in the park, I find myself daring people to look."

Anna said she was angry at her mother for being intrusive and angry at a friend for not being more attentive. This all sounded a bit different, more fierce, more fed up. I wondered what she was doing with me. Was she angry? Daring me to see it? I wasn't sure. I was intrigued. I began to wander.

As she continued, Anna broke off a long piece of her hair and played with it between her thumb and finger. I hardly took notice. But as she was talking, almost out of my awareness—except that it was right in front of my eyes—Anna took the strand of hair, put it into her mouth, ran it between her teeth like dental floss—and a spitty bit of food came flying across the room nearly hitting my leg!

There was a moment untouched in the room of stunned disbelief. And then I blurted "That's disgusting!" except I didn't say it, I closer to yelled it.

Anna squealed with delight.

There is one more thing about this moment that must be included: as soon as I had yelled at Anna, I realized that this was not the first time she had flossed her teeth with her hair. It was, however, the first time I had noticed. As soon as I reacted to her flossing I realized that this was something Anna had done before, although usually more languidly, and certainly, up to now, without capturing any food. Again, I wondered what Anna might be trying to say to me. It took her basically spitting at my leg for me to pay attention.

Only retrospectively was it apparent to me that Anna had been silently screaming at me to look for a long time.

For more than four years prior to the reported session, Anna had been progressing quite steadily in treatment with me. She had stopped stealing garbage from her apartment's incinerator rooms. This change had been, through the use of contracts, a major part of our early therapeutic focus. Anna was no longer vomiting and had been bingeing significantly less. She was dating for the first time in four years and had begun to embrace her career with a passion that had heretofore been absent. In general, things appeared to be going quite well.

And then suddenly, there was a plunge into the abyss. Anna returned to bingeing and vomiting, after four years of abstinence, with such severity that her face, usually beautiful and mystical, looked punched to a pulp. Her return to bingeing and vomiting was subsequent to a major disappointment with a man. And of no little importance, I was on my August break when Anna first vomited again. Still, looking back, I'm not sure, even knowing what I do now, that I could have foreseen the advent of the symptomatic regression. The reemergence of this old symptom, worse than ever before, was so absolutely unanticipated by both of us that it felt as though someone else had banged open the door to the treatment room and forced herself into our lives.

Our sessions were completely ineffective in stopping the binge-ing and vomiting, and ultimately Anna was hospitalized for several weeks' duration. For more than four years prior to the "spitting" session, Anna had been out of the hospital only two months. She was again free of the bulimia, but not without struggle.

Several sessions after the reported session, the following inter-action occurred: The office I was using at the time was in my home, where patients were seen in a study that was separate from the rest of the apartment. Without a formal buzzer system, I was required to answer the door directly, ushering patients to and from the office. In the foyer, a grand floor-to-ceiling mirror lined the wall. Anna usually would sweep back and forth through the hallway, often commenting breezily about the weather or, perhaps, making a final comment about the session we had just had.

This time however, upon leaving the session, Anna stopped and stood in front of the mirror.

"Do I look fat?" she demanded, looking over at me, not at herself. I found myself surprisingly uncomfortable with this now quite routine and familiar demand to look. Was I reluctant to look, or was my reluctance that of being seen? I stood sideways.

"I'm so fat," she again insisted.

I imagined telling her the usual: "Why now?" Or, "I can't determine how you feel about your body. You have to decide whether you're really fat or not" or, more likely, "We're going to have to end now. We'll talk about it next time." Instead, not quite conscious of my decision to attend to whatever needed to be seen, although it obviously played a part, I found myself saying, "Show me what you see." I turned hesitantly to face the mirror. The next several minutes were spent looking.

Another form of looking with Anna came in quite an opposite manner. Some time after our interaction in front of the mirror, I found myself wandering during sessions. Anna was talking about a new dress she had bought and was wearing to the session. It was a beautiful dress, and not unlike something I would buy for myself. I found myself thinking about a dress that had been given to me as a gift. It too had been beautiful—in fact, I thought, *more* beautiful than the dress Anna had on. The thought, though, was a bit more subtle, less formed than that. It was only later, when Anna was showing me a picture of a man she had begun to date, that the momentary horror of self-recognition emerged. In seeing the picture of a young man with a particularly striking face, I had thought, "I dated someone who looked like him years ago." And then, I was startled into awareness as I found myself shouting silently, "That's disgusting!!"

These vignettes are brief moments in a long and quite complicated treatment. They are not concretely reflective of my usual behavior or thoughts—in fact, this was the only time I've ever stood in front of a mirror with a patient, and the reveries I had with Anna have never been the same with other patients, nor again with Anna. What I would like to emphasize in these examples is my understanding of crisis with the eating-disordered patient.

Symptomatic regression, impasse, or even chronic malaise may well be an indication that something is hovering, something needs to be seen and experienced before words can be used to interpret what is going on.

Anna's spitting—both in the therapy room and in the privacy of her bulimic activities—alerted me to the possibility that something or someone was hovering here too. Sensitive to the question, Who really is in the room? and sensitive to the patient's need for active intervention, I believe I was liberated to enter the challenge of a less verbal, more active momentary interaction with Anna (in this case, looking in the mirror). This active stance may well have allowed me to be a fuller, richer presence in the room with Anna, and perhaps as well to be added to the broader, albeit less comfortable, range of thoughts that followed.

Ultimately, with Anna, I wondered openly about the role of competition in our relationship. What surfaced was a fierce rivalry that I think has underlined our work together over the years—a competition that had not been allowed consciousness in either of us. It was too nasty, too dirty, too unprofessional—and yet so transparently there when I allowed myself to look. Indeed, it became apparent that when facing the mirror, Anna was making me look not just at her "fat" but at her beauty. Her leggy, slim, exotic presence could not be disguised by any mirror.

What was important about these examples of looking was that I was indeed daring to look, both at Anna and myself. By daring to challenge the conventional restrictions imposed in the analytic frame, by daring to react openly and actively with Anna, our previously sterilized confinement was smashed. The more aggressive parts of me were more present, reacting to the parts of Anna that were often kept out of both of our awarenesses, and expressed through Anna's disordered eating. Only then could the link between action and reflection begin to take shape.

The treatment has since unfolded with a broader and more eclectic twisting and turning of affect and experience. The bulimia has been out of the picture for the last two years, and Anna's enriching and now significant relationship with her boyfriend endures the participation of parts of herself previously confined to the garbage room. Anna, for the moment, is not outside looking in, but inside the rocky, tumultuous realm of living, where actions are inevitable, but thoughtful and quiet consideration of self exists at its side. Will this progress stay steady? Likely not, but the range of possible experiences open to both of us has been significantly broadened. It is this ever-growing possibility of a capacious realm of experience, regardless of momentary behaviors or paralysis, that I believe defines therapeutic growth.

A QUESTION OF SAFETY REVISITED

Crisis is an opportunity for challenge, disruption, and catapulting shifts in ground. A step into the unknown allows for a moment of dare and vulnerability, a moment to disrupt the familiar and allow for change. This change occurs in both the therapist and the patient, as dissociated and/or unformulated parts of each participant emerge in action.

These are potentially dangerous waters, and the ever-present necessity of respecting the patient's boundaries and integrity cannot be emphasized enough. With the eating-disordered population, constraints must be adamantly respected; indeed, these are people exquisitely sensitive to intrusion, abuse, and control. Yet, at the same time, these constraints must be respectfully elbowed and nudged, with, as Hoffman (1998, p. 191) would urge, an ongoing "commitment to the long range goals of the analytic process."

In the treatment of the eating-disordered patient, the spit inevitably is going to fly. Bingeing, vomiting, and starving reemerge with a vengeance. This is not merely a regression or setback, but an opportunity to get to know who and what has just barged into the room. Likely there is more of the patient—and therapist—that needs entry into the treatment. An awareness of such an active use of internal experience and an openness to the use of action itself can allow for a greater play during these moments of symptom exacerbation and chaos, and allow for growth of both the patient and therapist in the treatment arena.

REFERENCES

Barth, F. D. (1998). Affects, language, and psychoanalysis. *Psychoanalytic Dialogues* 8(5):685–705.

Brisman, J. (1992). Bulimia in the late adolescent: an analytic perspective to a behavioral problem. In *Psychotherapies with Children*, ed. J. O'Brien, D. Pilowsky, and O. Lewis, pp. 171–187. Washington, DC: American Psychiatric Press.

——— (1995). Addiction. In *Handbook of Interpersonal Psychoanalysis*, ed. M. Lionells, J. Fiscalini, C. Mann, and D. Stern, pp. 537–552. Hillsdale, NJ: Analytic Press.

———— (1998). When actions speak louder than words: verbal and non-verbal wrangling in the therapeutic arena. *Psychoanalytic Dialogues* 8(5):707–714.

Bromberg, P. (1996). Standing in the spaces: the multiplicity of self and the psychoanalytic relationship. *Contemporary Psychoanalysis* 32:509–536.

———— (1998). *Standing in the Spaces.* Hillsdale, NJ: Analytic Press.

Davies, J. (1996). Dissociation, repression and reality testing in the countertransference. *Psychoanalytic Dialogues* 6(2):189–218.

Davis, W. (1991). Reflections on the boundaries in the psychotherapeutic relationship. In *Psychodynamic Treatment of Anorexia and Bulimia,* ed. C. Johnson, pp. 68–85. New York: Guilford Press.

Hoffman, I. (1998). *Ritual and Spontaneity in the Psychoanalytic Process.* Hillsdale, NJ: Analytic Press.

Levenson, E. (1983). *The Ambiguity of Change: An Inquiry into the Nature of Psychoanalytic Reality.* New York: Basic Books.

Mitchell, S. (1993). *Hope and Dread in Psychoanalysis.* New York: Basic Books.

Slavin, O. (1996). Is one self enough? Multiplicity in self-organization and the capacity to negotiate relational conflict. *Contemporary Psychoanalysis* 32(4):615–625.

5

Out of Body, Out of Mind, Out of Danger: Some Reflections on Shame, Dissociation, and Eating Disorders

Philip M. Bromberg

There is an animal—a strange looking sea creature called a holothurian—that is best known for its disconcerting ability when attacked, to divide itself into unlinked parts and regenerate from that which escapes death. "*Non omnis moriar*—I shall not wholly die!" Consider the following brief excerpt from a poem written by a woman in her late seventies who was awarded the 1996 Nobel prize for literature, the Polish poet Wislawa Szymborska. The title of the poem, "Autotomy," is the biological term for this capacity of certain living things to give up wholeness to preserve life.

In danger the holothurian splits itself in two:
it offers one self to be devoured by the world
and in its second self escapes.

In the middle of the holothurian's body a chasm opens
and its edges immediately become alien to each other.

On the one edge, death, on the other, life.
Here despair, there, hope.

To die as much as necessary, without overstepping
the bounds.
To grow again from a salvaged remnant.

Here a heavy heart, there *non omnis moriar,*
three little words only, like three little plumes ascending.

Wislawa Szymborska[1]
From "Autotomy" (1983)

"I shall not wholly die!" With these words in mind, now
contemplate a piece of advice offered over 140 years ago by George
MacDonald (1858), a Scottish clergyman and author whom C. S.
Lewis acknowledged as the primary source from which his own
capacity to bridge fantasy and reality was shaped. MacDonald wrote,
"The best way to manage some kinds of painful thoughts is to dare
them to do their worst, to let them lie and gnaw at your heart till
they are tired, and you find you still have a residue of life they
cannot kill" (p. 55). His words sometimes come to my own mind at
moments with certain patients when hope seems far away indeed.
But all too often it's just too damned hard to do what MacDonald is
proposing. It's hard even for those of us who haven't been seriously
traumatized as children. But for those who have, trying to hold
painful affects, letting them "gnaw away at your heart till they are
tired," and surviving it without dissociating, is an outright impossibility.

Laurie, age 26, had been obese as a child and became
bulimic during adolescence, at which point she shed most of
her weight, and for a brief period became anorectic. At the
point I first met her she appeared slightly underweight but not
anorectically thin. Her older sister, who was also obese as a
child, remained that way, never having developed a bulimic

---

1. The author wishes to thank Marcel Hudon for bringing Wislawa Szymborska's
writing to his attention.

solution. She became for Laurie the apotheosis of greed—an object of contempt and a constant reminder to Laurie of who she was *not*. Laurie entered treatment with a variety of symptoms along with the eating disorder. Some were classically dissociative, such as fugue states manifested in such things as her history of "forgotten" appointments, not going to class, not coming to work—all without awareness. She also suffered from flashbacks, traumatic nightmares, and a body experience that was sometimes blurred and always unstable. She would frequently start sessions by asking me either "What do I look like today?" or "Do you think I look different from last time?" She was also prone to sudden state shifts during sessions, preceded by attentional disturbances in which she seemed to "disappear" from whatever interaction was taking place between us. She also presented with other symptoms, less classically dissociative, but often found to accompany the former. The major ones were migraine headaches so severe that they could virtually incapacitate her, and compulsive hair twirling leading to a hair-pulling habit since age 14, at which age she also developed amenorrhea that lasted until she left home at age 20. The bingeing and hair pulling had both been described by her as reducing tension because they "make my mind a blank."

On this particular day she began her session, as she frequently did, sitting silently and staring, trancelike, into space. She then began to talk blandly and without affect about having pulled out her hair the night before. "I discovered I haven't stopped. *You* thought I had." As I listened to her I became aware of my own feelings—an odd blend of apathy and irritation. I might have ignored it and just launched into another dead-end inquiry about the details of what led to the hair pulling, except that I noticed her sitting back contentedly like someone settling in to watch a movie. I commented on this and her response was to remember a dream she had the night before about being at her sister's birthday party that was taking place in an insane asylum. "There was a big gooey birthday cake—my sister loves cake; I hate it—and she's getting mad at me because I don't want any. I finally start yelling at her to 'shove it.' I woke up just as I had my face up against hers, screaming, 'I don't have that body, it's yours, not *mine*, you pig!' "

I asked her what thoughts she had about the dream and she said in an offhand manner, "None! I don't like to come up with ideas. I'd rather wait for *you* to have some. That way I can either agree or disagree and I don't have to risk being wrong." There was a look in her eye as she spoke that made me feel she was trying to pull me into a battle. But unlike earlier in the session, I could vaguely sense she was conscious of what was going on between us at least to some extent, and contrary to the apathy and irritation I was feeling earlier, I was not put off by her manner this time. In fact, I was feeling kind of playful, and found myself saying to her:

Actually, what you usually do is agree *and* disagree at the same time, so I never can really be sure what you feel. It's like I slave over a hot couch all week [she in fact sits up, but she got the point]. I cook you my best interpretations. Do you eat them? No! You taste a piece here, a piece there. I throw out three quarters of what I cook. There are starving patients in Europe who would be grateful for what I throw away that you don't eat.

She began to laugh, and I could feel the atmosphere shift—lending some support to Michael Lewis's (1992) observation that laughter is a mechanism by which shame can be reduced or eliminated. "Laughter," Lewis says, "especially laughter around one's transgression as it occurs in a social context, provides the opportunity for the transgressing person to join others in viewing the self. In this way, the self metaphorically moves from the site of the shame to the site of observing the shame with the other" (p. 130). In my own preferred idiom (since I don't see the shift as metaphorical), it allows more of one's selves to get into the act. A part of her that was lively, animated, and almost enthusiastic was now clearly participating.

I said to her that at this stage of our work the odds of each of us being wrong were pretty high because there's so much we don't know yet. But the odds get better when we compare notes about what each of us are feeling about what we are doing. It reduces the amount of guessing. After a moment of silence she replied, "I think the insane asylum was your office. Sometimes I feel you want to make me fat like my sister. All these interesting things you say to me make me afraid to hear more. Yeah, I guess I was sitting back like I was getting ready to take in a great movie—like a great meal I could have without getting fat because I didn't even know I was eating it. I think I know what made me start pulling my hair out again." She then described an event that took place two days before this session. "I was walking to a restaurant with my father and he holds my hand in this weird way—he won't let go. I had to pretend I was fixing my hair to remove my hand." This was her first concrete association that could potentially shed some light on the hair-twirling/pulling behavior. Then, suddenly, in the voice of a preadolescent child, "He never touches Mommy that way. I wonder some times if people who see us think I shrunk."

"Who would they see?" I ask her.

Now back in the other voice, "They'd see a 10-year-old girl walking with her father. My husband lives with her most of the time. Most of the time he likes it. But he doesn't like it when I change. He says, 'Why do you have to be different people on different days?' "

"Well, I'm glad I had a chance to meet her," I reply, "even if it was only very briefly."

"Yes," she said pointedly. "She went away again as soon as you asked me to *tell* you about her." A bit dazed as the hour approached the end, I mumbled what I hoped would be a supportive response and a "good" note on which to stop: "Maybe if I talk to her more directly she will stay longer. Do you think so?"

Naively anticipating that this would be our "marker" for next time, I was shocked when she ignored what I thought were my obvious cues that the time was up, and she began what felt like a nonstop monologue. She began to talk about how afraid she is of offending people who she secretly scoffs at—people who think that what they say matters to her when it really doesn't. "It's so strange," she went on, "even though some people don't seem to get angry about it. I crash when it's over. I'll go home and binge and vomit."

I felt paralyzed at this point. Even though I felt she was talking about us and about what it feels like for her after she leaves sessions, I also wanted to end the session. I kept hoping that if I gave her just a little more time I would think of the "right" thing to say, so I let her go on . . . and on . . . and on . . . hoping that if I didn't stop her before she stopped herself it would end in the "right" way. Well, I finally abandoned that hope and stopped her ten minutes past the end of the hour.

She said, sounding a bit miffed, "I haven't finished yet." I replied, probably sounding a bit contrite, "I know, but our time is up for today and I'd love for us to have a moment to reflect on what just happened here. She retorted, "I never reflect on what I'm saying when I'm like this." I answered, now a bit more composed, "But later when you get home, a different part of you does think about it—all alone. And then you decide you were horrible and end up binging and vomiting." At that moment something clicked into place for me, and I added, "But in a funny way you only did what I asked you to do, didn't you? Remember when I said, 'Maybe if I talk to *her* more directly she'll stay longer?' I just didn't expect it to happen *now*! But why wouldn't it?" And then, shifting realities, "After all, you were just being you. 'Longer' means until *you've* finished, right?" She, stood up, grinned and left. I breathed a grateful sigh of relief.

Tronick and Weinberg (1997), in a seminal paper on research into affective regulation and what they call the architecture of mother–infant interactions, emphasize how disruptions in the mutual regulatory process create a break in the development of intersubjectivity. In the face of chronic failure to repair the interactions, the infant is unable to achieve social connectedness, and develops dysregulated affective states that he or she is unable to control. An early coping style begins to develop in which most of the infant's activity is enlisted into stabilizing out-of-control affect. Most significant is Tronick and Weinberg's conclusion:

> *Reparation* of interactive errors is the critical process of normal interactions that is related to developmental outcome *rather than synchrony or positive affect per se.* That is, reparation, its experience and extent, is the "social-interactive mechanism" that affects the infant's development . . . [because] the infant develops a representation of him- or herself as effective, of his or her interactions as positive and reparable, and of the caretaker as reliable and trustworthy. [pp. 65–66, italics added]

Much adult psychopathology may thus be the end result of prolonged necessity in infancy to control physiological and affective states without an experience of human relatedness *and its potential for reparation* that mediates it. With regard to those individuals for whom this state of affairs leads to an eating disorder, Harold Boris (1984, 1986) offers the view that eating disorders arise when the dysregulation of desire is linked in infancy with the dysregulation of appetite. This leads to what he calls an unevolved state of mind in which one wishes and hopes to have everything all of the time—a state of mind that is labeled, in the vernacular, "greed." Greed is a state that attempts to eliminate the potential for traumatic rupture in human relatedness by replacing relationship with food—a solution that is largely self-contained and thus not subject to betrayal by the "other." But it is by no means a perfect solution. The particular problem with greed is that its presence is inevitably tarnished by the existence of *choice* and the shadowy pressure of the need to make one. The realization of the need for choice, Boris writes, either stimulates a refusal to endure it, leading to the decay of appetite

* scientific study of mental disorders, inc. genetic, biological, psychological + social causes.

back into greed and an experience of vast frustration, or stimulates the making of the choice, leading to the satisfaction of appetite but always accompanied by the feeling of profound loss—loss of the thing not chosen. In Boris's words, "Appetite . . . makes manifest the infant's first encounter with actuality and, as such, makes actual experience for the first time a player in the process. The quality of the appetitive experience will now play a role in whether the feeling of loss is modulated by compensatory and consoling experience—or is not" (1986, pp. 48–49).

Boris is saying, in other words, that the essence of the human condition is having to recognize one's insufficiency, and that the degree to which one draws satisfaction from human relatedness will keep him from seeking nonhuman solutions (such as food) as a means of compensating for the experience of loss. For some people, because the recognition of insufficiency is unbearable, choice becomes unbearable, and in the infant who later in life develops an eating disorder, the capacity to make a choice is impaired because the experience of loss connected to appetite is not modulated by the compensation and consolation of human relatedness. That is, what in adulthood could develop into appetite and healthy, *regulatable* desire, because it is denied the relational context upon which that transformation depends, freezes the experience of being an affectively out-of-control infant, within a dissociated self state that takes on an imperious life of its own. The person who eventually shows up at the therapist's office, no matter how she chooses to define her presenting problem, is someone whose real problem is that she is totally at the mercy of her own feelings, someone who is enslaved by her felt inability to contain desire as a regulatable affect. The renunciation of desire is what we see as the hallmark of anorexia and, in a different way, of bulimia. But at its core, it is a loss of faith in the reliability of human relatedness.

I have found that in patients with eating disorders, the transmutation of desire into renunciation is most frequently mediated through the mechanism of dissociation. Sands (1994) suggests, "Dissociative defenses serve to *regulate* relatedness to others. . . . The dissociative patient is attempting to stay enough in relationship with the human environment to survive the present while, at the same time, keeping the needs for more initimate relatedness sequestered but alive" (p. 149). In other words, dissociative defenses are not designed simply as an impermeable suit of armor. No matter how walled-off the patient may be from intimate contact with others, the broadest purpose of a dissociative mental structure, including its place in most eating disorders, is not just insularity but regulation. It is above all else a *dynamic* mental organization designed for affective self-regulation—a mental structure tailored to anticipate trauma, but sufficiently permeable to be a potential doorway to therapeutic growth. Its insularity reflects the necessity to remain ready for danger at all times so it can never—as with the original traumatic experiences—arrive unanticipated; its *permeability* reflects a capacity for authentic but highly regulated exchange with the outside world and similarly regulated spontaneity of self-experience (Bromberg 1995). Let me put it in the words of a patient who did *not* have an eating disorder:

> When I was little and I got scared—scared because Mommy was going to beat me up, I'd stare at a crack in the ceiling or a spider web on a pane of glass—and pretty soon I'd go into this place where everything was kind of foggy and far away, and I was far away too, and safe. At first, I had to stare real hard to get to this safe place. But then one day Mommy was really beating on me and without even trying I was there, and I wasn't afraid of her. I knew she was punching me, and I could hear her calling me names, but it didn't hurt and I didn't care. After that, anytime I was scared, I'd suddenly find myself there. Out of danger and peaceful. I've never told anybody about it, not even Daddy. I was afraid to because I was afraid that if other people knew about it, the place might go away, and I wouldn't be able to get there when I really needed to.

As treatment progresses, a patient will often reveal the existence of an inner life dominated by a never-ending war between parts of the self, each denouncing the other around the issue of appetite

and desire—a war that more often than not manifests itself experi-
entially through the presence of internal voices, often sadistic and
unrelenting, that the patient desperately needs to still by finding
ways to give each some of what it wants. And the war between self
states never ends, because desire, as Boris writes, is undeniable and
durable, and for someone with an eating disorder it means that
everything else is obliterated.

How does this get expressed in treatment and how does it relate
to dissociation? Kathryn Zerbe (1993) writes, "Perhaps one test of
the integration of self comes from how consciously we hold varying
perspectives of ourselves and other people in full awareness from
moment to moment. The more easily we do this, the better we seem
to know ourselves and the more we experience self-cohesion" (p.
320). She goes on to say, "Given the frequency with which dissociative states and eating disorders may occur together, it behooves
clinicians to keep an open eye to making both diagnoses if one or
the other is found" (p. 321).

In bulimia, for instance, bingeing is by and large done in a
dissociated (not-me) state. John Muller (1996) states that such
patients "are attempting to set a marker at the edge of the self so
that they can experience a limit and not become fragmented in a
diffuse unnamable scatter" (p. 85). This purpose could not be
served if the bulimic were fully conscious because it would be a
self-experience that was being done *by me to me*, and thereby useless
in its ability to ward off autonomic hyperarousal of affect. The
trance state allows separate islands of reality to come into being
when the illusion of unity is too dangerous to be maintained. But
this protection comes at a huge price. It forces the self into a
dissociative structure that rigidifies what can be experienced as "me"
at any given moment, and creates a solution that then becomes its
own problem. It is in fact a perfect example of what I meant when
I wrote elsewhere (Bromberg 1996) that we do not treat patients "to
cure them of something that was done to them in the past; rather,
we are trying to cure them of what they still do to themselves and
to others in order to *cope* with what was done to them in the past"
(p. 237).

But the term eating *disorder* can become a real handicap to therapy if it is embraced unreflectively by the therapist as simply a handicap to the patient The therapist must simultaneously recognize and respect as an achievement the means by which a patient has constructed her eating disorder by finding ways to preserve its dissociative structure, and thereby give each part of self *some* of what it wants without unbearable conflict.

The therapist's own dissociative processes enter the picture in this context. If the patient's eating behavior is held by the therapist for too long a time as simply a piece of pathology to get rid of (and the patient, of course, makes it very easy for us to hold that view), nothing much changes, and what we have come to call "resistance" starts to fill up all the space. It becomes very easy to grow to hate the patient's eating disorder, and then without recognizing it, to hate that part of yourself that is trying but failing to cure it. The therapist begins to feel victimized by his own desire, and then feels the patient's pathology as an adversary. The mortal enemy of an eating-disordered patient, as Boris cogently observed, is desire. Because she does not wish to want, her solution is to stimulate desire in the *other*, to become object not subject—she wishes to be the object of other's wants. Where this leads in treatment is to a situation with which we are all painfully familiar. The patient–therapist relationship is pulled into the patient's internal drama that has become a substitute for living. The war over who shall hold the desire is externalized as an interpersonal war and fought out dissociatively, calling into play a constantly shifting array of the patient's and therapist's self states. It is a war that, in one respect, the therapist has to lose in order to win. A transitional reality has to be constructed in which trust in human relatedness begins to become possible, and this can happen only through the therapist's surrender to his own dissociated self-experience.

Not so simple! And especially not so simple at those moments when reality feels like a kaleidoscope. For example, after a session that seemingly went well, a depressed patient with a long-standing eating disorder leaves a message on my answering machine late that night: "Memories are beginning to come up that I've never had before and it's very disturbing. It's like I'm watching them from a different part of my brain," she says. "It's very weird." Her voice sounds upset, but not in a panic.

Next morning, someone I hardly recognize appears for her hour, and growls menacingly:

I'm the one you need to ask the permission from! Who do you think is going to pay the rent if you keep going the way you are going? You said that I would be able to carry on with my life and my work if we agreed to do this therapy. This is bullshit! There is nothing to be gained from this; this work changes nothing, it's expensive and a waste of time.

You remind her of how alone she is, how alone she has always been, and this is supposed to be of help? She's nothing but a fat, ugly, poor kid in pain, and she has suffered enough! I won't let her suffer anymore! She knows that no one will support her if I don't. Not even the shrink will be there if the bills don't get paid. WHO DO YOU THINK PAYS THE BILLS ANYWAY???"

I won't allow this! I will *not* allow this! I WILL NOT ALLOW THIS!!! As long as you threaten to disable me I will not allow this. I am not nice and I don't care what you think of me.

As an example of working with state-change phenomena this incident is not as dramatic as it may sound. I selected it because it puts into high relief the point made by Gerald Stechler (1998) that "the possibility of the emergence of new states and new organizations arising during times of disregulation and apparent disorganization or chaos, has become one of the hallmark principles of contemporary theories of self-organizing systems" (p. 8).

In therapy, it is almost entirely a renegotiation to try to facilitate the creation of new organizations and new states. [p. 10] . . . Whether that new state will be a richer, more complex, and more appropriate foundation for further development, or will be the less advantageous choice in the sense of narrowing via toxic adaptation, may depend on whether the partner in this self-organizing system biases it in one direction or the other. The more toxic adaptation can stem from an interactional partner who reacts as if his destabilization is toxic to him. That is, if the therapist's . . . primary aim is to reduce his own destabilization and its accompanying anxiety as if it were toxic and intolerable, it will bias the partner's choice in the same direction [pp. 16–17]. If the therapist can stay connected with his own and with the patient's destabilization, and can bias his own subsequent state choice towards openness and affective authenticity, then the patient's will be similarly biased. If the patient feels the freezing or the pretense of the therapist at those critical moments, the work of the therapy cannot proceed well [p. 17].

What Stechler calls openness and affective authenticity requires an abiding respect not only for a patient's autonomy, but also for what might be called, more poetically, a patient's autotomy—the dissociative unlinking of parts of the self in the face of potential trauma so that "*non omnis moriar*—I shall not wholly die."

REFERENCES

Boris, H. N. (1984). The problem of anorexia nervosa. *International Journal of Psycho-Analysis* 65:315–322.

———— (1986). The "other" breast: greed, envy, spite and revenge. *Contemporary Psychoanalysis* 22:45–59.

Bromberg, P. M. (1995). Psychoanalysis, dissociation, and personality organization. In *Standing in the Spaces: Essays on Clinical Process, Trauma and Dissociation*, pp. 189–204. Hillsdale, NJ: Analytic Press, 1998.

———— (1996). Hysteria, dissociation, and cure. In *Standing in the Spaces: Essays on Clinical Process, Trauma and Dissociation*, pp. 223–237. Hillsdale, NJ: Analytic Press, 1998.

Lewis, M. (1992). *Shame: The Exposed Self.* New York: Free Press.

MacDonald, G. (1858). *Phantastes.* Grand Rapids, MI: Wm. B. Eeerdmans, 1981.

Muller, J. P. (1996). *Beyond the Psychoanalytic Dyad.* New York: Routledge.

Sands, S. H. (1994). What is dissociated? *Dissociation* 7:145–152.

Stechler, G. (1998). *Affect, the heart of the matter.* Paper presented at the Paul Russell Symposium, Cambridge, MA, November.

Szymborska, W. (1983). Autotomy. In *Postwar Polish Poetry*, 3rd ed., ed. and trans. C. Milosz, pp. 115–116. Berkeley: University of California Press.

Tronick, E. Z., and Weinberg, M. K. (1997). Depressed mothers and infants: failure to form dyadic states of consciousness. In *Postpartum Depression and Child Development*, ed. L. Murray and P. Cooper, pp. 54–81. New York: Guilford.

Zerbe, K. J. (1993). Selves that starve and suffocate: the continuum of eating disorders and dissociative phenomena. *Bulletin of the Menninger Clinic* 57:319–327.

6

On Preferring Not To:
The Aesthetics of Defiance

Adam Phillips

My title refers to Melville's remarkable story, "Bartleby, The Scrivener: A Story of Wall Street," that was published in 1853. It would be daft to say that Bartleby was a story about eating disorders; but even the most cursory reading of the story makes it more than clear that hungers and compulsions are somehow the metaphorical heart of the matter. It is set in the offices of a law firm, and is rife with the language of appetite. The narrator describes himself as an "eminently safe man" who, oddly like a therapist, says that he seldom loses his temper, and much more seldom indulges in dangerous indignations at wrongs and outrages. When he describes his employees, he gives them telling nicknames—Turkey, Nippers, and Ginger Nut. Nippers, whose name is not as overtly food-like as the others, is described as the "victim of two evil powers—ambition and indigestion" (as I will discuss, I think of eating disorders as a form of ambition). When the narrator first hires Bartleby to join the office, Bartleby did, we are told, "an extraordinary quantity of writing. As if long famishing for something to copy, he seemed to gorge himself on my documents." Bartleby, like a starving man, is hungry for work.

But very soon there are problems, problems that are, I think, akin to the kind of difficulties therapists often have in working with people who are often called anorexics. People who refuse to eat can do something so devastating to the environment—the parents, the therapist, the hospital staff—that they often need to dissociate parts of themselves to manage it. The food refused, often unconsciously, engineers the possibility of a dissociation in the people who try to help. At first the boss takes it for granted, in a commonsensical way, that Bartleby will do the work demanded of him, just as, in a commonsensical way, one might assume that people will eat, simply in order to live, as though food only has a use value and not an exchange value as well, or to feel well. The boss assumes, in other words, that there is a kind of natural order in the office, that people are there because they have agreed to play the game:

> I abruptly called to Bartleby. In my haste and natural expect-
> ancy, I sat with my head bent over the original on my desk, and
> my right hand sideways, and somewhat nervously extended with
> the copy, so that, immediately on emerging from his retreat,
> Bartleby might snatch it and proceed to business without the
> least delay. In this very attitude did I sit when I called to him,
> rapidly stating what it was that I wanted him to do. . . . Imagine
> my surprise, nay, my consternation, when, without moving from
> his privacy, Bartleby, in a singularly mild, firm voice, replied, "I
> would prefer not to."
>   I sat awhile in perfect silence, rallying my stunned faculties.
> Immediately it occurred to me that my words had deceived me,
> or Bartleby had entirely misunderstood my meaning. I repeated
> my request in the clearest tone I could assume; but in quite as
> clear a tone came the previous reply, "I would prefer not
> to." . . . This is very strange, thought I. What had one best do?

Bartleby's refusal, "without moving from his privacy," reminds us that the refusal itself is a way of not moving from a privacy, and indeed might constitute that privacy; and that conclusion, "This is very strange, thought I. What had one best do?" is the refrain, albeit calmly put, of every parent whose child won't eat, and every therapist who works with people who would prefer not to eat. What Melville is fascinating about, and fascinated by, is what Winnicott (1965) would have called "the effect on the environment," the world Bartleby creates around him, by his phrase, the performative utterance, "I would prefer not to."

Winnicott's sense of what he calls "the nuisance value of the symptom" seems pertinent here (p. 126). "Nothing so aggravates an earnest person as a passive resistance," Melville's narrator remarks (on behalf of all parents and therapists).

The second confrontation between the Bartleby and the boss-narrator cannot help, I think, remind the earnest therapist of her forlorn endeavors:

"Why do you refuse?"

"I would prefer not to."

With any other man I should have flown outright into a dreadful passion, scorned all further words, and thrust him ignominiously from my presence. But there was something about Bartleby that not only strangely disarmed me, but, in a wonderful manner, touched and disconcerted me. I began to reason with him. . . .

"I prefer not to," he replied in a flute-like tone. It seemed to me that, while I had been addressing him, he carefully revolved every statement that I made; fully comprehended the meaning; could not gainsay the irresistible conclusion; but, at the same time, some PARAMOUNT CONSIDERATION PRE-VAILED with him to reply as he did.

The narrator concludes, like the exhausted therapist faced with this well-named paramount consideration:

It is not seldom the case that, when a man is browbeaten in some unprecedented and violently unreasonable way, he begins to stagger in his own plainest faith. He begins, as it were, vaguely to surmise that, wonderful as it may be, all the justice and all the reason is on the other side. Accordingly, if any disinterested persons are present, he turns to them for some reinforcement for his own faltering mind.

Psychotherapists treat a great variety of people who, in a great variety of ways, would prefer not to. When treating such patients, do we begin to stagger in our own plainest faith (in our therapeutic beliefs)? Are we able to experience, and to find useful words for, what I call the aesthetics of defiance, and what Melville calls the vague surmise that all the justice and all the reason is on the other side, that the person who refuses to eat is acting honorably, that the person who prefers not to is doing the right thing, the beautiful thing in the light of their own paramount consideration? It is Bartleby who, the narrator observes, "never went to dinner," who is quite literally the hero of the story, in a way in which people who refuse to eat are rarely the heroes and heroines of the case histories written about them.

In the story we find the narrator (who is Bartleby's boss) struggling to, as we say, contain himself; to remain kind, patient and pragmatic. Bartleby's "perverseness," he writes, "seemed ungrateful." In short, the narrator goes through the rigmaroles, the contorted ordeals of the dismayed therapist. After a fascinating meditation on the kinds of suffering in others that kills what he calls pity, he has recourse—again like many a desperate therapist—to something called common sense: "To a sensitive being, pity is not seldom pain. And when at last it is perceived that such pity cannot lead to effectual succor, common sense bids the soul be rid of it." Common sense equals getting rid of what you cannot effectually succor. It becomes, as it sometimes must, a situation in which the sufferer might seem to be driving the helper mad. "I thought to myself," the narrator writes, "surely I must get rid of a demented man, who has already in some degree, turned the tongues, if not the heads of myself and the clerks." As psychotherapy shows us, there are many ways of getting rid of someone (or something), one of which is dissociation. The therapeutic guideline is that what the patient wants to get rid of, the therapist must tolerate, hold, contain, consider, and redescribe. The patient is often puzzled about why the therapist is prepared to do this for him, why, that is, the therapist wants to so starkly suffer for someone else's well-being.

The narrator tries what family therapists call a bit of positive reframing: "I strove to drown my exasperated feelings towards [Bartleby] by benevolently construing his conduct." But *exasperation* is the term that recurs; the narrator refers to his "exasperated connection with . . . this intolerable incubus."

Ultimately Bartleby defies his boss's wish to get rid of him, and so the boss leaves instead; he moves into new offices. Refusing to move even with the arrival of the new tenants, Bartleby is carted off to prison. In one of the last scenes of the story, the narrator goes to visit Bartleby in prison, and finds himself talking to the prison cook, referred to as the "Grub-Man," whose abiding grievance is that Bartleby won't eat, that he "lives without dining."

"Ah, Bartleby! Ah, humanity!" are the famous last words of this great story. Bartleby, the narrator wants us to remember, is one of us, we are one of him. He has needed to live out, at whatever cost, his own personal aesthetic of defiance. "I would prefer not to," one might say, is a sophisticated version of Freud's paradigm for aesthetic/emotional judgment in "On Negation"; it is a spitting out of something. Bartleby dies, the narrator implies, from an obscure form of heroism, from an intransigent commitment to a personal preference. Preferring not to is both the means and the end of his personal ideal.

Therapists might wonder whether, or to what extent, the responses to Bartleby by the people around him were complicit with his predicament. One of the more intriguing aspects of the story is that Melville keeps distinctly unclear the question of what it would be to help or hinder Bartleby. Should he have been persuaded, one way or another, to prefer *to*, should he have been accommodated to, or should he have been, as he was, gotten rid of? In what sense and from which points of view was Bartleby's life a failure or a success? What would a persuasive account be of why it is a good thing not to eat, and of why preferring not to eat would be a good thing to dedicate one's life to? We are familiar with the religious stories about people trying to live what are, in their view, the best lives available to them in their time.

What we call symptoms—of which refusing to eat and being unable to stop eating are stark and frightening examples—I suggest are experiments in living. Children put out probes to their parents, samples of their internal worlds, as rudimentary forms of such experiments. "What kind of mother or father will I have, or create, if I say I'm not going to bed, or say I love my teacher more than my mother, or indeed, if I refuse to eat, or eat too much?" What we think of as eating disorders are elaborated versions of these common childhood scenarios, in addition to whatever else they are. Most children, in my experience, experiment with not eating and tend to get a rather vivid message back from their parents that, in its turn, modifies the experiment. Preferring not to creates a certain kind of relationship, a certain kind of atmosphere; it calls up something powerful, and sometimes almost demonic in the people to whom it is addressed. So one kind of paramount consideration is, "What kind of people will I have on my hands if I prefer not to eat?" And one straightforward answer is: You will be faced with people you would prefer not to talk to, people who are obsessed with food, frantic, bossy, manipulative, defeated, enraged, and concerned— and people, in other words, who might feel so intensely about you that they might have to dissociate some of these feelings in order to psychically survive. So what kind of experiment in living, what kind of ambition, from a psychoanalytic point of view, is refusing to eat? What constitutes a paramount consideration such that people might die for it, rather like they might die for their country or for their child? As Melville's narrator found, and as many a therapist has found, starting to reason with people who prefer not to has an ironic effect, because the other thing they prefer not to do is what is called reason. Indeed nothing exposes our fantasies of reasonableness than the refusal to eat. It explodes the categories of good sense.

When Freud described sexuality in the *Three Essays* as leaning on nutrition, he provided us with useful analogies and disanalogies between nourishment and sexuality; each can and can't be used to redescribe the other. Just as it became apparent to Freud that sexuality was sexual disorder, we might say something similar about eating. What would it be not to have an eating disorder? Who do we think of as being a normal eater, and what do our criteria, on reflection, seem to be for this reassuring assessment? These kinds of questions seem particularly pertinent in relation to eating because hunger as an appetite tends to make us essentialists, and tends to make us revert to biology. A person has to have a certain amount and quality of food in order to survive; the same thing could not be said, in the same way, about sexuality. When faced with behavior at the more extreme end of the so-called sexual perversions, we call the police; when faced with behavior at the more extreme end of the so-called eating disorders, we put people in the hospital. In the case of sexuality we are forcing people to behave themselves; in the case of self-starvation we are forcing people to survive themselves. Long-term work with people who starve themselves is an opportunity to think about what makes life worth living, and what might be worth dying for. It is for the therapist, and occasionally for the patient, a particularly grueling kind of moral education. It makes one wonder, in short, what a paramount consideration is, and why it might be worth having.

Working with anorexics is a graveyard for the more zealous forms of psychotherapeutic optimism. Therefore, it would seem to me to be rather promising ground, if one can be bothered to bare it.

The only sense in which I balked at Jean Petrucelli's invitation to write this chapter was that I have a temperamental aversion to diagnostic categories. I prefer not to; partly for old sixties-style ideological reasons, which I still believe in; but also, and more pressingly, I never seem to have acquired what people call clinical experience; if by that they mean a kind of accumulating inner archive of types of people which one recognizes and treats accordingly. And this particular issue is, I think, pertinent to the whole question of eating disorders.

The adolescents I have seen with an eating disorder as their designated symptom are exceptionally wary of the therapist's knowingness. After all, nothing could be more omniscient than the claim to know about someone else's appetite. In my many years of doing child psychotherapy, all sorts of so-called eating disorders, as peripheral or prominent symptoms, have been prevalent in the children I have seen. Perhaps unsurprisingly, it is my impression that most children have some kind of eating difficulty as they grow up, and this is pertinent to the more extreme predicaments of treating eating disorders. It is that continuum that I have in mind when I see people who are diagnosed as having eating disorders.

Chloe was referred to me because her parents, who had been divorced since she was 10, were concerned about her weight loss. She was 15, and so thin that others were worried about her, although she was not worried about herself at all. She told me that people eat far too much in the West, that she liked being "lithe and boyish," and she didn't want to come and see people like me who just "force feed people with their own weird ideas."

"Lithe?" I said.

She said, "You know . . . thin. You're lying if you don't know what that means."

I said, "What's lying got to do with eating," full, as usual, of good intentions. And then there was my first experience of the leaden silence that was to be the climate of many grueling sessions. She simply sat there practicing the great adolescent art of making the so-called adults feel stupefyingly redundant. After this brief interchange in the first session, which set the pattern, we settled into that most unpromising venture— enforced psychotherapy, the truly impossible profession. Her parents had given her a choice: me or the hospital. I had told them, and indeed her, my misgivings about this, but I suggested that we would see what, if anything, was possible. Chloe and I would meet for six sessions and then review it. One detail in her history that the parents recounted had struck me as both interesting and hopeful—that she had first, as her mother put it, "got difficult with eating" when her brother was born, when she was 6, and she had resumed eating normally again a year and a half later, after having a tonsillectomy. She came out of the anesthesia, her mother told me, and asked for strawberry ice cream, and, "I knew she was all right again." She ate normally for several years, until soon after she started menstruating at age 13. It was then that she had become "superpicky" about food, and was unable to eat what parents call proper meals. As a middle-class modern adolescent, Chloe knew, as she put it, "everything about anorexia. There's nothing you can tell me." I said, "So I have got nothing you want, either."

"Correct," she said, and the silence descended. Of course, if she would rather not eat, she also would rather not talk about not eating. Like Bartleby's boss, I went through my repertoire of silence, ingenuity, exasperation, patient kindness, impatient kindness, unkind patience, and so on. I reflected out loud, as one does, about the links, if any, between what I was thinking and feeling and what might be important to her. She was really very patient with me as I did my best, that sometimes terrible thing one is prone to do. But in this sparse and mostly unpromising encounter there were a few minutes in one session when we had a good conversation—when we wanted something from each other in a way that made us forget that that was what we were doing. There was, in other words, some mutual appetite that dissolved self-consciousness. I had been musing aloud, in a slightly fraught way, about what her mother had told me about the tonsillectomy: "I've been wondering whether you started eating again after that operation because the operation felt like a punishment you deserved." Usual silence, but she shuffled in the chair and rubbed her eye. So I carried on. "I imagine it something like this; when your brother turned up you were so upset you started hating your parents by not eating, or maybe it was a competitive thing, the baby was the best eater so you'd be the best noneater. Anyway, there was something that made you feel really bad, so you felt like a criminal who deserved a punishment, who went looking for one. And that's what the operation was like—you'd had your punishment and now you could go back to ordinary life, to eating. It's something to do with punishment." There was brief, but lighter silence, and she said, "Why do you put up with this?"

I said, "With what?"

"With me sitting in silence."

I said, "That's a very good question, why *would* anyone put up with this, what's the point? It's punishment."

She said, "Why don't you think about that for a change?" And that was the end of the session. She had made me think in a way that was quite unlike the dissociated, therapeutically intent so-called thinking I had been doing in and between the sessions.

The next day her mother telephoned to tell me that she and her ex-husband had decided that they were withdrawing her from treatment because the therapy wasn't making any difference. They were undissaudable, and I never saw Chloe again.

This termination may or may not have been linked to what seemed to me to be a minor breakthrough, and, as we know, families are acutely sensitive and responsive systems. But in actuality I do not know why that moment was chosen to stop whatever was or wasn't happening in the therapy. What I do know is that Chloe had left me "food" for thought.

In psychotherapy, as in ordinary conversation, the links between what one person says to another and what that other person then responds are obscure. It is possible, though, that something in what I had said in my musing had called up a thought in Chloe about her punishing me and others, her seeking punishment, and, most interesting to me, my seeking or accepting punishment from her. Taking a certain common therapeutic position vis-à-vis the patient—that is, accepting projections, containing them, and feeding them back—shows a strange willingness to suffer. What is being modeled, to use the old family therapy term, is a form of self-sacrifice, and this sacrifice that therapists routinely go through, and are trained for, requires, I suggest, a dissociation to make it possible. If one wanted to describe in short-hand what has to be dissociated—

what I was unwittingly dissociating with Chloe—it is, paradoxically, appetite. As Chloe's therapist I had a problem with my appetite—I couldn't bring it into play. To put it at its most extreme; the therapist humiliates the patient if he allows the patient to humiliate him.

At two developmental crises in her life—the birth of her brother and adolescence—Chloe had come up with the solution of not eating as an experiment in living; this evoked in the people around her a kind of exasperated collusion. They had to dissociate to manage their rage, and this meant that Chloe was abandoned by real people and left with ghosts. So the people around her, including me, became cross and helpful, but never really hungry enough. Just as with Bartleby, everyone's appetite failed him, including his own.

It is perhaps an interesting and obvious question to ask about clinical work: Which versions or parts of oneself does one feel under pressure to disown in the presence of any particular patient? Which parts of oneself need to be sacrificed—or at its most extreme, dissociated—in order to sustain a relationship with a particular patient? With Chloe I had to struggle neither to be a person obsessed with appetite, nor a person oblivious to my own appetite as a way of fostering hers. "The anorexic," the Lacanian analyst Nasio (1998) writes, "seems to be saying, 'No, I do not want to eat, because I do not want to be satisfied, and I do not want to be satisfied because I want my desire to remain intact—and not only my desire but that, as well, of my mother'" (p. 87). Anorexia is a cry against all satisfaction and an obstinate maintenance of the general state of "insatisfaction" (p. 87). In this version the anorexic is so in love with her hunger that she must not violate it by eating. What Nasio points out is that it is part of the idealization of appetite to refuse appetite, as though the anorexic is asking a profound and paradoxical question: How does one keep appetite pure? But what interferes with hunger is eating. My guess is that the wish to purify appetite is reactive to, or a consequence of, something already having been done to a person's appetite, that the refusal of appetite is a belated attempt to restore the viability of appetite.

There must be as many distortions of appetite as there are individual people; indeed the word *distortion* is misleading because it implies some kind of basic norm. But I propose, by way of a conclusion, that something can be done to one's hunger that is akin to what we call sexualization.

In some kinds of sexualization it is as though something traumatic is evoked by an object, and this is unconsciously transformed into sexual fantasy and desire as a form of self-cure. Perhaps something comparable is sometimes done by people with an eating disorder, but they have not sexualized the occasion or the relationship; they have, for want of a better word, appetized it. It has been translated into a question about eating and being eaten, about digesting and being digested. The need then to appetize trauma becomes, as in Bartleby's case, voracious. A world is created in which nothing can be eaten, nothing must be taken in.

In sexualization the person turns the trauma occasioned by the object—and desire for the object—into a scenario of sexual excitement, or sexual nullity. The person with an eating disorder appetizes the trauma occasioned by the object into a scenario of bingeing or refusal. Anyone who prefers not to, once very definitely preferred to; and it got them into trouble. And it is this trouble that we always end up talking about.

REFERENCES

Freud, S. (1925). On Negation. In *Standard Edition*. Vol. 19.
——— (1905). Three Essays on the Theory of Sexuality. In *Standard Edition*. Vol. 7.
Nasio, J. (1998). *Five Lessons on the Psychoanalytic Theory of Jacques Lacan*. Translated by David Pettigrew and Francois Raffoul. State University of New York, Albany.
Winnicott, C., Shepherd, R., and Davis, M., eds. (1985). *Deprivation and Delinquency*. New York: Tavistock/Routledge Publications.
Winnicott, D. (1965). *The Maturational Processes and the Facilitating Environment*. London: Hogarth Press.

III

On Being Stuck: Enactments, Mutuality, and Self-Regulation with Eating-Disordered Patients

7

Close Encounters of the Regulatory Kind:* An Interpersonal/Relational Look at Self-Regulation

Jean Petrucelli

*The author wishes to thank Janet Tintner, Psy.D., for her contribution to the title of this paper.

The therapist's sense of being stuck can be pervasive in treating a patient. But then there are moments where everything seems to come together.

My patient, Abby, was describing how she was feeling about her long-distance relationship with her father. She said, "I'm on cruise control and then all of a sudden there are these moments where I totally tune in. When my father brings the conversation to something about him and me, I feel like it grabs me, but I can't seem to sustain it. So it just slips away."

My attention had been drifting, but I felt jolted to seize the moment. "Yes," I told her, "I know just what you're talking about because I often feel like I'm on cruise control with you." In that moment I realized that part of my feeling stuck was also evident in my feeling a lack of motivation and inspiration to write about her. Realizing that I am often metaphorically driving on "automatic" with her, and knowing that in real life I will only drive a "stick" (the line I've always used with my friends is that I always need to have my hands on something), I found myself, in the session, thinking about the shifts in our mutual levels of involvement and how this experience of coasting might be serving some purpose for both of us. Reminding myself of how the use of the stick, while driving, helps me stay fully conscious and alert in the car, I wondered, how does a person who is more used to functioning with a stick work comfortably with a person who is used to functioning on automatic? Where is the precious and valued space that would allow us to be alert and conscious of our relationship while having our own subjective experiences?

I have found that there are powerful moments that often happen spontaneously that jolt us into a heightened state of consciousness or alertness that can set the stage for therapeutic change. By seizing these moments that catch us by surprise, we are offered an opportunity to see something from a new angle, a view we might not have ordinarily seen.

One example of such a moment occurred with Judy, a 34-year-old patient with bulimia and compulsive overeating issues. Judy, who is typically extremely contained and compliant, walked into my office one session, sat down, and with her eyes wide open in shock exclaimed, "Oh my God, what's that on your jacket?" Now, I'm thinking spider, huge water bug, dead mouse, the remains of lunch, until she burst out, "Are you wearing an ice cream cone pin?!!!" In my cool professional analytic stance I replied, "What? Am I wearing a what?"

"That pin . . . you're wearing an ice cream cone pin!" she retorted accusingly.

"No, I'm not," I replied defensively, now really throwing my analytic hat out the window, as I looked down to my turquoise and ruby stoned silver pin from Mexico. Within seconds she had leapt from her chair and came within inches of my face to get a closer look. "Oh," she sighed and then started to giggle.

Judy was 8 when her mother hanged herself. Her 3-year-old sister discovered the mother's body in the basement of their home. Judy, when she came home from school that fateful day had gone halfway down the stairs to the basement, called out to her mother, but then turned around and went upstairs instead to the kitchen where she made herself an American cheese sandwich on white bread.

Judy typically keeps a lid on all her feelings of aggression and has a Pollyannaish way about her, in the world and with me. This moment, where she misperceived my pin, caused a flood of aggression in her that allowed the two of us to approach her dissociated feelings of anger toward her mother and her assumption of my "sadistic" tendencies. She showed me the part of her that wanted to devour me as if I were "edible."

There is inevitably a moment I experience with almost all my patients, a kind of close encounter, where they take the risk of asking me this question: "Has anyone ever told you that you look like Cher?" The uniqueness of interaction around this question with each patient reflects the subtleties of components of self-regulation. How, when, and why they choose to ask and how I choose to respond becomes a unique moment with each patient. Some use humor, some check with me if it's okay that they're asking, some feel anxious in asking, some use it as a distancing question, some are very careful, some are convinced they are the first to ask, and one sang, "I Got You, Babe." I've come to think of this question as a diagnostic indicator of the degree of safety in relatedness in the room.

These moments allow us an opportunity to move toward greater shared intimacy where the relational field shifts into a momentary new configuration. Being able to sustain the shift is a far-reaching issue and struggle for all patients, but it is particularly interesting for the eating disordered or addictive patient who struggles with pervasive issues of regulation. This chapter explores some of the back-and-forth process and the moments when "the meeting of the minds" as Aron (1996) puts it, occurs in response to chance encounters with a patient who has difficulties with self-regulation.

Self-regulation can be thought of as the ability to successfully integrate external and internal demands, while at the same time sustaining a feeling of safety, self-continuity, and desire. Difficulties with self-regulation affect one's capacity for relatedness and create anxiety and an instability in one's multiple self-representations that lead to intrapsychic difficulties.

These issues of self-regulation, therefore, have an impact on the therapeutic dyad. The going back and forth within the relationship then becomes an arena for growth and change (Joseph 1989). The therapeutic action is about the negotiation and the interpersonal use of the relationship as a method of mutual and self-regulation. Meeting points between patient and therapist can often occur in a split-second exchange whereby the level of involvement and/or relatedness will shift back and forth between patient and therapist. The work of treatment then becomes a process of redirecting the eating-disordered patient out of the world of food and into the arena of human interaction.

I have been particularly interested in the moments in the relationship when these shifts occur. There is a distinction that can be made between how much work is involved to create these moments and how with some patients these moments occur naturally. Sometimes the patient invites the therapist into a moment. Sometimes the therapist invites the patient. Sometimes these moments just occur by chance.

There are many moments of intimacy between patient and therapist that cannot be adequately conveyed verbally. Words would ruin such moments, and those moments play a very important part in creating the mutative effects of psychoanalysis. But we cannot consciously strive for them. In this way, they share the quality that makes reflective consciousness authentic and, as Donnel Stern (1997) writes, "They must just happen" (p. 77).

These negotiations of patient–therapist boundaries, transferences and countertransferences, or overinvolvement or underinvolvement take on an added dimension when they happen to occur outside the treatment room. When such an encounter occurs, it provides a meeting point between the patient's real life and the patient's life with the therapist. It also allows the patient to see the therapist in a less rigid or one-dimensional way, and perhaps brings the split-off parts of the relationship, and the patient's inner life, into the room. This is particularly powerful when the difficulty in self-regulation that is manifest in every arena in the patient's life forces itself unannounced into the therapeutic relationship.

CASE VIGNETTE

One such example of a chance encounter occurred one spring afternoon with a 27-year-old female patient with a history of bulimia and an ongoing addiction to marijuana and alcohol. This patient, Abby, who I mentioned at the beginning of this chapter, has been in three times a week analysis, on the couch, for the past four years.

Our first chance encounter occurred one year into the treatment. It was a Saturday and I had my two daughters in the car and we had just come from the park. My youngest, age 6 at the time, announced with great urgency, "Mom, I have to go the bathroom now!" Given my daughter's history of waiting until the last possible second, I frantically pulled over to the first available space. Like a madwoman, I raced out of the car with my two daughters in tow and burst into the nail salon in front of me. With desperation in my voice I asked, "Can my daughter please use your bathroom? This is an emergency."

In my black leather fringed jacket with Led Zeppelin written on the back, ripped jeans, and pink high top sneakers, and my daughter holding her crotch with both hands, we were a sorry sight. We barreled through the pedicures and arrived at the bathroom in the back of the salon. All of a sudden, I heard a very calm, "Hi, Jean" only to look up and see my patient Abby. I smiled sheepishly and said, "Hi. When you gotta go, you gotta go." To make matters worse, while in the bathroom my daughter kept asking me, "Who is that, Mom? To which I replied, "Shhh, I'll tell you later." (Big mistake.) Her next question, in a very loud voice was, "Mom, is that one of your patients?" I cringed at the sound of nervous laughter on the other side of the door.

It wasn't until several months later that Abby could begin to process with me that chance encounter. My attempts to address it with her elicited no response other than, "It was fine." "How did you feel seeing me outside of my office?" "Fine." "Did you have any feelings or reactions to seeing me with a child, children, my daughters?" "No." "I was pretty crazed in that moment. It must have stirred up something to see me like that. It's not how you typically see me in the office." "It was fine." "Did you have any feelings about *me* seeing *you* at the nail salon?" "No." Appealing to her sense of fashion, in my frustration I even asked, "What about what I was wearing, any comments, feelings?" "No."

I felt that the chance encounter had overwhelmed her, stuffed her, by exposing her to too much information about my life, and she had quickly needed to purge and numb herself of the experience of having any feelings about me or with me then or in the room. Given that this encounter put more data "out there" in a direct way, my questions were meant to invite Abby to associate to the information presented to her. However, it was a meal that neither party had been invited to. She had not asked to take in or know that information. In that moment I could not claim my privacy by conforming to my professional analyst role. I had not made the choice to disclose the personal details of my life, such as having children, wearing pink high top sneakers, or looking frantic and "untogether." Given that the information had been disclosed, I was prepared to follow through on looking at it openly with Abby. To Abby, that didn't feel safe and the potential sense of safety derived from the agreement that anything can be openly addressed was temporarily suspended.

Persevering and hopeful that this chance encounter might open up avenues for exploration in the therapy, I kept at it with her until one day she revealed to me that she knew why she couldn't talk about the meeting in the nail salon. Having me be real and existing with my own life and experiences brought up strong feelings of loss and the realization that in that moment I am not there for her because I have my own life. She said, "When I saw you with your daughter, I had to face the fact that I wasn't your only child."

The notion of Abby being an only child has historical meanings. Abby has a sister, two years her senior, who outwardly rebelled, got in trouble, and was physically abused by their mother. This occurred mostly after their parents were divorced when Abby was 8 and her sister was 10. Abby's sister became overweight, Abby became bulimic. On the surface, Abby maintained a false self-identity as the "good girl" while behaviors such as enuresis until she was 12, setting a fire in a forest, smoking pot and drinking, crashing her moped when drunk, and stealing girlfriends' boyfriends and having sex with them went unnoticed and unaddressed. Limits and boundaries were never clear or set in a reliable way and deception was the rule.

Abby developed a style of deception and accommodation to the experience of being neglected. She did not reveal to me her addiction to pot and alcohol or the extent of her bulimia until a little over a year into her three times a week treatment. Looking back, there were many sessions where my countertransference response of feeling sleepy, dazed, disconnected, or on "cruise control" went unanalyzed in the sessions. It was clear to me that there was something going on but I didn't know what it was. What I knew was that something just didn't make sense. I couldn't seem to wrap my mind around anything with her. I was clearly caught in an enactment where, looking back now, I, like her mother, was okay with not knowing what was really going on with her. I realized I had also been okay with not knowing what it was I did not know.

Stirred up by this encounter in the nail salon and by the lack of her apparent reaction, I began to address my feelings of discomfort with the discrepancy of reactions between us. I told her that her blasé style now reminded me of how I had often felt in the room with her.

It was shortly after this that Abby came clean and revealed to me the extent of her bulimia, her getting high and drinking every day, and the level of her deception and guilt around it. When I told her how good she was at hiding and that she probably had many more secrets that she had decided she didn't feel safe enough to share with me, she told me not to feel too bad about it, this was something she was *really* good at. I was left feeling a mix of things: I felt foolish, because I had always considered myself very street-smart. How did I miss knowing she was purging and getting high? I felt betrayed, because hadn't I provided a safe-enough environment for her to be able to tell me what was really going on. At the same time, I felt excited, because we had finally found a door that could be opened. She had taken a risk, and I was given an opportunity to be there for her. In exploring this, we came to understand how Abby's bulimia and her getting high served as anesthesia to the more painful feelings of depression, neglect, guilt, and betrayal that she had learned to mask in order to function in the world and in the room with me. Her fear of falling into the bottomless pit of feelings served to keep a feeling of unsafety in the room. But it was this unplanned, chance encounter that somehow allowed what was split off to come in. It felt safer for Abby to be numb than to have a mutually shared experience. To regulate herself, she kept me out and I had stayed out.

Abby and I had a second chance encounter that occurred outside the treatment room. This one led to a different outcome. This time she was riding a bike with her son in the kid's seat and I was driving in my car. She saw me. I didn't see her. I was eating a sandwich while driving. She said she got great pleasure "seeing you stuff your face," and had wondered what kind of sandwich I was eating. This time she said she was saddened that I didn't see her, as she wanted me to see her with her child, being a good mother. It was an interesting response, given her concerns of who's a child, whose child is whose, and who's taking care of whom. She was also able to compare the two chance encounters and was able to admit that a part of her didn't want me to see her as happy with her son. Showing me that she could experience happiness would feel like a loss of my interest in her and a loss of me. Abby told me that she now knew even more clearly why she couldn't talk about the first encounter for so long. "I can now say to you, 'I only have you 45 minutes on Monday, Wednesday, and Thursday.' I want to have more than a therapist in my life."

With both of these encounters Abby had to deal with me "racing about" revealing aspects of my lifestyle that I don't necessarily feel comfortable in revealing. Perhaps it's a parallel process whereby being seen inadvertently in another way allows another part of Abby (e.g., her bulimia or addictive side) to be visible. However, in the face of this, her capacity for self-regulation has increased over time. Externally, symptomatically, the bulimia has stopped. She had several start-stops or slips with getting high until she was able to set a "clean date" and has been drug and alcohol-free for a year and a half. Moving along the spectrum, we then dealt with her brief episode of compulsive shopping. After several $30,000 credit card bills that she could actually easily afford, Abby began to identify for me how her shopping was another vestige of the same difficulty in sitting with the antsyness that her unpleasant feelings evoked. She went through the process of returning many of the unnecessarily purchased items. The act of returning demonstrated for me that there was another level of internal negotiation going on.

At the same time, similarly in our relationship, Abby began to feel less of an intense need for me to be in control of my own self-regulation in order for me to help her with her issues of regulation. My capacity for tolerating my own discomfort when things are revealed that make me feel uncomfortable has also increased.

This was tested most recently with a moment that occurred with Abby, this time in the treatment room. I had been informed that my ground-floor office had been broken into and vandalized. My electronic equipment was stolen and the office was trashed, but fortunately the session notes and patients records were untouched. From home I called my first patient, who happened to be Abby, and left her a message asking if we could please start thirty minutes later than her scheduled time. When I arrived at my office, with a new phone and fax machine in hand, Abby was already sitting in the waiting area, and apparently had not received my message. Seeing me with my hands full, she said, "Here, let me open the door for you." Before I could utter a response, she opened the door to my vandalized office and, as I saw the damage, I gasped, "Oh, shit."

I didn't know which felt worse, seeing my office in such disarray or having my patient see me seeing my office. Abby immediately offered to help me clean up my office. I thanked her for her offer and asked if we could just start 30 minutes later. After surveying the damage I was quite relieved, though I could feel that I was still in shock for most of the session. In the session, Abby spoke as if it were business as usual. Any attempts to elicit anything about her feelings about the break-in were met with, "I'm fine."

The next session she gave me a present. It was a beautiful, leather-bound, handmade journal. She said, "I'm giving it to you with two sessions to go before the holiday break because I know you'll want to talk about the meaning of this." I asked her about her reactions to the break-in and whether or not this gift had anything to do with that (given that we have gone through several holidays without gift giving being an issue).

Abby explained that she had felt good about feeling free enough to offer to help me clean up, and that just opening up the door for me was a positive experience for her. "Positive?" I asked. "Yeah, it made me feel that I could give back to you. And you had a nice attitude about it. So, you know, I went easy with you with the gift." (The reference to going easy referred back to her compulsive shopping days.) Abby then told me, "When you said you had a break-in and I saw the room, it still took me a minute to put it together. Then I thought, maybe you don't want me to see you vulnerable."

I was struck by how much she was compensating for my feeling so upset and violated by making her experience around this so nice and neat and all okay. After all, my office was a mess! I told her I felt she was adapting to what she felt I needed of her, and that I wondered if she was feeling lost in the moment. She said not until she saw the broken clock that she is always mindful of and uses in the sessions. She then said, "Oh, I wish I had bought you a clock instead."

We had one session left before the break and she brought me in another gift, this time in the shape of a dream. She said, "I dreamt about you and it was bizarre. It was very real. I was puking and I wasn't going to tell you I was puking." I guess I was having a lot more feelings than I realized and I never test that there's enough room for people to have shared reactions together. I always feel taken away from when I experience another person's strong feelings because there's no room for them. I take on theirs and hold back mine.

"Yes," I replied, "instead of feeling that shared emotions can add to a feeling of connectedness rather than distance." To which she quipped, "Being true to myself would be like sitting down to a nourishing meal and being able to share and digest good feelings with another." My break-in had led to a momentary breakthrough in Abby's understanding of what happens between us.

I was helping Abby regulate her affect by not forcing her to deal with more than she felt that she could deal with. This gave her the freedom to process some of the affect on her own through the buying of the gift when she left, and also with me when she came back. The gift was a statement of how she could feel for me, which spoke to the level of intensity of feeling in the room. She could still have her privacy but she could also share in the moment with me. For Abby, feelings are like things: there is a finite, too small, and fragile space in which they can be contained, so the strong feelings of another person push out her own feelings. The gift of the journal was rich symbolically as a psychic container—first, as a place where Abby learned how to put her feelings into words rather than project them onto food or shopping, and second, as a place for me to put my feelings.

DISCUSSION

Outwardly, Abby, like other eating-disordered patients, is keenly attuned to the needs of those around her. Abby quickly learned to adapt to what she felt I needed from her. She "behaved" as the good patient, while living a "double life" with me and all around her. For Abby, her work in treatment initially was not an attempt at change but an enactment of an old familiar pattern, where I was enlisted to play along through unacknowledged deception, manipulations, and control (Brisman 1994). She kept her "bad self" out of the room by adapting to what was needed of her and disavowing her potentially disruptive needs or experiences. As Brisman states, "Eating disordered patients focus attention on one piece of business (engaging in the analysis) while, covertly, something else (security, safety, the illusion of being cared for) gets taken from the scene. Inevitably the therapy is on one level gratifying and on another experienced and played out through body torment and destructive eating behaviors" (p. 69).

SUMMARY

To foster an environment for a "closer encounter," one may need to be comfortable working in a way that may feel "alien." It is important to recognize that I am not suggesting this be done by plan or as a technique. It is simply part of the basic interpersonal analytic stance of making full use judiciously of what is already there and not disguising it. Paradoxically, it may be that to help regulate the patient's level of anxiety associated with relatedness and impasses in the transference, the therapist has to go the opposite way—outside in and inside out; specifically, using what occurs on the outside as a way of entering the inside, and using what occurs for the therapist on the inside as a way of understanding what's occurring on the outside. The mutuality of the therapeutic relationship becomes the vehicle for change. The negotiation of safety in relatedness between therapist and patient is done largely on an unconscious basis with safety and disruption not ultimately being at odds with each other.

Eating-disordered patients want help, and yet they don't because moving out of their comfort zone is changing the only sense of security they have known and that is terrifying to them. Being able to move out of the comfort zone and into relative "unsafety" involves learning how to self-regulate both internally and in an interpersonal exchange.

Eating disorders can be thought of as a botched attempt at self-regulation, with the treatment relationship threatening this attempt with inquiry, confrontation, and interpretation. Chance extra-analytic encounters destabilize both patient and therapist, but also seem to open up the dialogue, allowing for more split-off affects to enter into the relationship, even as they threaten the anorexic or bulimic's "safety" in dissociation. And lastly, these things have to "just happen" and sometimes can't even be discussed directly for a long time (if at all); but they still work.

It is for these reasons that the demanding work of therapy with the eating-disordered patient involves the constant interplay between knowing what one is doing and a certain not knowing, a losing one's self in the language and experience of the patient and in the process of the session. Therapists can't approach this group with a locked-in template or they will just eat us up and spit us out.

REFERENCES

Aron, L. (1996). *A Meeting of Minds.* Hillsdale, NJ: Analytic Press.

Brisman, J. (1994). Learning to listen: therapeutic encounters and negotiations in the early stage of treatment. *Eating Disorders* 2(1):69–73.

Joseph, B. (1989). *Psychic Equilibrium and Psychic Change,* ed. M. Feldman and E. B. Spillius. London: Routledge.

Stern, D. (1997). *Unformulated Experience: From Dissociation to Imagination in Psychoanalysis.* Hillsdale, NJ: Analytic Press.

8

"No Matter How Hard I Try, I Can't Get through to You!"

Dissociated Affect in a Stalled Enactment

Frances Sommer Anderson

This chapter presents the care of an eating-disordered patient, focusing on stalled enactments. I begin by elaborating a pervasive, immobilizing enactment, which I refer to as "No matter how hard I try, I can't get through to you!" I then describe the floods, eruptions, and stagnant states that characterize the therapy's seventeen years of mutual and self-regulatory processes. I conclude with a recent session that illustrates a shift in the enactment.

I've been watching Marilyn get fatter and fatter. She's 5′4″", weighs 287 pounds, and wears size 24. In the last two years, her body has become so cumbersome that she needs the arms of a chair to help her sit and stand. Marilyn has been battling insatiable hunger and obesity since her early 20s. She's 55 now. When she came to see me seventeen years ago because of back pain, wearing size 14, she wistfully remembered getting down to size 8 several years earlier—that's still her benchmark.

Our accomplishments over these seventeen years seem outweighed by Marilyn's inability to regulate her eating and maintain a healthy weight. In addition to our work, she's reached out to familiar external regulators of quality and quantity—Weight Watchers, Jenny Craig, and even the lure of Fen-Phen. Eight years ago, bolstered by enthusiastic encouragement from a back pain therapy group I run, she lost more than seventy-five pounds and kept it off until the group ended, six years ago.

Since then, she has slowly, steadily gained weight, to everyone's dismay—even her family members, who are all considerably overweight. I've often felt like the self-righteous Spartan Food Police, envisioning clogged coronary and carotid arteries, as Marilyn describes a typical meal—stacks of juicy barbecued ribs glistening with fat, a couple of baked potatoes with globs of butter and drifts of sour cream, corn on the cob with more butter, and cheesecake and cannolis for dessert. The truth is—I eat ribs at Hog Pit Barbeque and savor a chopped liver and pastrami sandwich at the Carnegie Deli. BUT, I've said to myself smugly and reassuringly, at least I TRY not to go to those places REGULARLY!

I conceptualize Marilyn's binge eating and musculoskeletal pain as attempts to regulate affects associated with a life permeated with losses. In our first session, I learned that her musculoskeletal pain began a month after she'd begun living alone because her roommate, a close friend of many years, had become pregnant—out of wedlock—and needed to move into a larger space. Marilyn had dissociated feeling rejected, abandoned, envious, and enraged about losing her friend to the new baby, just as she'd dissociated when she lost her special place as her mother's favorite companion at age 7 when her brother was born. She became a competitive co-mother and bossy sister, forerunners of a lifelong coping style. Caregiving over the years has left her chronically enraged because she's unheard, unseen, unappreciated, and taken for granted. She medicates her fury by eating herself into a stupor at the end of the day.

Marilyn's father died of metastatic stomach cancer in the spring of her senior year in high school. She quickly stepped into his shoes, trying to hold the family together by playing sports with her brother and providing discipline. Her mother, who had lost her father when she was 19 and her mother when she was 21, plummeted into a major depression which became established pathological mourning. Thirty-eight years later, Marilyn's mother still doesn't seem to notice that Marilyn explodes with rage when she feels completely obliterated by her mother's involvement with her dead father.

Marilyn is haunted by the following scene: Her father had been terminally ill for about a year, in and out of the hospital. One spring day, Marilyn came home from school to an empty house. Running from neighbor to neighbor, she finally found someone who told her that her mother had rushed her father to the hospital, where he had died. She's never forgiven her mother for leaving her alone with overwhelming emotions. Her mother hadn't remembered her, hadn't thought about what she might be feeling, and didn't let her say good-bye to her father.

Despite this disruptive loss, Marilyn left the family to get training as a health care professional, which she completed after a rocky beginning. Identifying with her father's exacting standards, she became highly skilled in her specialty.

Like her mother, and others who suffer with complicated bereavement, Marilyn has been dedicated to preserving every area of her life in a state of suspended animation, because change has been associated with traumatic loss. Until the last few years, each time she entered my office she'd survey the premises carefully, instantly detect any additions, and remark on the slighest rearrangement of books on my shelves. For the first several years of the treatment, she always got a disabling bout of back pain during my vacations.

In addition to actively mistreating her body by overeating, Marilyn also neglects her body. A chronic fungus on her feet since childhood deformed her toenails. It was never successfully treated, despite numerous excruciatingly painful medical procedures without anesthesia when she was young. Memories of those procedures are retraumatizing. Even the mention of further care of her feet brings acute shame and floods of tears, making me reluctant to pursue the discussion and contributing to her stagnant state regarding her care of her body. Until five years ago, when she experienced severe gastric pain, she hadn't had a medical examination in twelve years. My concern increased as Marilyn minimized that pain for weeks, while I made ineffective interventions about her father's misdiagnosed stomach cancer and her announcement in our first session that she wouldn't live past age 45. A diagnosis of gastric ulcer made her concerned enough to give up her two-pack-a-day smoking habit.

I was often doubtful that we would survive her explosions of frustration and rage as she withdrew from smoking's oral incorporative, expulsive, and soothing properties. She ate more than before. It seemed like she was expanding to the next garment size each session. After the ulcer healed and she weaned herself off the nicotine patch, Marilyn's bouts of depression and frequency of angry outbursts increased so sharply that I was afraid that she'd have a stroke or heart attack. Seeking additional regulatory support, I referred her for a medication consultation. An antidepressant and anxyiolytic helped temporarily. Within six months, however, she learned that she had Graves' disease due to an overactive thyroid. Buffeted by two more years of emotional turbulence before her thyroid was regulated, my minimal goal was to help her maintain her job and not totally destroy her professional, personal, and family relationships.

Since early this year, I've become even more alarmed and incensed by my impotence. Marilyn has developed diabetes, had all of her upper teeth removed because of periodontal disease exacerbated by smoking, and had two automobile accidents because she was driving in an agitated and distracted manner.

To help me regulate my own eruptions and torpor during the treatment, I went for consultation at three intervals. I enumerated Marilyn's and her mother's traumatic losses. I described her impotent rage at her mother: for not having regular medical checkups, and for the foul smells in her mother's house coming from decaying meals, months of empty cat food cans, and cat shit everywhere that her mother doesn't seem to notice. As I watched my consultants' eyes glaze over, I realized that I had infused the consultant with the refuse of our analytic space. I had re-created my experience with Marilyn and her experience with her mother—that repugnant, enraging, immobilizing, despairing entanglement.

From time to time, when I couldn't regulate my apprehension, hopelessness, and fury with interpretations or a detailed inquiry, I would blast at Marilyn, "After how hard you've tried to get your mother to take care of her health and to clean up the cat shit in the house so that you can tolerate going inside, can't you see that you're doing the same thing to your body that your mother is doing to her body and her house? The squalor keeps people away, and that's terrifying and infuriating. I think I know how you feel with your mother. No matter how hard I try, I can't get through to you!" Recognizing that I was onto something crucial, Marilyn would associate to times that she and her brother, in exasperated fervor, cleaned up their mother's noisome space and gave her orders to keep it that way. Their directives didn't work, just as my inflammatory, judgmental outbursts didn't work with Marilyn.

In preparation for writing this chapter, I began to examine, relentlessly, my stuck, stagnant state with Marilyn. I experienced disturbing cravings for carbohydrates unlike any I'd had since my first analysis, when I had discovered a relationship between my own food escapades and dissociated fear and rage over abandonment and loss. Much as Marilyn has done, I began to medicate my feelings about being stalled with her by eating cakes and pastry, such as a four-inch wedge of German chocolate cake AND a similar serving of Coconut Cake, evocative of the 1950's layer cakes my mother, a proud Southern cook, used to make—great soothers!

No matter how hard I was trying with Marilyn, nothing different seemed to be happening. How could I write a paper about our predicament without feeling like a failure? The Tuesday following Memorial Day weekend I was in the office trying to recover from bronchitis, which had beset me at the beginning of the badly needed holiday weekend. I was furious that I was sick, and didn't seem to be getting better, AND I'd been unable to start writing this paper.

Marilyn, always at least fifteen to twenty minutes late, arrived only two minutes late, entering with, "Am I on time?" Matching her humorous disbelief, I said, "Actually, just about!" She began a ritual of telling me the events of the day in great detail, including reexperiencing all of the associated affects. I thought, "Oh, no, here we go again. I hate this because I can't ever do anything different. What's the use in trying?" Then I noticed that she had her upper teeth in place, having survived three weeks of the humiliation of going to work without teeth until her gums healed from the extractions. Her expression signaled that she knew I'd noticed. She smiled and said, "Oh, I got my teeth." I rejoined, "I see, how do you like them?" She replied, "I like them. They look more natural than I expected." I offered, "They look great."

She smiled appreciatively and returned quickly to a recurrent theme—the multitude of ways in which her supervisor never acknowledges her hard work and excludes her from important policy-making decisions. I was alternately bored and alert, saying to myself hopefully, maybe *this* time something different will happen. But I could feel that I was drifting off, worrying about how sick I was. Then I heard Marilyn breezily say, "And all I had time to eat today was a spoonful of peanut butter and some crackers." Ever vigilant about her diabetes, and mindful that *not* eating could be dangerous, I was aghast. To my surprise, I heard myself uttering words I've spurted out before. But this time, I queried very calmly, "Do you realize that you're damaging your body by eating so little?"

She recoiled in her chair, as if I'd hit her. Faltering, and flooding with tears, she shouted, furiously hurling it back at me, "Are you saying that I'm trying to slowly commit suicide? All these years, you've never said anything like that to me before. Why haven't you?" She knows I can be an overly responsible caregiver, like her, so I felt guilty immediately. I said something mealy-mouthed about suicide not being my word, that maybe *she* was feeling suicidal in some way. Disgusted with my defensive deflection, I stopped and said, "I don't know why I never said it to you in this way before. I've certainly felt it many times and I know that we've talked about it in various ways for years. I hadn't planned to say it today, but something happened. I don't know what. I just couldn't believe that you could do that to yourself when you know what happens to your blood sugar when you *don't* eat, as well as when you eat too much. Somehow, I think I finally got through to you!"

In an uncommon silence, astonished, we assimilated what had happened. After a while, I asked, "What do you feel inside when you make yourself think about what's happening to your body when you don't eat?" She asked, "What do you mean?" I repeated my question. She started weeping again, in desperation, wailing like a helpless little girl, "I know that I'm doing bad things to my body because of my diabetes. But I'm tired out. I feel like giving up. God has done bad by me—first the ulcer, then the thyroid, then the diabetes, then losing my teeth, then the skin thing on my feet, then two car accidents in six months. And I have to get my food. It's so much work." Feeling her anguish acutely, I said, "It *is* so much work."

After another rare silence, I said, "Marilyn, God *has* done bad by you with all those things. And I'm amazed that you keep surviving—despite all those things, despite the part of you that wants to give up, that does give up and doesn't take care of yourself well. Maybe next time we can talk more about how you keep surviving, despite all the ways you don't take care of yourself."

We felt reverberations of that encounter for weeks. In this session, Marilyn and I experienced an aerated, mobilizing state that brought authentic connection in contrast to our stagnant, collusive entanglement, as described by Levenson (1983). Among the many questions my work provokes, I will address two: Why has this enactment been so inescapable and enduring? And what made the shift in the enactment possible?

As Maroda (1998) notes, overlapping elements of the therapist's and the patient's pasts foster the emergence of inevitable, desirable enactments in a mutative treatment. The greater the severity of traumatic experience in the overlap, the more likely an unyielding, stalled enactment will occur. Long ago, I realized that, like Marilyn, I had shouted at people I care about, "No matter how hard I try, I can't get through to you!!" It is no coincidence that we use the same language and intonation when we explode because we can't get through to impervious, self-annihilating people who abandon us. Along the lines Brisman (1995) has suggested, we overeat and shout, rather than experience fear and despair about our powerlessness.

I'm well suited to be Marilyn's persevering, exasperated therapist in that I've developed a "hovering countertransference," delineated by Looker (1996). Looker and I (1996, 1998) have each discussed how this hypervigliant stance keeps the analyst and patient stuck. Like a broken record, I keep trying to get through to Marilyn rather than tolerate experiencing the affects that we both were dissociating—the dissociation that was mediating her self-destructive course and our impasse. The return of my carbohydrate cravings meant that I could no longer smugly differentiate myself from her. Viscerally experiencing how she's coped with despair and rage for thirty-eight years in trying to get through to her mother broke through my dissociation, an essential precursor to the mutative session described above. Elsewhere (1996, 1998) I have substantiated that the therapist's visceral experience of the patient's dissociated affect is essential in the treatment process.

In the session described above, I was sick as a result of overworking, which forced me to confront my tendency, like Marilyn's, to ignore my body's needful states. Because I was integrating responsiblity for my own somatic functioning, I was less hypervigilant about her, as Looker (1996) has observed. Brisman (1995) would say that I was disengaged from the familiar pull to be the caregiver. In a more autonomous, fluid state, I could hear the dissociation in Marilyn's near-gleeful statement about how little she'd eaten. I was free to speak spontaneously, without trying, in a tone that penetrated her dissociation. Using words uttered many times, I was speaking from a more integrated stance. We had shifted from a stagnant to a lotic state, with its image of freshly flowing water—a state in which Marilyn had to integrate her cavalier disavowal and abandonment of her body.

REFERENCES

Anderson, F. S. (1996). *Psychic elaboration of chronic physical pain and suffering in an analytic dyad.* Paper presented at the annual April meeting of the Division of Psychoanalysis, American Psychological Association, New York.

———— (1998). Psychic elaboration of musculoskeletal back pain: Ellen's story. In *Relational Perspectives on the Body*, ed. L. Aron and F. S. Anderson, pp. 287–322. Hillsdale, NJ: Analytic Press.

Brisman, J. (1995). Addiction. In *Handbook of Interpersonal Psychoanalysis*, ed. M. Lionells, J. Fiscalini, C. H. Mann, et al., pp. 537–552. Hillsdale, NJ: Analytic Press.

Levenson, E. (1983). *The Ambiguity of Change.* New York: Basic Books.

Looker, T. (1996). *Impinging anxiety and bodily experience: a treatment enactment.* Paper presented at the annual April meeting of the Division of Psychoanalysis, American Psychological Association, New York.

Maroda, K. (1998). Enactment: when the patient's and analyst's pasts converge. *Psychoanalytic Psychology* 15:517–535.

9

The Destabilizing Dyad: Psychoanalytic Affective Engagement and Growth

Emily Kuriloff

Analysts have always been emotionally engaged with patients. In a letter to Jung, Freud (McGuire 1974) comments that "the neurotics" are driving him "crazy." He adds, "I believe an article on countertransference is sorely needed; of course we could not publish it, we should have to circulate copies among ourselves" (pp. 475–476).

It is only recently that we began to openly acknowledge our feelings as therapeutic tools, alongside our more cognitive, interpretive work. Across theoretical lines, today we applaud the analyst who responds more personally, who is moved by the process. Countertransference has become the mark not of pathology, but rather of professionalism.

In a true two-person model, this means considering not only the push and pull of the patient's mentalized and/or somatized affects, but also that the analyst's feelings can be remobilized in a particular therapeutic moment, and deserve attention. Perhaps this is because such grappling and integrating within the analyst serves as both model, and moreover as relational catalyst for the patient's own grappling with feeling. The analyst's struggle results in a change in the quality of relatedness within the dyad, which in large part determines what becomes possible for each participant. This chapter discusses embodied affect and struggle in psychotherapy, and demonstrates some aspects of shifting relatedness in a case example.

Analysts are not trained to engage their bodies. We engage in the talking cure. We may sit where the patient cannot see how we move or how we hold ourselves. We yearn to symbolize in order to contain and explain our sensations, we use words to capture what feels disorganizing and meaningless or primordial. For many years this was the fire and iron that analysts acknowledged most often and easily—words for clarification and awareness, in order to excavate, integrate, titrate, and sublimate.

Yet from the start of our profession, since Freud espoused the primacy of insight and Ferenczi of affective experience, we have struggled to find the balance between what we feel and reason. There have been times when we may have become as disembodied, as split off from feeling as are our psychosomatic patients, the alexythymic ones for whom the connection between affect and word is severed. Here the mind is of no use in understanding the body, and bodies are of little use in understanding minds. In the past we have often called alexythymic patients unanalyzable, left to wander in the hinterlands because everything for them was too literal and they couldn't use our language. But maybe our interpretations were of little use to these patients. Conceivably our formulations, like dried up, dead leaves fallen from supple trees, were merely repetitions of their deadened, isolated affects. In the name of clarity and communication, perhaps we were also saying, or at the very least were experienced as saying, "I cannot bear this either, I must detach, I must separate from the moment with words."

In the case of my patient, Penny, a 25-year-old bulimic, it felt as if she herself were a caricature of a 1950s American ego psychologist. She had a magnificent command of language, and used words to avoid anything spontaneous between us. "I always apologize before I can be accused," she'd tell me after she spoke, and then she'd home in for the interpretive zinger, "I'm probably rageful, and envious, and sadistic, sadomasochistic, actually, towards everyone. But I transform it to guilt and shame, and project my impulses onto you." Between these barrages much transpired, what I might term juicy comments and interactions ripe with potential for uncovering. And yet my patient didn't want to dig in; she didn't even want to skim the surface.

For example, Penny spoke glowingly of her mother, blaming her troubles on an unkind world out there. Yet after the two saw a movie, Penny reported to me, somewhat sheepishly, that she wasn't sure how she felt about the film at first. "I have to wait for my mother's opinion, and, then, somehow, it all makes sense." I expressed great interest and tried to inquire about this, of course, but Penny shrugged it off and became stiff and remote when I persisted. Her mother called and wrote to me the first week of Penny's treatment, neither informing her daughter nor asking her permission to do so. She said she was ready to "kill" Penny for not eating, she was so beside herself after pleading with her to stop abusing food. Penny claimed she didn't mind that her mother had called.

I tried everything. I joined Penny in her interpretive zeal, making connections between her formulations and her overbearing mother who couldn't tolerate her aggression. Then, when it felt useless, I waited and listened. I soothed and reassured, I mirrored. I figured I needed to hold, contain, detoxify. I respected the power and life of the symptom, so I asked about the food, wondered about her keeping logs, charting patterns, noting sensations of hunger and satiety and their relation to upset. I suggested medication, nutritionists, I insisted on internists—all the while wondering and asking what this felt like to her, how she experienced my interventions into her disturbed eating and feeling. At still other junctures I confronted her, because things felt so stuck, with my experience of her in the moment as frustrating, thwarting, of taking me in but spitting me out. I asked her how she felt about me, about my ideas, about my body. When she started treatment she claimed that she threw up once a week. After two years of analysis she was throwing up five to ten times each day, and passed out on the street more than once. After three years, she had to be hospitalized repeatedly for electrolyte imbalances, and the next day would go home to binge and purge all over again. She missed so many workdays that she was demoted, and was often ill with viruses and gastrointestinal upset. And she felt terrified of her mounting symptoms, out of control of her life. The only hope was that she still attended sessions, although I worried that she would drop out, a part of me wanted her to.

One day she came in and spoke about how angry her mother had been at her the previous day. She added that she figured that I, too, must be angry, because she was still so ill, and such a burden. This comment came in the midst of a stream of verbiage, and I would have had to interrupt her monologue to respond. I didn't want to. In the past she blew me off when I tried to examine her fantasies about my reactions. "I don't think about you that much," she'd say, "I was just stating the obvious." She acted victimized if I copped to any of her presumptions about me. "I feel burdened by your feelings," she'd tell me if I agreed that her throwing up was dangerous and scary, for example. "I am too guilt ridden. I have a harsh superego," she'd explain, evenly. So in this particular moment I felt tired, fighting sleep. But suddenly I experienced a shooting pain in my mouth. I unclenched my jaw, and realized I'd broken a tooth. I wondered if Penny saw me wince.

In our next session, myself having just returned from the first phase of root canal therapy, Penny noticed my slightly swollen lip. "What happened?" she inquired, somewhat uncharacteristically. I paused for a moment, resisting the impulse to say "I was enraged at you and so I was clenching my teeth." I felt exposed, out of control of the treatment. I was literally falling apart in front of my patient, and instead of my prized version of myself as healer, I wanted to bite. As if Freud and Ferenczi were the cartoon angel and devil on each of my shoulders (to be both banal and grandiose at the same time), I was full of feeling, alive and responsive in the moment, but unnerved and suspicious about what I felt, worried I would lose my professional edge. I would placate or harm instead of understanding. Perhaps I was not doing real analysis. "Yesterday I bit down very

hard on a tooth and cracked it," I began. Penny's eyes lit up. "You bit
down very hard?" She rejoined, excitedly, "I thought I saw you doing
something with your mouth yesterday. You grind your teeth!" She
exclaimed emphatically, "So do I! Do you know that when I was a kid
they had to make me a mouth guard because I did it so much, I kept
breaking teeth!" I noted that this may have been the first historical
reference Penny made that was not immediately followed by an
interpretation. Instead, she ended, "I hated wearing that mouth
guard. It hurt. But my mother made me. I hated that she made me."
I nodded with genuine empathy.

There are too many case reports of analysts finally doing the
"right" thing with a patient, as if there is one correct and defining
moment in treatment, something between a television drama and
what Greenberg (1999) has referred to as a morality play. I don't
really think I'm describing *the* crisis in which Penny and I began to
do good work together. All that transpired before was not mistaken
and misguided. Penny herself explains how meaningful the first
three years of sessions were, as she pushed the limits of her
self-destructiveness. "Although I didn't know at the time, it was a
test," she explained recently, "because if you stayed with me through
the worst, I knew you wouldn't reject me for my worst feelings." And
our work continues to be a stormy challenge, although Penny rarely
binges, and now lives separately from her mother. While there is no
perfect technique in our ever-changing interaction, I do think
something important happened with Penny when I broke my tooth,
something in the quality of the relatedness between us that was
powerfully therapeutic.

What is this quality between us, this particular relatedness? In
retrospect, I can see that I felt an identification with Penny, an
identification that I was more than ambivalent about acknowledging, lest it knock me too far off my perch. But after all, she, the
rational, analytical one, was defending herself in ways that were all
too familiar to me, an analyst who is the child of a psychoanalyst, a
child who asked the kid in preschool who punched me in the nose
if she was upset about something. In my family we talked instead,
and all the talking sometimes protected us from feelings, from our

dirty little secrets wrapped in jargon. My only recourse was to develop stomachaches on the way to school, aches I never spoke of to anyone. How similar in flavor, if not degree, this feels to Penny's resisting my inquiries with reason and level-headedness while she secretly puked her guts out. It was only after I somatized in Penny's presence that I embraced this identification, what Dodi Goldman (1999) refers to as this "overlap between our mutually resonating areas of vulnerability."

In using and acknowledging my body with Penny, I saw myself in Penny's eyes. I considered my fellowship, my communion with Penny's fear of her rage and her helplessness, her need not to know what seemed too dangerous to feel, prompting the misuse of her body, rather than any lively engagement with it. Because I became receptive to the overlap between us, these were no longer only odd or shameful sentiments, verboten corporeal urges, ghosts of my past dangerously beyond the pale, come to attack my analytic self, or to place me in the line of fire. And, in the "interactive matrix" (Greenberg 1995), the swirling interpersonal ooze that forms a feedback loop between both analyst and patient, Penny, witness to my behavior, felt able to embrace more of these feelings, and to be interested in herself with less defensiveness and disapprobation. "You grind your teeth? So do I!" And then, for the first time, she went further, expressing hate in relation to her mother.

Such a turn suggests that in order to tolerate and take responsibility for feelings (perhaps among the prime and universally embraced goals of an analysis), the affective struggles inevitable in negotiating problems in living need to be shared. In this way the fear of being cast out as a pariah is diminished. Harry Stack Sullivan, who knew the pathologic impact of loneliness, eloquently espoused this requirement for commiseration when he cautioned that patients and therapists remember that "we are all more human than otherwise" (White 1977, p. 343).

Yet this is not the whole story. An analyst cannot be stuck in one relation to the patient, but must allow for ongoing destabilizations in order for change and growth to occur. Analysis is not only a safe nest, or a shared sensibility necessary for optimal working conditions. The patient must also experience him or herself more than privately, or idiosyncratically. In the light of the other, new possibilities emerge. Therefore, inasmuch as I feel a kinship with Penny when I break a tooth, I also become acutely aware that she is the one I am angry at, she is the reason for my clenched jaw, for the rage and frustration I am loath to own. I know something about *her* capacity to provoke and frustrate, perhaps an inkling about her own rage, lurking out of her awareness.

When I broke my tooth and want to break her, or at least to scream at her, I also connect with her mother, the heretofore villain in the story whom I imagined Penny would need to exorcise from her psyche in order to go on living. Finally, when I became the angry, controlling mother, the one who wished to "kill" her daughter, I see myself not just *in* but also *through* Penny's eyes (Goldman 1999). I understand her transference to me.

It is this shifting relatedness, experiencing myself as both the subject of the struggle and object of Penny's affects, that I believe is essential, an admittedly destabilizing journey that is both point and counterpoint to Penny's efforts to identify and differentiate. Penny struggles to feel that her affects can be received and shared without censure and pressure, but also to have her own opinion of a movie, eat what she wants instead of swallowing everything, only to be sickened. In this way she can know herself not only as a victim, the object of her mother's impingement, surrendering to her urges to binge, but also as subject, as maker of her life, even evoking murderous, tooth-cracking rage.

When Freud cautioned neutrality and abstinence he relegated us as objects, disavowing our personal sway. Fearing undue influence—seduction—he chronicled the patterns of the other, eschewing our impact in the mix. And when Ferenczi experimented with mutuality, wanting to literally and figuratively "touch" his patients in the spaces beyond reason, he relegated us as subjects, caught in the impossibly consuming web of idiosyncratic experience, flavored by our histories. So Freud denuded the mutative power of affective engagement, and Ferenczi allowed his famous test case, R.N., to maniacally and relentlessly consume him, as both doctor and patient nearly drowned in the myasma of psychic life. We struggle to hold onto both of these fathers of our field (and mothers, to speak in a postmodern, ungendered tongue), as the pendulum swings back and forth between them. This age-old effort at a dialectic in psychoanalyis informs my fluctuating journey with Penny as much as my personal history and my actual mother and father do.

Finally, if one knows oneself in relation, as both subject and object, and can best take responsibility for oneself when feeling related to the other, each analysand requires a fellow traveler, in body, mind, and spirit. Penny, alienated from dreaded emotions disguised in bodily preoccupation, required a destabilized, somatizing analyst in order to embark upon a more emotionally alive analytic journey. This paradox is a departure from the previously held logic that a focus on the analyst's visceral and affective responses detracts from a fuller recognition of, and impact upon, the patient's inner life. In a two-person cosmos, therapeutic change may in part require that the analyst tackle the interactive, affective mountains and valleys alongside.

REFERENCES

Goldman, D. (1999). Creative turbulence and the growth of the analyst. *Contemporary Psychoanalysis*, in press.

Greenberg, J. (1995). Psychoanalytic technique and the interactive matrix. *Psychoanalytic Quarterly* 64:1–22.

———— (January 1999). *The analysts participation: a new look.* The New York University Postdoctoral Program in Psychoanalysis Annual Bernard Kalinkowitz Lecture, New York.

McGuire, W., ed. (1974). *The Freud/Jung Letters: The Correspondence between Sigmund Freud and C. G. Jung.* Boston: Harvard University Press.

White, M. J. (1977). Sullivan and treatment. *Contemporary Psychoanalysis* 13:3 317–346.

10

Narrative, Affect, and Therapeutic Impasse: Discussion of Part III

Lewis Aron

Jean Petrucelli, Frances Sommer Anderson, and Emily Kuriloff presented some very moving and disturbing clinical stories in their chapters. For me, reading these stories has been both troubling and uplifting, and has made me feel proud of being an analyst, while also reminding me of the caution with which we must proceed in our work. Imagine telling a managed care reviewer that you are in the fourth or fourteenth year of work with a bulimic patient and that the symptoms may be worse now, but you are in the midst of a breakthrough and any session now. . . . We need to struggle with this, not because I am serious about even beginning to explain any of this to a managed care company, but rather because we need to recognize the seriousness of purpose of our therapeutic endeavor. We are talking about life and death stories, the narratives of hope and despair, and we just cannot think in terms of the number of sessions being authorized or of the specific treatment goals of any given sequence of sessions. These stories inspire a feeling of awe as to the magnitude of what we are trying to achieve as well as to the inherent obstacles in our path. This chapter highlights how therapists get stuck in their clinical work when, because of their own fears of identification with aspects of their patients' stories and characters (counterresistances), they lose their ability to keep the therapy moving fluidly and get bogged down in analytic stalemates and impasses.

Stories play an important role in psychotherapy. Eli Wiesel, a great storyteller who uses stories with great seriousness of purpose, has told a Talmudic story that begins with the question, Why did God create people? He answers, because God loves stories.

Storytelling to children before they go to sleep is a particularly relevant kind of storytelling for us as therapists because it has to do with helping a child learn to negotiate and move from one mental state to another, which is very much a way of thinking about what goes on in therapy as patient and therapist are mutually regulating each other's states of consciousness and one way of doing that is by telling stories to each other. Elsewhere I describe this aspect of therapy in terms of the mutual regulation of states of consciousness (Aron and Bushra 1998).

I heard of a storyteller who experiments with his own child by telling him bedtime stories to see what kind of stories he likes best before going to sleep. What the storyteller found is that of all the stories he could tell, the story that the child liked most was the story of what the child did that very day. The child loved to hear, for example, that Timmy had gotten up that morning and had orange juice, and after breakfast went to school where he saw his friends and so on. I see this as relevant to what therapists do in that we are always constructing and deconstructing the narratives of our patients' lives. There are schools and traditions of psychoanalysis based on this, the so-called narrative tradition (Schafer and Spence) as well as in deconstruction of narrative (as in the work of Levenson). These narrative and deconstructive approaches have in common an emphasis on working with stories, specifically psychoanalytic narratives, as being at the heart of psychoanalytic work.

Within the more general field of psychology, the cognitive revolution made it possible to begin to explore how knowledge and experience is organized. Since language is the most powerful tool for organizing experience and constituting our worlds, the social sciences moved away from positivism and toward an emphasis on interpretation, narrative, deconstruction, and dialogue. Bruner (1986) systematically described two modes of thought, each of which provides distinct ways of organizing experience and constructing reality, and each of which is irreducible to the other. Put simply, the two modes may be described by the differences between the good story and the well-constructed argument; more technically, they may be referred to as the "narrative" and the "paradigmatic" modes.

Specifically within the area of moral development, Vitz (1990) criticized contemporary approaches to moral development for their reliance on propositional thinking and logical reasoning (the paradigmatic mode). Vitz points out that stories (the narrative mode) are often better guides to behavior than are rules and maxims, as is evident by the oldest forms of moral literature going back to the parables and anecdotes of the Bible and religious literature (such as the Midrash within the Talmudic tradition). As summarized by Hermans and colleagues (1992), "Rules and maxims state significant generalizations about experiences, but stories illustrate these maxims in a concrete, understandable fashion and locate them in space and time. In other words, stories appear to be natural mediators between the particular and the general" (p. 30).

The recognition of the value of stories over and above propositional thought has particular relevance to therapy because rather than formulate systematic rules of technique, I think that we are much better off learning from stories by examining and reflecting on them, rather than relying predominantly on the logical-scientific model of propositional thinking. Contemporary relational and constructivist psychoanalysis has eschewed the technical-rationality of older psychoanalytic models (see Hoffman 1998). The interpersonal approach to psychoanalysis has long been critical of a rule-governed model of psychoanalytic technique, and I certainly view my contributions to this topic as well within the interpersonal tradition of the William Alanson White Psychoanalytic Institute.

Elsewhere I have elaborated this approach to the rethinking of psychoanalytic technique (Aron 1999).

Recent work by Charles Spezzano, Mitchell, Maroda, Ehrenberg, Fonagy, and Stern among others has attempted to highlight the centrality of affect in psychoanalysis. A new book by Nancy Chodorow, however, entitled *The Power of Feelings* (1999), makes the additionally important and subtle point that in psychoanalysis affects are always embedded in narrative constructions. "The feelings that concern psychoanalysis" she writes, "are always feelings enmeshed within stories" (p. 239). This understanding highlights the recognition that as therapists we never encounter abstract feelings or affects in pure form; rather, feelings are always found within stories, within the context of feeling-based themes or proto-stories. Feelings both condense and express complex stories or what traditional psychoanalysis has referred to under the rubric of "unconscious fantasy."

One way of thinking about how we utilize narrative, both construction and deconstruction, is that as therapists we are always helping our patients and ourselves move more freely from one story to another, from one affect to another, from one self-other relation to another. To do that, both patient and therapist have to be able to move somewhat freely from one character in a story to another, to identify with different characters and with different levels of story making, from identifying with the character to identifying with the narrator, the author, and the editor of the story. We even need to identify with the nonhuman background figures of the story such as the setting, the background, and the props. (I'm thinking here of a clinical methodology that is often associated with Jungian dream interpretation.) We are able to maintain contact with all of the mental parts of the patient only by being able to identify momentarily with each aspect of their story. It is the patient's inability to identify with each aspect of their story that we often refer to as dissociation.

The Part III chapters discuss being stuck—the impasses and stalemates in treatment. We get stuck by not being able to identify with important aspects of our patient's stories. We help our patients and ourselves to resolve impasses by freeing ourselves to move from one identification to another with greater fluidity. The Part III chapters have a common theme: the ways that the therapists found, after years of struggle and difficulty, to identify with a part of the patient they had been resisting identifying with previously.

The central difficulty holding us back when we are stuck in an impasse is that there is some aspect of the patient that we are counterresisting. There is often something that we are terribly afraid to see in ourselves, and sometimes we hide that by becoming overly identified with the patient, but there is always some kernel, some aspect of the patient, that we cannot bear to see in ourselves. In our counterresistance, we find ourselves blocked from playing all of the roles in patients' stories, and we cannot help them move because there is a part of them to closely linked with a part of ourselves that we are not seeing.

In Jean Petrucelli's chapter, the "close encounter" had to do with Jean's struggling with being seen and known in a way that she felt vulnerable in herself, regulating being more open or closed and regulating being more comfortable, as she put it, with what was alien. In Fran Anderson's chapter, I think that her being so overly identified with being the overly good caregiver, like the patient, was also getting in the way of her recognizing the ways in which she was not taking care of herself, which in a deeper way was more similar to the patient. She had to get to that and struggle with that in herself to see it in her patient. Perhaps most obviously, in Emily Kuriloff's chapter, the wonderful example is of her clenching her teeth, and both she and her patient recognizing in that an aspect of herself that was similar to her patient and that they could explore. This is a particularly rich illustration because Dr. Kuriloff was not attempting to model behavior for the patient. Rather, it brings to the fore an identification with the patient that had to surface and be dealt with by both patient and therapist. These chapters illustrate the therapists' struggle over long periods of time with their own inner resistances to identifying with some aspect of their patients. It is the relative progress that they make in this struggle, always with help from the patient, that allows them to make deeper and broader contact with the patient and thus to overcome therapeutic stale-mates.

Elsewhere I have outlined how both patient and therapist must overcome the dissociation between their subjective and objective senses of self, between the "I" and the "me," and have reviewed the literature on dissociation, mentalization, psychosomatic states, and catastrophic trauma, which reveals that trauma disrupts the capacity for self-reflexivity by severing the links between the self-as-subject and the self-as-object (Aron 1998). Left unable to move freely back and forth among different aspects of self, unable to utilize their bodily sensations and their skin membrane to mediate between their subjective and objective awareness, traumatized patients are unable to reflect on their traumatic experiences; self-reflexive functioning fails, and the body is left to keep the score. Approached from the point of view of those coming to treatment with psycho-somatic illness, self-mutilation, addictions, perversions, and other destructive enactments, especially patients with eating disorders, we see patients who utilize their bodies for the concrete expression of their affective lives because they have no way to process these affects through self-reflection and mentalization.

If the patient is not capable of using symbolic or metaphoric thought, the therapist may receive communications only in nonver-bal form, such as bodily communications, a change in the climate or the air (mediated by the breath), or a change in the feel of things (mediated by the skin). Here, the therapist must be attuned to the nonverbal, the affective, the spirit (breath) of the session, the feel of the material, and to his or her own bodily responses, so that these may be gradually utilized to construct metaphors and symbols that may be verbally exchanged between therapist and patient, gradually permitting the differentiation of the more primitive shared skin ego and the construction of a more developed, articulated, and differ-entiated personal attachment and interpersonal connection. At moments when patients are unable to utilize reflexive awareness, the analyst must carry much of the analytic work, psychosomatically processing the patient's communications and utilizing his or her own transcendent function to bring together conscious with unconscious, body with affect, unformulated experience with words and symbols, self as subject with self as object. At moments when both patient and therapist lose this capacity, they may mutually help each other to regain, reestablish, sustain, and improve reflexive awareness through ongoing oscillations, enactments, role reversals, projections, and introjections. All of these are aspects of the analytic task of constructing and deconstructing analytic narratives with all of the complexity and depth that this entails.

Much of my thinking regarding impasses derives from the training that I had with Benjamin Wolstein, an analyst long associated with the interpersonal school and specifically with the White institute. Dr. Wolstein died in 1999, and I want to honor his memory by noting his contributions to our understanding of analytic impasses. He wrote about this as early as the 1940s and later developed the idea of transference–countertransference interlocks, which he believed developed out of the enmeshments of the patient's and analyst's personalities. Wolstein inspired my thinking about the idea that we get stuck when there is an area of the patient's character that we avoid identifying with because we are resistant to experiencing and acknowledging that very aspect of ourselves.

As early as 1959 in his work on countertransference, Wolstein described a therapist who was overly giving, nurturing and maternal toward his patients. He identified a particular therapist "type"—therapists who are deeply afraid that they are really incapable of loving, and because they want to cover up these doubts about whether they can love at all, they attempt in an overcompensating manner to cure through love. But picture these therapists working with a patient who is afraid that he is unlovable, where this fear itself reflected the underlying feeling that he is incapable of giving love. Here might begin a vicious cycle in which the more the patient feels unlovable the more the therapist must prove how loving he or she is. All the time the therapist could miss the most critical dynamic because of his or her own reluctance to see this same aspect in the patient.

The Part III chapters are great stories about the various ways in which therapists have struggled with these mutual anxieties and resistances and found some means to move beyond these mutual resistances to processes of identification and to allow themselves to become better integrated with all aspects of their patients and of themselves. Thus, the heart of the analytic process requires a mutual struggle with anxiety and counteranxiety, resistance and counterresistance, transference and countertransference, so as to attain increased affective access to all aspects of self and other and a meeting of minds (Aron 1996).

REFERENCES

Aron, L. (1996). *A Meeting of Minds.* Hillsdale, NJ: Analytic Press.

———— (1998). The clinical body and the reflexive mind. In *Relational Perspectives on the Body*, ed. L. Aron and F. S. Anderson. Hillsdale, NJ: Analytic Press.

———— (1999). Clinical choices and the relational matrix. *Psychoanalytic Dialogues* 9:1–29.

Aron, L., and Bushra, A. (1998). Mutual regression: altered states in the psychoanalytic situation. *Journal of the American Psychoanalytic Association* 46:389–412.

Bruner, J. (1986). *Actual Minds, Possible Worlds.* Cambridge, MA: Harvard University Press.

Chodorow, N. (1999). *The Power of Feelings.* New Haven, CT: Yale University Press.

Hermans, H. J. M., Kempen, H. J. G., and van Loon, R. J. P. (1992). The dialogical self: beyond individualism and relativism. *American Psychologist* 47:23–33.

Hoffman, I. Z. (1998). *Ritual and Spontaneity in the Psychoanalytic Process.* Hillsdale, NJ: Analytic Press.

Vitz, P. C. (1990). The use of stories in moral development: new psychological reasons for an old education method. *American Psychologist* 45:709–720.

Wolstein, B. (1959). *Countertransference.* New York: Grune and Stratton.

IV

To Eat or Not to Eat: The Psychic Meanings of the Decision

11

The Male Experience of Food as Symbol and Sustenance

Margaret Crastnopol

Among the earliest archetypal scenarios depicting the desire for food, there is the sale of Esau's birthright to Jacob, his twin brother, for a bowl of red lentil stew (Plaut 1981). In this story from Genesis, Esau, the elder of the two brothers, is a huntsman, an active, "hairy" man who is beloved by their father Isaac. The younger, Jacob, is less active, "smooth-skinned," likes to remain in camp, and is preferred by their mother Rebecca. When Esau returns famished one day from the hunt, he bargains away the benefits of his firstborn position to assuage his hunger. In so doing, Esau has fatefully renounced the opportunity to represent the people of Israel in their covenant with God.

What does this story convey about the psychic significance of eating for men? A classical psychoanalytic interpretation might emphasize the overwhelming and, in this case, self-defeating pursuit of oral erotic gratification associated with the primitive biophysiological cycle of hunger and satiation. It is also a drama of oedipal strivings, where we can imagine that the elder twin, having failed to stand first and foremost in his mother's affections, is compelled to try to outdo both father and brother in masculine accomplishments. The bootless striving for his mother's admiration leaves Esau unutterably "starved," and he succumbs to the lure of lentil stew.

Another layer of interpretation suggests that the desire for food and drink—in this instance, Esau's decision to trade his birthright for it—exemplifies the effort to secure an attachment. The lentils would represent Esau's potential intimacy with his mother, which along with her approval, affection, and other emotional "goods," might be purchased by foregoing the firstborn's hegemony. The man-to-man activity-based bond with father must be forsworn in order to obtain connection with the mother and the maternal "nourishment" that would accompany it.[1]

From a third perspective, the act of eating reflects one's sense of identity. Apparently as early as biblical times, the type of food acquired, prepared, and consumed expressed how one consciously or unconsciously saw oneself and wished to be seen. Jacob cooked lentils (which presumably required little aggression to grow and less to prepare), while Esau, who is said to "have a taste for game," roasted venison he himself trapped and slaughtered. This difference in one's identification in relation to food and cooking seems to reflect the biblical authors' view of a meaningful characterological difference (Plaut 1981). In the contemporary Western family, food provision is probably still de rigueur for the female gender role, while males have more latitude. Because his behavior is less clearly defined by his sex role, a man's tendencies vis-à-vis food preparation communicate much about his own unique intrapsychic and interpsychic world.

---

1. I would argue that, notwithstanding the modern Western ideal of androgynous development, there is an inherent conflict of interests between the archetypal masculine and feminine attributes and values in their fullest expression, in that full-bore agentic self-assertion runs counter to a more receptive, community-oriented mode. The hypermasculine male thus may sacrifice an emotionally intimate and open type of relationship with his mother, though he may well obtain a different kind of connection centered around his gratification of her displaced "phallic" urges.

For one thing, a man's patterns of parental identification as well as separation/individuation are writ large in his culinary habits. Preferring or shunning a food associated with one's parents—eating or cooking as they did or didn't—can represent the wish to be or to avoid being like the parents, to symbolically ingest the parents' nectar or poison and make it part of oneself, or conversely to spit it out and establish oneself as distinct.

To these fairly standard psychosexual and object relational understandings of eating, I'd add a fourth perspective. An important part of food's allure, in my view, is that it represents other crucial psychic supplies and resources, many of which are concrete and factual—one might even say, practical—rather than being primarily affective or attitudinal. In other words, hunger and thirst symbolize our longing for enhanced knowledge, wisdom, emotional and sensory experience, physical and cognitive skill, and so on—elements that are essential ingredients for enriching, energizing, and replenishing the self. These are tangible acquisitions that in turn add to one's healthy self-regard; they pertain more to the self's private integrity and individuation than to its relational context, though the two interweave. "If I am famished and near death," says Esau, "what use have I for a birthright?" Understood symbolically, Esau is speaking of his psychological and spiritual impoverishment. He lacks the necessary psychic wherewithal to lead his people, a failing that then defines his current existence and determines his destiny.

As I see it, this type of appetitive drive—whether for physical satiation or for intellectual, spiritual, or affective nourishment—is just as compelling a motivator of human functioning as the pursuit of sexual gratification, attachment, or anxiety reduction. What, I wonder, would a drive-based theory of psychic functioning have looked like if the model had centered around varieties of *nourishment* rather than varieties of *libidinal gratification?* Perhaps the human lack that Lacanians (see Fink 1997) point to as a source of psychic struggle and pain is not the difference between who we are and how we "speak" ourselves, or between what we have and what we desire. Perhaps instead that gap is created by the fact that each of us is unable independently to manufacture his or her own food, relying solely on his or her own bodily resources to do so. Our inability to be self-sustaining in this respect may be at the core of that pervasive human feeling of being inadequate.

An obvious place to look for a developmental understanding of the psychic significance of food is the earliest relationship of infant and mother as the "nursing couple." Elise (1998) presents this nursing relationship as the prototype for bisexuality, wherein "the infant is the recipient of the mother's penetration and becomes a penetrator by identification with the mother" (p. 361). The male, in Elise's view, later defensively identifies solely with the penetrating (that is, masculine) role. He rejects being penetrated as part of his renunciation and disidentification with the mother. This difference between the sexes in their nursing relationship and its developmental course presumably helps create the substrate for gender-related character differences.

I largely concur with this view, but it is important to give each phase of life its particular due in terms of psychic significance. To imbibe the mother's breast milk or formula is of unquestionable emotional import in infancy, but so too is a toddler's experience of gnawing on teething crackers, the elementary school child's concern about the contents of the school lunch box, the adolescent's desire to eat in a fashion consistent with newly fledged sociopolitical values, and the adult's careful construction of the menu for a dinner party. Each of these experiences has its own cumulative psychic importance, as eating becomes increasingly laden with complex meanings across the life span. Also, I think it a mistake to reify the dichotomous gender-role–related stereotypes by implying that all men are principally phallic—that is, impenetrable penetrators. I find it more appropriate to speak of a range of patterns within one gender role.

Selecting one's food and chewing, swallowing, and digesting it are inherently gratifying. But eating is also importantly an act of psychic self-recognition and self-furtherance, first, because eating allows oneself to be both penetrated and penetrator, following Elise's view; second, because it brings together the identification with a "like subject" and "love object," in Benjamin's (1995) terms[2]; and third, because eating, though prototypically and fundamentally a relational act, is at the same time an act of illusory self-sufficiency. After all, notwithstanding my earlier point about each person's inability to manufacture his or her own food (and our consequent inability to be self-sufficient), nursing and later forms of eating *are* in a certain sense "feeding oneself," particularly after the food enters one's mouth. There is an interweaving of the subjective with the objective, where the individual is the self being gratified and, at the same time, the early parent gratifying the self. This gives the person an internal experience of wholeness, ephemeral and chimerical though that may be. I am being "like my parent" in feeding myself, I am "loving myself as the parental me" for feeding me, and I am also "feeling loved by the parental me" in the act of feeding myself.

Much of what I've said so far is equally applicable to both men and women. But there are distinctive features of the male experience. A man's identification with the mother while feeding himself may have a particular poignancy as distinct from a woman's. It both enables him to recover the renounced experience of being penetrated (a passive/receptive identification), and it compensates him for having had to give up the mother as part of the oedipal drama. The intensity for men of the appetitive drive to eat may be attributable to the combination of these compensatory maternal/feminine identifications with the attachment to a mother who can confer "feminine" psychic resources. The man may be in shorter supply of these than a woman would be, since he has been raised to be "masculine."

In the parable of the lentil stew, it seems to me that the biblical writers, those ancient psychoanalysts par excellence, were interested in formulating gender-role–specific personality patterns. Among

---

2. Benjamin emphasizes that in the course of development, the child identifies not only with the same-sex parent (the "like subject"), but also with the opposite-sex parent who, in the normative heterosexual scenario, is also the object of his or her desire (the "love object").

the panoply of biblical character types, we can recognize Esau as the boy and then man who is excessively predisposed toward action, assertiveness, and physical self-expression. As a result, this kind of masculine-typed man, to borrow a term from personality theory (Spence and Helmreich 1978) also sacrifices a more nuanced affective life related to interpersonal closeness. A relatively masculine son and his relatively feminine mother react against early symbiotic and oedipal/erotic pulls by too heavily disidentifying and too severely separating from each other. The son misses the opportunity to develop an enhanced emotional vocabulary via closeness with mother and her potentially more nuanced affective life.

I propose that such a man may develop an overemphasis on the world of internal sensation and biophysical drive. The sensations and physical gratification of eating and perhaps preparing food becomes a replacement for a more richly articulated affective life.[3] But an especially intense involvement with food can also conversely become a *conduit* to a more elaborated emotional life. Men who procure or prepare food for others get a consistent opportunity to develop and hone their empathic skills, as they consider and get feedback about how their own food predilections mesh with the eating patterns of their significant others. Cooking thus becomes a symbolic expression and extension of the feeding parent, expressing either maternal or paternal generativity.

Some men I've encountered in my practice, while not necessarily disordered in their eating, do have a particularly intense food preoccupation. These men, having a guarded fascination with emotional life per se but a rather restricted access to their own, tend instead to experience emotions vicariously through their mates and close friends, or through indirect channels like the arts (including gastronomy). My impression is that many of these men were ambivalently identified with their fathers, the father–son relationship being hostile and competitive. Their mothers were affectively

---

3. I am grateful to Emmanuel Ghent, M.D., whose comments stimulated my thinking along these lines.

unavailable due to their own personality constriction, low self-esteem and anxiety, or emotional isolation. Serious friction or shallowness marred the parents' marital relationship. So both mother's and son's constricted feeling life went in part into the provision and consumption of food, a mutual displaced pleasure. The redirection of affect into sensation may also have led to an intensification of sexual interest and desire, with the sensations of lust and orgiastic satisfaction being craved as a substitute for the gratifications of emotional intimacy.

However, as is characteristic of compromise formations, these men's extreme if not obsessive interest in food only partially resolves the problem it addresses. The taste, texture, and quantity of food become the focus, imperfectly representing elements of affective life. The man is symbolically ingesting bits and pieces of his parents, friends, and lovers. He may get preoccupied with finding the right food and fixing it in just the right (that is, psychically satisfying) manner. This is a subjective judgment that he can control, creating an especially strong sense of self-sufficiency that temporarily shores him up. He establishes his own quasi-affective environment by his specific food choices and their associate links. The man in a sense becomes his own ideally attuned lactating "mother," a covert feminine, maternal identification. Even when he himself is not the food provider, the man experiences but need not acknowledge the pleasures associated with the relational context of his eating. This yields the regressive and gratifying experience without its attendant sense of dependence, and hence, vulnerability vis-à-vis the feeding "other."

It may be that such men feel inadequate and insufficiently powerful (especially in communal as opposed to agentic pursuits) because unlike many of their peers, they are sensitive enough to perceive the limits of their own emotional competence. An overinvolvement with food and eating rituals may compensate these men for their inability to work through such feelings of inferiority, which in circular fashion is due to their lacking the kind of bonds that permit the daily therapeusis of intimate contact with others. Such contact is curative both in providing the missing relational experiences that generate emotional competence, and in revealing our human commonality, insofar as each of us is inherently flawed.

Yet, a food preoccupation can reinforce the issues it aims to resolve. The extreme focus on food can shield an emotionally detached male from anxiety-provoking occurrences that might otherwise round out his affective life and provide other forms of comfort. If the man were to become more self-attuned to his affective needs, the overreliance on food could diminish.

Imagine, for example, that Esau had had the internal capacity to recognize his growing hunger earlier while out on the hunt, perhaps in identification with a "good-enough" mother. Suppose he had been able to place self-nurturance above bagging further game that day. Perhaps he would have returned to camp sooner, and feeling less physiological urgency, he might have had the patience to negotiate more productively and less self-destructively with his brother.

These food-related psychic issues manifest themselves clinically in complex ways, as the following case demonstrates.

CASE VIGNETTE

George, an obese 40-year-old unmarried man, sought therapy primarily because of depression, but also to get help for his inhibitions in the areas of both love—he had never had a long-term relationship—and work—his capacities far exceeded his actual achievement level. He worked as a paralegal, although he did have significant managerial responsibility. George was the self-elected protector of his passive-submissive, doting, overly loquacious mother, who lived under the thumb of a domineering, inadequate husband. A culturally sophisticated man who had all but given up trying to slim down, George was surprisingly ignorant of even the most basic elements of dietary control. Instead, he ate as his mother had always fed him—large portions of hearty foods that were laden with the fat of her own childhood cuisine. George modeled his self-feeding on his mother's habit of compulsively and inexorably giving him another serving before he'd finished the last. This pattern of self-feeding now made it impossible for him to lose much of his girth. George's internalization of his mother's excessive feeding style reflected the unconscious wish to remain his mother's baby boy and also her narcissistic extension, providing her with one of the few sources of self-esteem she possessed as the purveyor of food for her son.

The father, himself seriously overweight, decided at some point during George's adolescence that he disliked his wife's "comfort food." He took control of the kitchen, ostensibly to make healthier food, but in fact to cook quirky things that the family found inedible. He would secretly substitute supposedly healthy ingredients that made the dish unpalatable to his family, and afterwards spring the truth on them triumphantly, believing incorrectly that he'd succeeded in deceiving them. The mother thereafter lost her culinary touch and also many of her recipes, which the patient imagines his father to have thrown away. The father, unable to provide an adequate living for his family, had enviously usurped his wife's role as food provider. Moreover, the father's habit of repeatedly "dressing down" both his wife and his son, and his refusal to tolerate any expressions of upset (much less anger) from either one, contributed to the squelching of George's affective life.

Reverberating throughout this case material we hear the oedipal issues, attachment-seeking, identity strivings, and effort at psychic self-replenishment that constitute eating's psychic significance for men. I believe George's need to bottle up his unacceptable rage and frustration made him turn even more avidly to the act of eating. It was an effort to assuage his own humiliation and fury by substituting positive bodily sensations for dangerous feelings. George's involvement in eating the food associated with his mother also acted as a covert, forbidden, metaphoric alliance with the mother and rebellion against the father. The comfort food may have fortified him through its association with his mother and her heritage, thereby symbolically shoring up his depleted self. I believe this food also represented psychic self-replenishment, as it stood in for various kinds of intellectual and creative input that his familial environment had failed to provide. In this respect, George's heightened involvement with food represented not only regressive but also progressive psychological movement, to the degree that it signified the possibility of an affectively richer and more delicious existence. The unfortunate irony here was that the bodily effects of too much comfort food—George's obesity—blocked his ability to pursue his longing to have an active sexual and romantic life, which would have much more effectively nourished and enhanced his self.

A brief sample of our clinical interchange will illustrate how these eating-related themes surfaced both in the manifest content of George's associations and in the transference–countertransference matrix. In a session occurring a year into our work, the patient was complaining about the number of administrative issues being brought to him by his co-workers. The sheer volume of them made it difficult to accomplish his own work. Yet, he felt unable to refuse to tackle them, and to do so immediately. We compared his compulsive submission in this regard with the earlier bind of how to react to his mother's overfeeding. He was afraid that even if he objected, his co-workers would keep "serving" him inexorably just as his mother had. Equally disturbing was the possibility that they'd stop approaching him at all for help, which would cause their shared work performance to deteriorate.

What became painfully obvious was the underlying risk for George either of having his protest overridden or of losing all and being "starved" (through the loss of his sense of identity, a rupture in the connection with his colleagues, and so on). This accounted also for his customary passive-submissive posture of "overeating"— that is, being hypercompliant and nice. We later linked this with his tendency to "take too much grief" from his friends and lovers, to the degree that the resulting sense of violation often led him into a period of phobic avoidance and hermitlike seclusion. We spoke about his need metaphorically to carve out appropriate-size servings and set desirable mealtimes for himself.

At the close of this session George involuntarily winced with back pain, which he then dismissed as "just" stress-related. Mindful of its potential symbolic meaning, I asked George whether perhaps he was feeling overfed by *me* at that very moment. Not surprisingly, he demurred, saying that we had indeed covered a lot of ground that day, but that he would take it in bit by bit. This demurral was not, I think, to be taken at face value. At this point in the work we had not yet clearly differentiated between when George was reliably in touch with his true appetite for my analytic offerings, and when we were perhaps reenacting the shared scenario of "the good eater" who makes it look like he's cleaned his plate in order to please his gratified and gratifying mother. Again speaking metaphorically, I had to be alert to the bits of food he might have surreptitiously "slipped to the dog"; I needed to recognize that these analytic bits were in fact "indigestible" for him and adjust my feeding of him accordingly. In this material we see how a patient's eating-related emotional issues may infuse the analytic relationship itself. Attunement to the nuances of the patient's relationship to food and feeding on the bodily level can also shed light on his relationship to other more psychological types of "food" and feeding.

CONCLUSION

Food and food rituals give men the opportunity to be penetrated and to penetrate, to pursue connection and self-assertion, and to be passive/receptive as well as dominant. The traditionally feminine aspects of relatedness and dependency are present and enacted, without their being highlighted in a way that would create self-consciousness and therefore shame. For many men, an over-involvement with food results in the creation of an illusion of self-sufficiency and the partial recovery of whatever had been renounced in the maternal identification. Especially for men with intense feeding preoccupations, eating activities may act as a sensory substitute for—but also a means of accessing—aspects of affective life that would otherwise be left unarticulated.

REFERENCES

Benjamin, J. (1995). *Like Subjects, Love Objects: Essays on Recognition and Sexual Difference.* New Haven, CT: Yale University Press.

Elise, D. (1998). Gender repertoire: body, mind, and bisexuality. *Psychoanalytic Dialogues* 8(3):353–371.

Fink, B. (1997). *A Clinical Introduction to Lacanian Psychoanalysis.* Cambridge: Harvard University Press.

Plaut, W. G., ed. (1981). *The Torah: A Modern Commentary.* New York: Union of American Hebrew Congregations.

Spence, J. T., and Helmreich, R. L. (1978). *Masculinity and Femininity: Their Psychological Dimensions, Correlates, and Antecedents.* Austin: University of Texas Press.

12

The Meaning of the "Body" in the Treatment of Eating-Disordered Patients

Ann Kearney-Cooke

Slade (1988) describes body image as the "picture we have in our minds of the size, shape, and form of our bodies and the feelings we have concerning these characteristics" (p. 20). From such phenomena as phantom limb, eating disorders, body dysmorphic disorder, and depression, we know that body image is based on the physical self but is not synonymous with it. We know the translation from the physical body to the mental representation of the body is a complex and emotionally charged developmental process.

Based on scientific research and clinical work, I have developed a model that describes how the processes of internalization, projection, identification, and sociocultural forces play in the development of body image disturbance (Kearney-Cooke 1998, Kearney-Cooke and Striegel-Moore 1997). This model includes exercises to use with a therapy group to demonstrate the processes that affect body image.

Dimen (1998) states, "Body matters are so weighty, so deeply important, [that] they often cannot be spoken. Untellable, they can be shown like much that happens in consulting rooms" (p. 66). We can learn about a patient's body image by attending to those aspects of the transference that actualize the patient's early representation of body-self. But the disturbed structures of body experiences are not always directly accessible to psychoanalytic discourse. Therefore, I have developed experiential exercises to help patients understand the complexity of body image. Each of these exercises was developed in response to psychodynamic issues that emerged during group therapy with eating-disordered patients. Themes focused on aggression, entitlement, sexuality, and connection. Initially patients would talk about these conflicts in a dissociated way. The experiential exercises enabled the patients to connect with their affect and to understand the deeper meaning of body obsession and the connection between psychic distress and their shifting body images.

To help patients understand that body image is based on interactions between the self and others, I introduced the following guided imagery into a group of patients struggling with anorexia nervosa and bulimia nervosa.

After a brief relaxation exercise, I asked the group members to imagine that their parents were sitting at a holiday meal with the extended family. They were told to imagine that their mother is pregnant with them and she begins to daydream about the baby. What sex does she want the baby to be and what does she imagine the baby will look like? Their father also begins to daydream about the baby. What sex does he want the baby to be and what does he imagine the baby will look like? They are then asked to imagine the delivery room in the hospital where they were born. Their parents are in the room. As the baby comes out and they say, "It's a girl," what happens to their father? Mother? What happens to their bodies? How do they respond to the baby?

One woman responded:

> I always remember hearing that my dad wanted a son to carry on the family name. Since I was the second and the "last hope" I imagine he was disappointed that I was not a boy. Maybe I felt like I had to be the boy dad never had. He hated how Mom complained about menstrual cramps, and was moody because

of her hormones—so I never complained. I always stayed pleasant around him. I knew Mom was happy I was a girl, yet I still feel I disappointed her because I am not very attractive. I had to make it up to them somehow. So I tried to achieve in school, be a good athlete, and the thinnest at my school.

Her response evoked another woman to speak:

My parents were fighting over me in the delivery room. Their bodies were tense when they picked me up. Both wanted me. I felt guilty if I was with one; I felt I was cheating the other. Fighting not so much because they wanted to take care of me, but because both wanted something from me. The image of my body is one of being pulled by the two of them at once.

Then Mary responded. Mary was diagnosed with bulimia nervosa and borderline personality disorder. She had been sexually abused by her father from the age of 5 until she was 8, and she manifested symptoms of posttraumatic stress disorder. I met with her two times a week for seven years in individual therapy and led two groups that she participated in during this time period:

In the delivery room, "it" came tumbling out and Mother was ambivalent and Father [a physician] was very clinical. It was cold in the delivery room. No one caught me or welcomed me into the world. I have no images of being touched, being held by them.

Aron (1998) states that in infancy our bodily sensations are greatly affected by the qualities of holding and handling that we receive from caregivers. He suggests that our self is first and foremost a body in relation self. Madhulik A. Gupta, at University of Michigan Medical School, found that women who are dissatisfied with their body or obsessed with being thin tend to have few memories of being touched or cuddled in childhood.

Mary began another group therapy session by saying that she wanted to talk about problems she was experiencing in her marriage. Two other women acknowledged they needed time to talk about issues in their life. Members of the group became anxious because there was a limited amount of time and several people wanted to present their issues. In an attempt to help patients understand their anxiety and not avoid conflict, I invited them to participate in the following exercise.

I asked group members to sit on the floor in a circle. I put a piece of paper in the middle of the circle. Then I gave the following instructions. "Imagine this piece of paper represents the time available to the group, and you are having a crisis and want all of the time. When I clap my hands, go after the piece of paper the way you usually go after what you want." When the paper was gone, the clients were instructed to draw how their bodies looked and felt to them.

The exercise was then repeated, but this time patients were encouraged to go after the paper in a different way from the way they did the first time. Here are some examples of responses from patients.

Amy, who struggled with anorexia for ten years and was now in her first year of treatment, stated:

> This was a strange experience for me. I thought we would all very politely reach for the paper and share it. I didn't know everyone would be so aggressive here. But I know I wanted some—so I went after it, but when I got it I gave most of it away. Then I felt depressed. This happens in my life a lot. I want something, but I don't want to feel guilty and upset people. The thought of having people angry at me, or thinking I am selfish makes me nauseous. I can't stand that, so I am willing to give up what I want to avoid it. But then I end up feeling deprived and sorry for myself. Then I don't want people around.

She draws the image of her body which she titled, "Me Inside the Box Where I Live."

This is where I retreated when you said, "Close your eyes and be aware of your body and what's happening to it." I was getting smaller and going inside the gold box where I have lived the last ten years. I feel protected inside there; I'm kind of crouched and lost in my thoughts. I'm feeling deprived and unreachable. All this stuff outside the box is glitter and action around me. I can't get at people or the action out there, even though I sometimes want it. I feel lonely and isolated. My body is thin and preadolescent, almost like a child. It's a gold box because gold is a precious metal, a metal that is not real strong, kind of soft substance—so it can be easily damaged, wounded or pierced. A metal box has the illusion of being safe, but it's not.

Here is Amy's response a second time when she was encouraged to do something different:

I thought for sure this time that everyone would take one-fifth of the group time. In a neat, rational, calm manner I started to go toward the paper to cut it into five pieces. That didn't happen. I felt shattered. My picture is of a thin body being broken up. My soul, needs, and me (the interior me) are trying to stay held together. The exterior me felt frayed. I felt like I tried to go about it nicely but it didn't happen. I don't hold up in the real world—this cushy part of me will be exposed out there. I can't get what I want. Even if I employ new systems, will they work or will I end up getting nothing at all (like I did the second time)? At least in the first picture the gold box is the anorexia and it's something. I may get nothing in the real world.

Mary grabbed most of the paper the first time around. She said:

I was really embarrassed the first time around. I kept thinking of how aggressive I was, like I got a lot but destroyed the rest of you in the process. I hate to take things from others or destroy things to get what I want. After I grabbed this paper and there was silence, I felt horrible. I wanted to break the silence and tell you, "Don't be mad at me." I wanted to justify getting so much. I want to be allowed to go directly after time like this, to win once in a while, but I was afraid you'd say, "You selfish pig." I felt competent being able to get what I want but then I felt bitchy, bullish.

She drew the image of her body. She titled it, "Large Marge from Pee Wee's Adventure."

When I got so much of the paper my body felt large, overflowing, piggish, aggressive. My middle is very big. My heart is on the outside—I'm vulnerable. Then this is my "razzmatazz" stuff going on all the time. I'm a showgirl; this stuff is pretty, shiny, exciting—but not me.

Here is Mary's response a second time when she was encouraged to do something different: "This time I didn't grab any time. I couldn't stand to be "Large Marge" again. I am a stick figure, just there. I went from big to nobody at all."

The unique closeness of the individual's body to his or her identity maximizes the likelihood that the body reflects and shares in a person's most important preoccupations. Fisher (1996) states that the body, like all significant objects, can become a "screen" on which one projects one's most intense concern. In the exercise above, it is clear that eating-disordered patients' conflicts about aggressively going after what they need effect their perceptions of their bodies.

In another session, Mary entered obviously upset after an appointment with her gynecologist. She told the group she had been diagnosed with genital warts and her boyfriend denied giving them to her and blamed it on her. She cried and shook as she reported this to the group. I asked her if she wanted to hold someone's hand for support while she told her story. She held the hand of the patient next to her for one minute, and then let it go. She asked her to give her the Diet Coke can instead to hold on to. In this vulnerable moment when she felt shame and despair, it felt safer to hold onto an inanimate object rather than a person's hand. Her body shook with fear as she tried to let people help her at this moment of shame. But people in her past had been so dangerous and toxic for her that after one minute she had to go back to the safety of the Diet Coke can. The image of the "it" tumbling out in the delivery room and the despair about ever being able to be cared for were written all over Mary's body in this session.

In another session, Mary sets a goal to eat more meals with others, so she would eat more. She sets up a dinner date with her sister and brother-in-law. They were supposed to pick her up at 6:00, but do not show up. By 6:45 she is feeling hungry for Chinese food, hungry to be with people. An appetite for food and people makes her feel out of control. She reports looking down at her stomach. It's out of control—she's gained too much weight. She calls her sister and leaves a message that she already ate, they don't need to pick her up. She jumps on the treadmill and goes at high speed for one hour. She is sweating and begins to feel better. She regains control of herself through exercise.

It is clear how for Mary and others suffering with eating disorders, psychic distress is projected onto the body. Instead of feeling "I'm out of control because I feel abandoned, neglected and alone," she looks in the mirror and sees herself as fat and believes fatness is the cause of her distress. She then focuses on changing her body. Thus in a desperate attempt to seek active mastery, she focuses on something concrete (the body) which she could effectively control. She converts helplessness into action. A transient sense of mastery occurs and the action (excessive exercise) regulates the self.

DISCUSSION

Patients with eating disorders speak a language about the body that we must help them to decode and understand. This requires paying attention to our own somatic responses as well as helping the patients pay attention to theirs. It involves therapists sometimes offering an interpretation, but sometimes using other methods to help a patient gain insight. For example, at a particularly difficult time in the therapeutic relationship, I asked Mary if she would be willing to sculpt with clay the way she was experiencing her body in the session. This allowed Mary to access information within herself about important early relationships and their impact on her body image. It allowed me to understand the source of her psychic pain and how it was being acted out in our relationship. Relationships heal, not techniques. But in treating the body image disturbance of eating-disordered patients, we may need to be creative and use experiential techniques to help the patients "decode" their endless talk about their body and develop a richer vocabulary for expression of the self.

REFERENCES

Aron, L. (1998). The clinical body and the reflexive mind. In *Relational Perspectives on the Body*. Hillsdale, NJ: Analytic Press.

Dimen, M. (1998). Polyglot bodies: thinking through the relational. In *Relational Perspectives on the Body*. Hillsdale, NJ: Analytic Press.

Fisher, S. (1966). Body attention patterns and personality defenses. *Psychological Monographs: General and Applied* 80:1–29.

Kearney-Cooke, A. (1998). Understanding and treating body image: a holistic approach. *Journal of Independent Practice* 18:35–38.

Kearney-Cooke, A., and Striegel-Moore, R. (1997). Etiology and treatment of body image disturbance. In *Handbook of Treatment for Eating Disorders*, ed. D. Garner and D. E. Garfinkel, pp. 295–305. New York: Guilford.

Slade, P. D. (1988). Body image in anorexia nervosa. *British Journal of Psychiatry* 153(suppl. 2):20–22.

13

The Armored Self:
The Symbolic Significance of Obesity

Stefanie Solow Glennon

While much of the psychoanalytic literature on compulsive eating has addressed the defensive function of the activity of eating and/or bingeing, less attention has been paid to the psychodynamic meanings of the oftimes resultant fat. In this chapter, I will attempt to show how the symptom of obesity unconsciously serves to symbolically protect the psyche from feared penetration and annihilation. Bromberg (1991) said, "It is in the nature of the human condition that the experience of 'insideness' helps to protect the self from excessive external impingement." I am fascinated by the notion of a self in need of protection from "excessive external impingement." What does this mean? What is the actual danger that is feared and protected against? Bromberg and others speak of the self or psyche protecting itself from being overwhelmed by affects it "knows" cannot be processed or integrated, that somehow if allowed access to center stage, these affects could annihilate the self. But again, what does this mean? What sort of death or annihilation is being avoided through the defensive maneuvers that we observe so frequently in our offices? Freud's (1895) ideas about the overstimulation of neurons and their capacity to go on overload and become dysfunctional are appealing in this context and give some credence to his conclusion that the psyche is always seeking equanimity, quiescence, safety from electrocution, so to speak. This chapter focuses on the ways in which the self seeks protection from "excessive external impingement" through the erection of a fat barrier as a symbolic boundary as well as through the more commonly understood act of anesthetizing and shoring up the internal self through the compulsive ingestion of food; in addition it addresses the unconscious defensive function of the meanings of being fat that I have repeatedly seen in my practice.

It is often thought that compulsive eating and obesity are synonymous. They are not. Although compulsive eating frequently results in varying degrees of overweight, there are patients who do not need to be fat, or are afraid of being fat, who either purge after binges or return to eating normally or sparingly and so never get heavy. These people do not have a need to be fat or, put differently, do not possess a fear of being thin which I have seen in my practice over and over again. Even patients who are afraid of being thin can, after considerable analytic work, frequently differentiate the times that they are binge eating to anesthetize themselves from the times that the eating has been stimulated by some occurrence in their lives that kicks off their fear of getting thin or need to be fat. I am distinguishing between the act of eating as anesthesia and the act of eating unconsciously designed to produce fat, and I have found this distinction to be an extremely important one. In numerous cases of long-term intensive analytic treatment, patients have lost thirty to fifty pounds, still have another thirty to fifty pounds to lose, but no longer binge eat. The eating disorder in that sense is no longer present. Never before, even in childhood, had they been the same weight for any length of time. They were always either gaining or losing weight but never maintaining. The work is now focused on their fear of being thin, and they are once again losing weight. One of these patients said, "I could no more cook up a pound of pasta and eat it than I can go to the moon. I am no longer a binge eater!"

The act of eating obsessively, as differentiated from the need to be fat, not unlike other obsessive-compulsive behaviors, serves to ward off anxiety, to anesthetize people to what they unconsciously and sometimes even consciously fear are potentially overwhelming affects that they cannot metabolize, to use Eigen's (1992) terminology. One patient found herself in the subway shaking, feeling extremely pressured and anxious, and so stopped to buy a bagel and two large cookies. She then described feeling as if she had taken a Valium. One woman has been able to get in touch with an inner voice that says at such anxious moments, "I gotta eat, I gotta eat," and she finds herself in front of the refrigerator indiscriminately eating anything to push down or numb the feelings.

The sources of anxiety, the specific affects that are feared (anger, sexual desire, envy, a fear of being envied, competition, a fear of being competitive, etc.) differ based on patients' unique psychodynamic histories. But how does obsessive eating quell anxiety? Patients can fairly readily become aware that they are eating to "push down feelings." What does this mean? It seems to be a metaphoric representation of affects concretized and able to be physically pushed and kept down and out of awareness by the actual press of food. In addition, there is the metaphoric representation of food filling an internal emptiness or shoring up the self by filling the stomach with the food as symbol for nurturance, love, strength, and even passion. These phenomena reveal a fascinating interplay of the concrete and the symbolic. Understanding the shared symbolic or metaphoric meanings of fat and being fat can further our efficacy in working with eating-disordered patients.

One young woman said about her compulsive eating and intermittent obesity, "The fat barrier protects me from me and me from the outside world." That is, the anesthetic function of eating keeps feelings down and out, and the fat provides protection from occurrences out there that threaten to kick off feelings that could be overwhelming. There is a metaphoric or symbolic way in which the literal, concrete fat exterior of the body, a thickened outer layer, is experienced by the person as a thickened outer layer of their psyches. Now, this cannot be literal, it is clearly irrational. They are speaking metaphorically for sure, but it feels literal and we as therapists "know" what they are talking about. The internal experience of self feels overwhelmable by affects. Many patients who have been violated sexually, physically, or psychically (such as through invasive, narcissistic parenting) are ever watchful of their outer barrier, their moats against further penetrations. Their psyches frequently accomplish this mechanism of defense by coating their bodies with fat so that they symbolically experience themselves, their psyches, as reinforced and impenetrable. They are therefore able to go out into the world in their armor of fat. This mechanism is a symbolic representation of a desired inner state of protection. Fat cannot protect one's psyche, but it feels like that unconsciously. I often find myself picturing a one-celled animal, a paramecium or amoeba, whose boundary or protective membrane is in danger of being punctured and its life contents in danger of spilling out. Interpretations that I make with this simile in mind are almost always understood and responded to by patients, and produce a bonding between us based on my having articulated something for them that they have always "unthought known" (Bollas 1987). In speculating on the existence of an internal "one-celled psyche," I recall that Richard Feynman, the nuclear physicist, was asked, If all scientific knowledge were lost in a cataclysm, what single statement would preserve the most information for the next generation of creatures? How could we best pass on our understanding of the world? Feynman proposed, "All things are made of atoms, little particles that move around in perpetual motion, attracting each other when they are a little distance apart, but repelling upon being squeezed into one another" (quoted in Gleick 1992, p. 39). Is it possible that our psyches operate similarly, like atoms being attracted to and needful of one another, but requiring the necessary distance or boundary to survive, remaining always vulnerable to the intrusion of noxious affects produced by noxious, interpersonal happenings in our lives, dissociated affects that do not fade, do not go away, that may, according to Miller (1990), live in our cells?

Interpretations that are informed by this way of thinking frequently lead to the patients' understanding the irrationality of their eating behavior when consciously they so desperately want to be thin, wear lovely clothes, engage in physical and sexual activities, and have a normal life. However, like all interpretations, they may be accurate and may make intellectual sense to the patient, but cannot be integrated until the fear of the attendant affects and fear of being overwhelmed by affects is lessened. And, as with most patients, this mainly occurs through an in vivo, affective experience with the analyst. To quote Levenson (1993), "Ultimately, the patient does not learn from us how to deal with the world. The patient learns to deal with us in order to deal with the world." Winnicott (1969, 1974) also addresses this issue. Many of my patients have in fact experienced a severe trauma that constituted a breakdown in the psyche that they have already lived through but are terrified, unconsciously, that affects surrounding that trauma will be kicked off again, or emerge full blown for the first time and be overwhelming. And this is the unconscious reason why some of them need to anesthetize themselves to their affects and coat themselves with fat as a symbolic protection from reexperiencing the old traumas.

The psychodynamic, defensive function of blocking affects, either stuffing them down with food or symbolically protecting oneself psychically with a fat barrier, serves to protect the psyche from feared affects or invasions that will kick off affective responses. But when the affects are successfully defended against or are never allowed to "formulate" (Stern 1987), the person is left with a depleted inner life and frequently feels and is experienced as "deadened." Ogden (1997) says, although not specifically about people with eating disorders,

> I believe that the analytic task most fundamentally involves the effort of the analytic pair to help the analysand become human in a fuller sense than he has been able to achieve to this point. This is no abstract, philosophical quest; it is a requirement of the species as basic as the need for food and air. The effort to become human is among the very few things in a person's life that may over time come to feel more important to him than his personal survival.

To become human means to be more affectively responsive, more able to be in the present. Green (1996) said that there is in all of us, along with the need for self protection, a desire/drive toward experiencing. And experiencing, after all, means affects. Without affects there is no experience. Eigen (1992) said, "Our productions far outstrip our ability to handle them. We are taxed by the inner and outer worlds and must grow capacities to handle our creations." Bion (1963) noted, "The human race is ill-equipped to tolerate its own experiential capacity." Thus we see our patients, eating disordered and others, utilizing whatever mechanisms are available to them as defenses against the feared to be lethal affects, but paying the life-robbing price of feeling unreal or deadened in the present.

CLINICAL ILLUSTRATIONS

A 49-year-old obese woman, about sixty pounds overweight with whom I have been working three times a week (once in group and twice individually) for three years, tells me about not having yet heard the outcome of a job interview. She has told me repeatedly how much she wants this job because it will bring her back into New York City from the wilds of Westchester. I begin to feel myself numbing out, and getting annoyed with this very verbally effusive and affectively disconnected woman. I think, why is she telling me this again? This is not new information she is imparting. I interrupt her and say, "Do you really think that I don't know how much you want to return to the city? How many times do you think you have told me exactly what you have just said?" The patient is somewhat stunned, but I continue. "Why do you think you do this?" She responds, "Well, my mother never listened, so I repeat myself. Other people have told me that too." But this, though true, is also a repetition. Many times she has used this formulation to explain her verbosity and repetition. I then remember her admission in the group the previous evening that she hates silences, that they scare her and make her extremely uncomfortable. And in fact, in the group, she rarely lets a silence persist. I say to her that I think there is a relationship between her discomfort with silences and her need to fill the air with verbiage, verbiage that is not in the service of communication. The patient is a very intelligent woman who has by now developed a trust in my not wanting to hurt her. So, nondefensively, she asks me what I mean. I say that I think her fear of silences is related to a fear of being invaded, penetrated, as she repeatedly was by her mother, and that her words serve the function of keeping people away, since they are not communications that would draw them near to her. Similarly, I say, "I think that your being fat serves the same function, to keep people away and to protect yourself." She is stunned into the first long-lasting, introspective silence that I have experienced with her. This is a woman who has the most egregiously invasive, infantilizing mother I have yet heard of. A mother who lives in another city but still buys and sends cans of tuna fish, toilet paper, underwear, matzohs for Passover, that is, care packages, for her adult daughter, a high-powered executive who makes more than $130,000 a year. When the patient was a child, the mother never knocked on a door, including bathroom doors. (The patient says she did not know that people were supposed to knock on doors until she went to college.) Each day the mother chose the clothing and dressed the daughter until she was 11 years old. The patient is now so sensitive to invasion that she cannot allow a cleaning woman into her home for fear that her things will be touched, moved, or broken. She has had anxiety attacks when the super has entered her apartment to fix something without her knowledge. When repairs were going to be made on the outside of her building and she was advised to keep her windows closed and blinds down so that construction dust and debris did not enter her apartment, she emphasized the severity of her depression and the out-of-control eating that was connected with it. When I interpreted her reactions to these "invasions" as feeling like internal penetrations, from which she protects herself with the act of eating and the external barrier of her fat, she associated to her mother's not knocking on doors, thus making the connection between her fears about being psychically violated and her apartment being entered, doors not being protection against invasion etc, and so on—all symbolic representations of psychic penetration and the resultant feared loss of self. The patient had only one sexual experience in her life, at age 25, which ended with her returning home at 10 P.M. to her "hysterical" mother, who, over the telephone, had threatened to call the police if she did not come home.

Just as there are people who use the ingestion of food as an anesthetic, but do not psychically need to be fat, there are people who eat in order to get heavy but do not psychodynamically experience their external boundary of fat as a symbolic protection from psychic invasion. Their overweight can instead be the result of an unconscious desire to solidify their internal, psychic selves through body size. I have found this symbolic meaning of body size to be a less frequent, though no less powerful, psychodynamic than the unconscious utilization of fat as insulation. Patients, through the large size of their body, feel rooted to the ground, strong, and in that sense experience themselves as less fragile internally, as if their outer physical size were a symbolic representation of their inner or psychic self, which is experienced unconsciously and concretely as either being big and strong or vulnerable and weak depending on the size of the body.

Another dynamic has to do with the unconscious or sometimes conscious idiosyncratic meanings attached to being fat or being thin. For example, a lesbian woman believed that if she were thin, other women would "hit on me," and she would not be able to resist. She would thus be in danger of losing her highly significant relationship in which she felt loved for the first time in her life. She knew that her relationship would not survive if she were not monogamous, so she rapidly gained weight from the time she and her partner decided to have a marriage ceremony. She blew up to over 300 pounds.

Another woman, an uncommonly beautiful woman who often reminded me of Snow White, knew from experience that if she were thin, men would pursue her avidly, and if pursued, she would risk kicking off her mother's envy and malevolent power (not unlike the evil stepmother in the story). So she gained weight until men stopped expressing interest in her. She had to be over 250 pounds for that to happen. And it did.

The psychodynamic explicated in these examples is different from the need to be fat as a protective barrier against feared penetrations, although some of these patients also ate to anesthetize and also unconsciously used the fat barrier defensively. I have found that this careful titration of the differing dynamics of eating and obesity, even in the same person, is crucial to the patient's understanding of, and eventual change in their symptomatology.

I want to emphasize once again that the work with the patients I have written about here is, technically speaking, no different from my work with other patients. I am always listening for derivatives having to do with what's going on in the room between us; I am always monitoring myself for reactions to my patients that can help me understand how they are feeling and how they are reacted to in the world. Since I firmly believe that immediate experience constitutes the major component of therapeutic action and is the route to overcoming a fear of experiencing affects, I am always looking and listening for the transference–countertransference choreography as it develops and plays out between myself and my patients. I have not gone more deeply into transference and countertransference issues because I wanted instead to focus on the multiple psychodynamic and symbolic underpinnings of the specific symptoms of compulsive eating and obesity that have greatly informed the contents of interpretations that I make, including transference interpretions. I also wish to emphasize the effectiveness of these interpretations, especially those involving symbolic thought.

It is interesting to think of Feynman's description of atoms always being attracted to one another but repelling upon being too close, when listening to this statement from a patient during our final session. This patient, though not obese, was fifteen to twenty pounds overweight at the beginning of our work. She had been seriously alcoholic but was now no longer drinking, had lost the excess weight and had secured a fulfilling, creative, high-powered job in the field in which she is gifted. At her final session, in response to my asking her what she thought had been most effective in our work together, she said, "I was transformed by being heard or listened to with such carefulness without being either suffocated or feeling like I was with an impersonal, clinical non–human being. I felt, feel, liked but without any expectations of what I should do or not do." I was so pleased by this assessment and wrote it down verbatim not only because it was narcissistically gratifying to me, but because I thought it so well illustrated the crucial importance (as in the case of Feynman's atoms) of the balance, the dialectic between distance and presence in the analytic engagement.

REFERENCES

Bion, W. R. (1963). *Elements of Psycho-Analysis*. London: Heinemann.
Bollas, C. (1987). *The Shadow of the Object: Psychoanalysis of the Unthought Known*. New York: Columbia University Press.
Bromberg, P. (1991). On knowing one's patient inside out: the aesthetics of unconscious communication. *Psychoanalytic Dialogues* 1(4):399–422.
Eigen, M. (1992). *Coming Through the Whirlwind*. Wilmette, IL: Chiron.
Freud, S. (1895). Project for a scientific psychology. *Standard Edition* 1:281–397.
Gleick, J. (1992). *Genius: The Life and Science of Richard Feynman*. New York: Pantheon.
Green, A. (1996). Has sexuality anything to do with psychoanalysis? *International Journal Psycho-Analysis* 76:874.
Levenson, E. A. (1993). Shoot the messenger: interpersonal aspects of the analyst's interpretations. *Contemporary Psychoanalysis* 29(3):396.
Miller, A. (1990). *The Untouched Key: Tracing Childhood Trauma in Creativity and Destructiveness*. New York: Doubleday.
Ogden, T. (1997). *Reverie and Interpretation: Sensing Something Human*. Northvale, NJ: Jason Aronson.
Stern, D. (1987). Unformulated experience. *Contemporary Psychoanalysis* 19:71–99.
Winnicott, D. W. (1969). The use of an object. *International Journal of Psycho-Analysis* 50:711.
——— (1974). Fear of breakdown. *International Review of Psycho-Analysis* 1:103–107.

14

When the Self Starves:

Alliance and Outcome in the Treatment of Eating Disorders

Kathryn J. Zerbe

The emerging data on treatment outcomes of eating disorders demonstrate that there is a great need for psychotherapy services among these patients, as they might be refractory to short-term, behaviorally based interventions and psychopharmacological therapies.

In an age where the value of understanding human beings and their symptoms has come under attack, the William Alanson White Institute holds firm to its beliefs in the necessity of treating the patient as a whole and in depth. It is to be commended for developing novel, cost-effective means of rendering psychoanalytic and psychodynamic care. Examples of these creative ways of attuning our ears to the dynamics of an eating disorder can be found throughout this book.

Over the years, the Menninger Clinic and the Topeka Institute for Psychoanalysis have had a felicitous relationship with the White institute, and our approaches to patients have much in common. The Topeka institute made its mark in treating seriously disturbed patients. One cannot do that kind of work without being cognizant of the relational sphere in which patients reenact their problems, make new and (it is hoped) healthier identifications, and gradually reshape their own identities based in large degree on the treatment relationships they have experienced.

In synchrony with Harry Stack Sullivan's assertions that a modified psychoanalytic approach where direct contact with another person is a vital, intrinsic ingredient in the process of change and growth (Mullahy 1970), Karl Menninger (1959, 1963) wrote:

It was not the treatment technique of psychoanalysis that changed psychiatry; it was the new understanding of men's motives and inner resources, of the intensity of partially buried conflicts, the unknown and unplumbed depths and heights of our nature, the formidable power each of us holds to determine whether he lives or dies. . . . It was the realization that we must encourage each individual to see himself not as a mere spectator of cosmic events but as a prime mover; to regard himself not as a passive incident in the infinite universe but as one important unit possessing the power to influence great decisions by making small ones. [1963, p. 399]

Menninger always believed that a patient could improve, no matter how serious the disability or tenacious the symptoms. He challenged trainees to avoid diagnostic categories that stereotyped people, instead insisting that we enumerate their strengths, even as we assimilated the biological, psychological, social, and family contexts that led them to seek out treatment. To alleviate human suffering was for Menninger the preeminent goal for the practitioner. To do so, he believed that you must first instill in the patient a sense of hope, in part by communicating that the patient is accepted and understood. Together, clinician and patient work to restore the "formidable power" inherent in charting one's own life course based on overcoming "partially buried conflicts" and gaining new appreciation of the patient's inner resources.

WHAT THE THERAPIST LEARNS FROM
THE OUTCOME LITERATURE

The psychiatric outcome literature indicates the unpredictability of the course of illness and, for a substantial number of eating-disordered patients, a poor prognosis. Even clinicians not psycho-dynamically oriented are confounded by studies that look at how poor long-term recovery is for these disorders, especially anorexia nervosa. For example, in Sweden, Theander (1970, 1983a,b, 1985) found an 18 to 30 percent mortality rate over a 30-year course for anorexic patients. Citing the research of other investigators, he notes that most patients who recover continue to suffer from various mental problems, including depression, anxiety, psychosomatic disorders, substance abuse, and characterlogical problems. He emphasizes that the prognosis in any one case is impossible to predict. Some patients do well, especially if the disease is diagnosed and treated early. However, the older the age of onset, the more disturbed the body image, and the greater the fluctuating eating symptoms (such as purging and restriction), then the more likely it is that the patient will have a poor outcome.

There is a consensus that severe eating disorders tend to become chronic, but "at the present time there is not enough evidence to guide any attempt to match patients to different treatments" (Treasure and Schmidt 1999, p. 172). Based on a more than ten-year follow-up of patients at the Cornell Medical Center, Halmi (1989, 1998) writes that partial hospitalization treatment helped a high percentage of subjects with eating disorders maintain adequate weight. Unfortunately, these patients continued to have other symptoms, including poor interpersonal relationships and preoccupation with staying slender.

For a significant number of patients, outcome is abysmal (Rodin 1991). No doubt progress has been made over the past twenty years in our appreciation of the metabolic effects of disordered eating. New medications and refeeding plans can initiate and sometimes help maintain recovery. There are numerous cognitive-behavioral and interpersonal therapies available for patients. But even the most optimistic outcome reports reveal that between 40 and 60 percent of patients have significant eating symptoms after treatment. The majority of reports look at results only in the short-term, with limited follow-up assessment (Herzog et al. 1991, Mitchell et al. 1996, Walsh and Devlin 1998).

Clinicians of every theoretical persuasion are perplexed by the sheer fortitude of the symptoms' tenacity and the long-term personal suffering and medical risks that accrue to the patient (Jarman and Walsh 1999, Srinivasagam et al. 1995). Yet even the most refined statistical studies do not tell the story of any one afflicted individual. Reams of comorbid diagnoses, symptomatic behaviors, and treatment options are listed and investigated, but little mention is made of what actually constitutes improved quality of life of the person who has an eating disorder diagnosis. Manifest symptoms may improve in the short run, but does the person find meaning, fulfillment, and pleasure over the long run?

In the late 1990s, quality of life measurements became a much-touted research tool to assess the benefit of what we do and how we do it—especially in order to argue to third parties that our methods are cost effective. In other words, better outcomes, including quality of life, not only help us gauge if we are helping patients but also help pay the bills. Intuitively, quality of life improvement has always been what psychodynamically oriented clinicians have set out to do for our patients. And improved quality of life inevitably means so much more than mere symptom control. Ultimately, it means growth in the development of the self and the transformation of the human soul. In the case of eating disorders, it means that patients must shift from the narrow focus on the eating disorder as a way of life to a much broader conception of what constitutes their life. Menninger said that such patients must begin to probe the "depths and heights" of themselves as individuals. In order to be transformed, so that they see themselves not as "a mere spectator of cosmic events but as a prime mover," they must begin by making those small decisions of reckoning with the disordered eating so they can begin "to influence great decisions," (p. 399) meaning the development of a sense of voice, purpose, meaning, and direction in their lives.

Recovery usually begins by making behavioral interventions regarding the patient's intake of food (if anorexic) or helping the person curtail modes of purging (if bulimic). Inevitably, these behavioral steps take on enormous psychological meaning. They are the first small steps, which if understood and worked through in the patient–therapist dialogue, have the ultimate effect of initiating great and lasting intrapsychic and interpersonal change (Zerbe, 1992, 1993a,b, 1995a,b, 1996, 1998).

Much can be learned from taking a look at the eating disorder outcome literature. Garfinkel and Garner (1982) described how anorexic and bulimic patients struggle to do the kinds of things that most of us take for granted as the cornerstones of a meaningful life. These researchers discovered, with respect to interpersonal relationships, that people with eating disorders have a plethora of difficulties that lessen their capacity to engage and to be intimate even after symptoms are partially or altogether curtailed! Eating-disordered patients often have difficulty getting "life off the ground." They have trouble completing school. They do not achieve at work to the highest level they believe possible, and they complain of difficulties getting along on the job. They describe how their preoccupation with eating interferes with just about everything. They do not marry as often as those without eating problems. They have fewer friends. They struggle with loneliness.

These patients often do fairly well with respect to short-term symptom remission, but they are unhappy in the long term in other areas, which hints at the perils and pitfalls of an excessive focus on symptom control to the detriment of discerning and ameliorating the plight of the person as a whole. But this point often gets missed in the psychiatric literature, which focuses on whether the patient achieves or maintains target weight, stops or at least diminishes the tendency to purge, is able to stay out of the hospital, or is less obsessed with body image and appearance.

One of my analytic patients, a practicing pathologist with a long-standing pattern of food restriction and self-recriminative tendencies (who reads broadly in philosophy, theology, and psychiatry), put it best: "You know, your journals say people like me are 'alexithymic.' Frankly, I think your literature is alexithymic." Her capacity to fantasize and to mentalize (Fonagy and Target 1996, 1997) are aptly captured in her quick, conceptual critique of psychiatric literature. She knows where she would fall if given a traditionally designed research protocol that was based solely on ascertaining the longevity of her symptoms and the plethora of eating-related problems with which she has struggled for more than 20 years (e.g., overexercising, brief periods of bingeing and purging, compulsivity, severe body image distortion).

This insightful woman mistrusts how "good" and "poor" outcomes are relegated to checklists of symptoms. She resents being labeled and pathologized. She is well aware that publishing in books and journals may do more to advance the egos and careers of authors and investigators than to advance a reasoned, sympathetic insight into what constitutes adequate patient care. Naturally, her thoughts on these matters have led to many fruitful discussions in her analysis because she knows I have published! These powerful manifestations of the negative maternal transference notwithstanding, this patient has something to say to us about ourselves, and her capacity to do so says much about her ability to open her mind, to question, to reflect. This patient is confronting our tendency as mental health professionals to think we have understood something because we have been able to name it. Naming a problem on a checklist may solve a researcher's problem. It never solves the patient's problem

HOW CAN OUTCOME RESEARCH BE INFORMED BY THE PSYCHOANALYTIC METHOD?

To consider what light the analytic perspective might throw on outcome research, let us focus on several instructive papers published on eating disorders in the late 1990s. One of the most thorough studies, a case-control design, compared patients to a community sample. Sullivan and colleagues (1998) found that therapeutic approaches that exclusively focus on weight gain but that neglect detection and treatment of associated psychological features may be inadequate. These researchers state that patients need more help than they are getting because even after treatment on an eating disorders inpatient service, patients persisted long-term in perfectionism, major depression, anxiety disorders, body and shape concerns, and alcohol dependence. Other studies assessing outcome from different vantage points (Herzog et al. 1999, Jager et al. 1996, Kaplan and Garfunkel 1999, Keel and Mitchell 1997, Mitchell et al. 1996, Wilson 1996) also report that recovery occurs in a significant proportion of patients only to be accompanied by other psychological issues that affect the patient's ability to engage meaningfully in life and, quite possibly, to achieve full recovery over time with respect to the specifically enumerated disordered eating and body image concerns.

One might reasonably wonder what a survey of the outcome literature reveals to be the most commonly associated psychological features that afflict our patients. In assessing the long-term course of anorexia, Pike (1998) found problems with psychological adjustment in 50 percent or more of patients. She opines that this finding warrants further study. Her analysis of a broad array of outcome literature supports the notion that long-term anorexic nervosa patients have a high incidence of major depression, fail to achieve normal body weight, are afflicted with the comorbidities of alcoholism, obsessive-compulsive disorder, panic disorder, separation disorder, and overanxiousness. Pike's survey further reveals that anorexics do poorly on the Global Assessment Functioning (GAF) Scale and have a persistent focus on thinness and lower body mass index over time. Finally, she notes numerous refractory psychosocial problems for both anorexic and bulimarexic patients.

As in Theander's earlier review, Pike concludes her critique of the outcome studies she reviews by boldly stating that treatment of anorexic patients is unusually challenging, often long-term, complex, and in need of more systematic follow-up. Given the chronicity and morbidity of the disorder, clinicians must "derive more carefully and consistently the milestones of initial treatment response, re-lapse, remission, and recovery" (p. 473). Although shorter, behav-iorally based, and pharmacological outcome studies could make us feel sanguine about the recovery of a majority of patients, Pike's careful analysis reminds us that the best results to date are limited by methodological issues, length of follow-up, and how one defines recovery.

Writing from the vantage point of expertise in addictive disor-ders, Peter Miller (1996) argues that the criteria for overcoming an eating disorder have been too narrow and simple. After reviewing more than fifty studies, he concludes that psychological health must be considered as important as defining improvement by changes in weight or bingeing. Viewing the recovery from an eating problem as a long-term issue where one must take into account the stages of success, Miller asserts that in addition to medical health, eating habits, and exercise moderation, treaters must emphasize helping the patient find solace in making "progress, not ['being] perfect'" (p. 749).

Most analytically oriented clinicians would concur that a goal of any analysis or psychodynamic psychotherapy would be to have a more "loving and beloved" superego (Schafer 1960) that eschews perfectionism and rigidity. Here is just one example of how the phenomenological (e.g., addiction, psychiatric) literature and the psychoanalytic literature converge by making the same point. We must begin to talk to each other in a commonsense language that spells out when and why we agree on an important point. In this case, both clinicians and patients have much to glean from holding less rigid perspectives on what constitutes progress. When both are more content to consider progress, not perfection, as a reasonable benchmark of change, patients inevitably feel less need to defen-sively hold on to the symptoms as one harbinger of personal autonomy. The world becomes a livelier, friendlier place when patients can tolerate their foibles and come to expect that backslides and forward moves are part of every person's life journey. This is one reason that all clinicians, regardless of theoretical persuasion, usually subscribe to individual treatment goals that include "making progress, not 'being perfect.'"

The non–analytically oriented clinicians and researchers who published their studies may prove to be a potentially friendly audience for those of us working from an analytic model. Although analysts must not dismiss the pharmacological, patient educational, and cognitive behavioral treatments used for most patients with an eating disorder, this literature demonstrates that clinicians "must begin to view outcomes as a continuous process rather than a definitive end product" (Miller 1996, p. 752). Various kinds of outcomes must be considered, including the overall physical and psychological health of the patient, regardless of absolute changes in weight or bingeing. There is also an implicit subtext to the conclusions of the authors I have reviewed. They are telling us, in effect, "We're missing something and people are suffering." They are covertly asking, "Why aren't our efforts paying off? How might we be of more help?"

Because current methods of treatment offer limited prognostic value, many clinicians can benefit from our consultation, and many patients can benefit from an analytically oriented approach that promotes sustained but often slow progress over time. Menninger used to challenge his staff and trainees when we were preoccupied with making a definitive diagnosis or were overly ambitious when seeking a cure. He would remind us: "We [psychodynamically oriented clinicians] are in the growth and development business! (Menninger and Freeman 1973, pp. 61–62). We must see mental illness as a degree of disorganization in a particular person and discover ways to help them improve organization" (Menninger et al. 1963, pp. 156–157).

BUILDING THE ALLIANCE: CONTEMPORARY PATIENT EDUCATION MODALITIES AND THE PSYCHODYNAMIC METHOD

When working with patients and their families, I provide them with some of the above data. One must use judgment and timing, and provide information that fits the situation. Overall, I want patients to know the medical and prognostic facts about their illness. Some might see this metaphorically as an attempt to confront and/or feed the patient. I do not conceptualize the papers as "food," although there is plenty of "food for thought" in them. I initially conceptualize this tool as simply empowerment through knowledge.

Patient education concretely addresses the dynamic of omnipotence that McDougall underscored in Chapter 1. Recall her mention of how, in the addictions, patients come to us with the delusion of omnipotence; in the transference, patients unconsciously want us to be the omnipotent mother or father. They then delight in rejecting us—exhorting our defects, deficiencies, and paltry value. This need to defeat is based in part on the patient's thwarted search for identity and autonomy. Thus, when attempting to help the patient who has an eating disorder (or other addiction), the therapist quickly learns not only that she is not omnipotent, but also to value and rely on her own imperfections as a tool in the treatment process. The eating disorder is held on to with a fierceness even as the patient seeks another person (e.g., the therapist) who will fulfill the role of the original object—the total, need-gratifying, omnipotent mother of the early preverbal period. By using patient education modalities that particularly emphasize the poor-prognosis portion of this outcome literature, we immediately take a defeatist, nonomniscient position with the patient. But we also tell the truth. We are saying: "You have won. I don't have a perfect tool to cure you. Only a certain percentage get better. What can be done?"

This stance immediately begins to challenge the transference that the patient brings with her—that she will find in me her answer. Because the patient is compelled to defeat that notion, therapists who provide concrete information become powerful agents of transformation. We are saying to the patient that she is an adult and that we can only *share* power with her. It is her responsibility to engage if she has enough *desire* for change.

This approach also has the potential to empower the patient by creating a dialogue. Following Kearney-Cooke's perceptive advice regarding the use of psychotherapy groups for eating-disordered patients, it increases leverage to say, "We are a team." Kearney-Cooke steps back and invites the patient to join her. In a psychodynamic context, this intervention can be conceptualized as a concrete interpersonal invitation to a mature dialogue, and is aimed at decreasing the fantasy of the therapist as omnipotent. We can further deconstruct these interventions by saying Kearney-Cooke is inviting her patient to have an experience of a parent in the transference who is eager for her to grow and to have her own ideas. In essence, shepherding the patient's autonomous desires is key to therapeutic progress.

The therapist will be sensitive to fantasies of abandonment as the patient improves because implicit in the team metaphor is the first adult model of how to work together while being separate people. A team works because it is made up of individuals who have different jobs. For patients who have often had impinging environments (like so many of our eating-disordered patients), where mother "knew" and was experienced as constricting or symbiotic, it is a crucial developmental experience to say to them in the metaphor or concretely, "There is another world out there. I can let you see it and have a little bite of it." This intervention gives tacit and explicit permission to grow, although the patient will invariably test the therapist's resolve to endure this paradoxical position of separateness and togetherness.

Regressions are expectable when the patient experiences growth away from the therapist or fantasizes abandonment if she makes progress. These concerns must be interpreted and the alliance preserved especially during periods of improvement, lest the patient reinitiate eating symptoms to avoid losing the therapist prematurely. Indeed, one might reasonably speculate how many exacerbations of eating disorders occur because a treatment relationship has been severed for financial reasons, family resistances, or the patient's desire to desert the therapist because she (the patient) imagines she will be left.

STRENGTHENING THE ALLIANCE: HELPING THE PATIENT COME TO KNOW HER OWN MIND

An example from the case files of an adolescent in the Menninger Eating Disorders Program illustrates therapeutic change when the patient increases her capacity to develop primary reflective functioning (Fonagy and Target 1997).

Valerie was a 15-year-old girl admitted with a four-year history of bulimia and anorexia. A particularly ominous symptom was a thought disorder found to be refractory to antipsychotic medications from several different classes (even after her weight had been restored). Valerie reported continuously hearing voices, but the hospital team wondered it anyone had ever listened to what Valerie's voices might be saying to her. A review of the records revealed numerous attempts at treatment from a behavioral perspective but no conceptualization of what might have caused the symptoms to develop in this particular person in her particular family at the time that it did.

After taking a detailed family history and making a multigenerational genogram, the social worker ascertained that Valerie was the only survivor of triplets. The multiple pregnancy was the product of in vitro fertilization after her parents had undergone a long and torturous infertility treatment. Valerie's biological father was not known. Her parents never spoke to her of any of these facts, but other members of the family and friends knew the entire story. Her father sobbed as he told the social worker he "was impotent because of severe juvenile diabetes mellitus," and he never wanted his child to know he "was not a real man or her dad."

In our initial interview, Valerie told me she heard a man's voice saying, "Don't speak it. Don't speak it." When I felt it was timely to do so, I posed the question, "What is it that you shouldn't be speaking about?" She told me she had no thoughts about this. She would follow the orders of this voice lest she face severe recriminations. Naturally, I wondered what Valerie "knew" but was "not supposed to know" (Bowlby 1979). In essence, might her voices (and her eating disorder) be conveying that she "knew" more than she could let us know? What pressured her so to exclude information from consciousness? Interestingly, hospital team members reported that her mother and father had "whispered their secret" about the father so often that all the staff knew. In effect, everybody knew, but supposedly not the patient. Valerie's hallucinations served a protective function for her parents: the male voice instructing her not to speak represented an internalization of her father's wishes not to have his shame acknowledged by his daughter.

Bowlby (1979) describes how messages that are shut off from conscious awareness are transmitted to people. Especially in troubled families, children have knowledge "about events that parents wish they had never observed" (p. 405). Case records of a group of so-called learning disabled children were studied in great detail. What the children had in common was significant loss. The surviving parent did not talk to the child about the deceased parent's murder or suicide. A collusion occurred between parent and child because the memory of the traumatic death caused suffering and seemed too horrid to broach directly.

The process of grief was thus thwarted. However, when it was discussed and worked through in therapy, the surviving parent was able to mourn the loss and help the child face what he knew but was not supposed to know. In many cases this proved a turning point in the child's psychological treatment and education progress.

The emotional and learning problems these children experience can be understood as deriving from memories that "have been shut away from conscious processing" but that continue "to influence what is thought and felt" (p. 405). The surviving parent was unable to allow the child to speak about the loss, so "their private world" became shut away and unavailable for the psychological work of grieving. Even when messages to repress are less noxious, such as a parent who wishes a child to acknowledge only strengths rather than any flaws, psychological damage can be significant. Bowlby suggests, based on his clinical experience, that psychopathology diminishes when the pressures on the child to repress are diminished.

Clinicians often wonder why our work is so exhausting. We are providing a safe place for helping patients to come to know what they already know and to feel what they already feel. Because patients feel disloyal or hurtful toward their family if they tell their story, they resist coming to grips with their memories and private worlds. We can teach our students to become better listeners, but for each of us the capacity to listen is always a work in progress. One is constantly on the leading edge with the patient who is sharing the nuances and vicissitudes of personal history. The patient must elaborate the affects that have been shut off, disconfirmed, and unexpressed. Sometimes the therapist must be quite active in facilitating the patient's capacity to bear what she knows and what she feels.

The hospital team put Bowlby's conceptualization to work in Valerie's care. Helping the patient elaborate her secret knowledge led to intense, emotional meetings with her therapist and concentrated family sessions. After years of living with this defensive mode of functioning, the parents needed a great deal of support in being more open and direct with Valerie. Gradually, they were able to see the cost of secrets in the family and began to discuss sexuality and the circumstances of Valerie's conception more forthrightly. Valerie's voices and eating disorder symptoms almost magically melted away. She could talk with her parents directly and not repress what she already knew. We also assumed this change in their interactions had an indirect benefit in lessening her guilt about her own emerging sexuality. She could think her own thoughts and have her own feelings about how she came to be (see Fonagy and Target 1996, 1997). Most likely, Valerie's symptoms took form at the time they did because adolescence is the developmental period when sexual issues are in the forefront and when family conflicts about these concerns can interrupt or impede normal psychological development. The father's wish "not to say it" not only encompassed the family secret of infertility but also affected this child's emerging sexuality, which she experienced as harmful and conflictual for her father. Self-reflective function provides internal space where she can think about all that has happened to her and place her world in context, thereby leading to recovery and resilience.

TALKING ABOUT FOOD: OTHER ESSENTIAL INGREDIENTS FOR BUILDING A SELF

Dr. S. is the 40-year-old pathologist with the protracted course of anorexia whom I mentioned earlier. No one would argue with the notion that her chance for recovery is guarded. Yet she is quite bright, engaging, and articulate. One day when she arrived for her analytic session, she started off by quoting Kohut at length: "Kohut wrote *The Analysis of the Self* (1971) and *The Restoration of the Self* (1977). . . . What happens if you don't have a self to begin with? What can be done to build one?"

When Dr. S. was 13 years old, she found an internal medicine textbook and brought it to her parents. She turned to the chapter on anorexia and said to them: "Read it. This is who I am and what I have." They refused. They also refused her pleas for treatment. When she wanted to eat some ice cream or peanut butter, these otherwise indulgent parents would re-mark: "I can't believe you want *that*. Are you ever going to stop eating?" Sometimes Dr. S.'s mother would lock the kitchen cabinets in order to keep her daughter away from food, even though the patient was always thin and athletic. Her mother did not seem to realize that a child needs more food than an adult. The impingements in this patient's family of origin are severe but not unlike others who carry an eating disorder diagnosis.

One day Dr. S. nearly collapsed at work. She was given an ultimatum by her chief of staff—to either get treatment or lose her job. Because of the distance she needed to travel, we began meeting twice weekly. Despite her emaciated state and obvious malnutrition, it was an expressive treatment process: The patient was verbal, insightful, and invested. But whenever she came in, she told me how starved she was. She politely refused suggestions for additional support such as nutritional counseling or hospitalization. As Freud (1909) (fed the Rat Man when he said he was hungry), one day I was so concerned she would faint I asked her if she needed something to eat. She said she would take anything I had, so I took out a candy bar from my desk drawer. She was shocked not so much that I kept food but at the type of food I kept and that I would offer it to her. She exclaimed: "You have chocolate? In your office?"

We can conceptualize this intervention in various ways, including (1) an enactment, (2) use of a transitional object (Aronson 1996), (3) an extension of the space, and (4) a manifestation of the real relationship because the patient had a desperate need for food. Certainly, this "close encounter of the regulatory kind" (Petrucelli, Chapter 7) announced that neither the patient nor I could live without food. A quotient of idealization was shattered as she came to grips with the fact that even I ate chocolate! Acknowledging the need to eat regularly further shatters the patient's treasured belief that self-sufficiency is possible (see Crastnopol, Chapter 11). In effect, narcissistic issues came to the fore as this patient began to reckon with what it means that both she and her therapist cannot survive without food. But most importantly for us, as it turned out, was that for the first time the patient and I were able to discuss food. From Dr. S. I learned that an eating disorder therapist must find food as worthy of interest and curiosity as any other psychological construct, such as a dream, a fantasy, an incident, or a transference manifestation.

Dr. S. has engaged me in a form of play by talking about food. Rather than focus on the multidimensional meanings of this particular incident, I want to stress how it can lead to an opening up of a whole new range of discourse. Discussions about eating took on enormous significance in our relationship. Gradually, we expanded our talk about food into realms such as what she thinks about eating pancakes or her elaborate fantasies about going out to dinner with friends, colleagues, or me.

For example, Dr. S. elaborated the notion of what it might be like to have her session at a local breakfast spot and actually eat pancakes with syrup. One day I found myself asking, "And would you have bacon?" On reflection I realized I was trying to introduce the paternal function of the "other." Pancakes and bacon together is a more complicated world with a mother and a father than a mere pancake alone. Over time, Dr. S. would let herself get into this and expound on all kinds of meanings and ideas she had about eating particular foods.

In summary, talking about eating and permitting fantasies of eating enabled this patient too "taste the forbidden fruit" of a relationship in which she had not heretofore partaken. Two years into treatment, Dr. S. went to a conference in Boston, where she ate some delicious clam chowder. I heard her report of this meal as indicative of her increasing capacity for enjoyment and of her growing ability to partake of even more differentiated objects. As she described the creamy broth, chewy clams, and squishy potatoes, she observed: "Your stomach just growled. I made you hungry." I silently reflected on how, when I lived on the East Coast, delicious clam chowder was more readily available than in the Midwest. I replied, "It must feel good to hear that you're not the only one with hunger in the room." But she rejoined, "Yes, but have you observed, Dr. Z., it's only ten in the morning?"

And I interpreted, "So what's your understanding of the hole you found inside your therapist?" And she said: "I love this. You let me talk about you and food and I don't quite know what to say. Maybe I found a place inside you that needed to be filled up. Maybe even a memory of food or sex or something happening in your life." I replied to her: "Well, you may be right about some of that. It seems to me that you're also trying to get at a notion of greed and how I deal with greed and envy between us. After all, you're the one who had the clam chowder."

Eating-disordered patients need to know they are not the only persons with greed or envy in the room. Their thoughts about food and their fantasies about how the therapist deals with food are ways they get to understand and to master these human issues.

Themes about food are essential issues to deal with directly, interpretively, and compassionately. The eating-disordered patient has little experience with normal eating or family meal time. The eating-disordered patient has many ideas about food but has not been able to speak about them.

Our patients want to know that we can at least speak about these things, and that they can comment on our ongoing commentary. Our patients give us some of the best interpretations of ourselves that we will ever receive. Ninety percent of any treatment is for them, and ten percent is for us!

To treat eating-disordered patients, you have to like food and enjoy talking about food. You have to see that depth psychology is embedded in stories about eating and food. You have to think food is lively and sexy. When my patient and I talk about clam chowder, we're talking about clam chowder, but we're also talking about lots of different objects in her world now. On the surface, it might seem as though only a physical need was filled. After all, she is no longer starving. However, this is not just about being soothed or nourished. These discussions take on the additional significance of having a differentiated, sensual experience that's all one's own and on as many psychological levels as the patient is able to elaborate at a particular juncture in the treatment.

I close with a comment from New York Yankees manager Joe Torre. After the second game of the 1999 pennant series, Mr. Torre was humble when he waxed philosophic about how and why his Yankees keep winning. He said, "We're a team. We know how we play our game. We're not big home-run hitters. We hit the singles. We bunt. That's how we get our runs. That's how we get them to home plate. That's how we win" (Torre and Dreher 1999, pp. 266–280).

And I thought to myself, How much like doing psychotherapy! Even though senior training analysts such as Schlesinger (1995, 1996) remind us that small increments of interpretation are often all the patient can use, why is it that I still find myself eager to hit that grand slam? But this rarely happens on any given day, and when it does the patient is just as likely to cry, "Foul ball." Therapy is a series of singles and bunts, and the season is long. Every day we must face down our longing for omnipotence and remember that those hits and bunts can win the day, save a life, and restore hope. For the patient with an eating disorder, Torre's wisdom might be reframed as a dietary analogy: start with a tidbit or an hors d'oeuvre. Save the smorgasbord for later. Sometimes a bite is enough to drive home a powerful message of hope and resilience.

REFERENCES

Aronson, J. K. (1996). The use of the telephone as a transitional space in the treatment of a severely masochistic anorexic patient. In *Fostering Healing and Growth: A Psychoanalytic Social Work Approach*, ed. J. Edward and J. B. Sanville, pp. 163–178. Northvale, NJ: Jason Aronson.

Bowlby, J. (1979). On knowing what you are not supposed to know and feeling what you are not supposed to feel. *Canadian Journal of Psychiatry* 241:403–408.

Fonagy, P., and Target, M. (1996). Predictors of outcome in child psychoanalysis: a retrospective study of 763 cases at the Anna Freud Centre. *Journal of the American Psychoanalytic Association* 44(1):27–77.

—— (1997). The problem of outcome in child analysis: contributions from the Anna Freud Centre. *Psychoanalytic Inquiry* Suppl:58–73.

Freud, S. (1909). Notes upon a case of obsessional neuroses. In J. Strachey (Ed. and Trans.), *The Standard Edition of the complete psychological works of Sigmund Freud* (Vol. 20, pp. 153–318). London, Hogarth Press. (Original work published 1909)

Garfinkel, P. E., and Garner, D. M. (1982). *Anorexia Nervosa: A Multidimensional Perspective.* New York: Brunner/Mazel.

Halmi, K. and Licinio, E. (1989). Outcome: Hospital program for eating disorders in CME syllabus and proceedings summary, 142nd Annual Meeting, American Psychiatric Association, Washington, D.C.

—— (1998). A 24-year-old woman with anorexia nervosa. *Journal of the American Medical Association* 279(24):1992–1998.

Herzog, D. B., Dorer, D. J., Keel, P. K., et al. (1999). Recovery and relapse in anorexia and bulimia nervosa: a 7.5-year follow-up study. *Journal of the American Academy of Child and Adolescent Psychiatry* 38(7):829–837.

Herzog, D. B., Keller, M. B., Labori, P. W., and Sacks, N. R. (1991). The course and outcome of bulimia nervosa. *Journal of Clinical Psychiatry* 52(suppl 10):4–8.

Jager, B., Liedtke, R., Kunsebeck, H. W., et al. (1996). Psychotherapy and bulimia nervosa: evaluation and long-term follow-up of two conflict-oriented treatment conditions. *Acta Psychiatrica Scandinavica* 93:268–278.

Jarman, M., and Walsh, S. (1999). Evaluating recovery from anorexia nervosa and bulimia nervosa: integrating lessons learned from research and clinical practice. *Clinical Psychology Review* 129(7):773–788.

Kaplan, A. S., and Garfinkel, P. E. (1999). Difficulties in treating patients with eating disorders: a review of patient and clinician variables. *Canadian Journal of Psychiatry* 44:665–670.

Keel, P. K., and Mitchell, J. E. (1997). Outcome in bulimia nervosa. *American Journal of Psychiatry* 154(3):313–321.

Kohut, H. (1971). *The Analysis of the Self: A Systematic Approach to the Psychoanalytic Treatment of Narcissistic Personality Disorders.* Madison, CT: International Universities Press.

——— (1977). *The Restoration of the Self.* Madison, CT: International Universities Press.

Menninger, K. (1959). *Hope.* Academic lecture given at the 115th annual meeting of the American Psychiatric Association, Philadelphia, April.

Menninger, K. A., and Freeman, L., eds. (1973). *Sparks.* New York: Thomas Y. Crowell.

Menninger, K. A., Mayman, M., and Pruyser, P. (1963). *The Vital Balance: The Life Process in Mental Health and Illness.* New York: Viking Press.

Miller, P. M. (1996). Redefining success in eating disorders. *Addictive Behaviors* 21(6):745–754.

Mitchell, J. E., Hoberman, H. N., Peterson, C., et al. (1996). Research on the psychotherapy of bulimia nervosa: half empty or half full? *International Journal of Eating Disorders* 20(3):219–229.

Mullahy, P. (1970). *The Beginning of Modern American Psychiatry: The Ideas of Harry Stack Sullivan.* Boston: Houghton Mifflin.

Pike, K. M. (1998). Long-term course of anorexia nervosa: response, relapse, remission, and recovery. *Clinical Psychology Review* 18(4):447–475.

Rodin, G. M. (1991). The etiology of eating disorders: lessons from high risk groups. *Psychiatric Annals* 29:181–182.

Schafer, R. (1960). The loving and beloved superego in Freud's structural theory. *Psychoanalytic Study of the Child* 15:163–188. New York: International Universities Press.

Schlesinger, H. J. (1995). The process of interpretation and the moment of change. *Journal of the American Medical Association* 43(3):663–688.

——— (1996). The fear of being left half-cured. *Bulletin of the Menninger Clinic* 60(4):420–448.

Srinivasagam, N. M., Kaye, W., Plotnicov, K., et al. (1995). Persistent perfectionism, symmetry, and exactness after long-term recovery from anorexia nervosa. *American Journal of Psychiatry* 152(11):1630–1634.

Sullivan, P. F., Bulik, C. M., Fear, J., and Pickering, A. (1998). Outcome of anorexia nervosa: a case-controlled study. *American Journal of Psychiatry* 155(7):939–946.

Theander, S. (1970). Anorexia nervosa: a psychiatric investigation of 94 patients. *Acta Psychiatrica Scandinavica* Suppl 214:1–194.

——— (1983a). Long-term prognosis of anorexia nervosa: a preliminary report. In *Anorexia Nervosa: Recent Developments in Research*, ed. P. H. Darby, P. E. Garfinkel, D. M. Garner, and D. V. Coscina, pp. 441–442. New York: Alan R. Liss.

——— (1983b). Research on outcome and prognosis of anorexia nervosa and some results from a Swedish long-term study. *International Journal of Eating Disorders* 2:167–174.

——— (1985). Outcome and prognosis of anorexia nervosa and bulimia. *Journal of Psychiatric Research* 19:493–508.

Torre, J. I., and Dreher, H. (1999). *Joe Torre's Ground Rules for Winners.* New York: Hyperion.

Treasure, J., and Schmidt, U. (1999). Beyond effectiveness and efficiency lies quality in services for eating disorders. *European Eating Disorders Review* 7:162–178.

Walsh, B. T., and Devlin, M. J. (1998). Eating disorders: progress and problems. *Science* 280:1387–1390.

Wilson, G. T. (1996). Treatment of bulimia nervosa: when CBT fails. *Behaviour Research and Therapy* 34(3):197–212.

Zerbe, K. J. (1992). Eating disorders in the 1990s: clinical challenges and treatment implications. *Bulletin of the Menninger Clinic* 56:167–186.

——— (1993a). *The Body Betrayed: Women, Eating Disorders, and Treatment.* Washington, DC: American Psychiatric Press.

—————— (1993b). Selves that starve and suffocate: the continuum of eating disorders and dissociative phenomena. *Bulletin of the Menninger Clinic* 57:319–327.

—————— (1995a). The emerging sexual self of the patient with an eating disorder: implications for treatment. *Eating Disorders: Journal of Treatment and Prevention* 3:197–215.

—————— (1995b). Integrating feminist and psychodynamic principles in the treatment of an eating disorder patient: implications for using countertransference responses. *Bulletin of the Menninger Clinic* 59:160–176.

—————— (1996). Feminist psychodynamic psychotherapy of eating disorders: theoretic integration informing clinical practice. *Psychiatric Clinics of North America* 19(4):811–827.

—————— (1998). Knowable secrets: transference and countertransference manifestation in eating disordered patients. In *Treating Eating Disorders*, ed. W. Vandereyken and P. J. Beumont, pp. 30–55. London: Athline.

V

Creativity and Addiction

15

Melancholy and Addiction?

Joerg Bose

Depression lurks in the shadow of many addictive states and addictive behavior staves off the crash. It is astonishing, in retrospect, that it took so long to develop the concept of dual diagnosis in addiction cases, but it is common now to associate depression with addiction. One may ask whether there is more than an associative relationship between the two diagnoses. Can depression present like an addictive phenomenon in its own right?

Despite the current emphasis on the biological aspects of depression, it is important to continue to study it as a reactive phenomenon, a response to current or remembered trauma, loss, injury, or humiliation. The reaction is essentially a defensive phenomenon, a means of avoiding the mourning process (Bose 1995). Depression is a restricted affective state in which the ability to feel and perceive painful reality is blunted, sparing the patient the perception of overwhelming pain, and replacing it with a more diffuse and ongoing numbness, which is painful in its own way. But perhaps there is more to this state than a self-administered anesthetic. Clinical theorists have observed that the depressive mental state can be put to a number of secondary uses, as when the person wrests support from others manipulatively through helplessness (Sullivan 1953), or takes a more angry, reproachful stance, demanding reparation from the other. These tend to be seen as preconsciously chosen stances, and are often discussed in the analytic literature in pejorative terms, with the patient characterized as indulging in self-pity. But this somewhat moralistic attitude fails to recognize that in many cases the extreme magnitude of the trauma cannot possibly be dealt with by the individual alone. The resulting depressive stance is thus often an indirect expression of an ongoing essential need for the other. In this way, I think we can understand some depressions as an incomplete or failed effort at finding or refinding a lost or absent connection with the other.

For this chapter I'm invoking the ancient term *melancholy* because it has long been associated with the strange lure of depression that I'm addressing today. The *Oxford English Dictionary* notes that "in the Elizabethan period and subsequently, the affectation of melancholy was a favorite pose among those who made claim to superior refinement." As an example of this sense of melancholy as an attractive and desirable state, particularly among artists, the dictionary cites a line from Milton's poem "Il Penseroso": "Sweet bird that shunnest the noise of folly, most musical, most melancholy." In a comic mode, Shakespeare portrays a kind of craving for melancholy in the character of Jaques in *As You Like It*, who calls again and again for a sad song: "More I prithee, more. I can suck melancholy out of a song, as a weasel sucks eggs. More, I prithee, more" (II.3. 12–14). In contrast to the play's love-sick melancholy hero, whose condition is cured by his lover, Jaques is an incurable melancholic whose artistic tastes have a lot to do with his insistence on his own sad disposition. He is resolutely, even tenaciously, melancholy, even in the face of the play's happy ending, and seems to draw considerable pleasure from his own sense of misery.

A feeling state that is very close to this addictive kind of melancholy is that of nostalgia. The nineteenth-century Swiss physician Johannes Hofer used this word to describe the problem of homesickness, noting, "The mind in nostalgia has attention only for a return to the Fatherland." He had coined the term *nostalgia* from the Greek words *nostos* (a return) and algos (pain) to describe a depressed state of mind that he found among a great number of immigrants to the New World (Michaelis 1998). Of course, the term now applies to much more than homesickness. Often, it suggests a yearning for some idealized version of a past that never was. Interestingly, the German word for nostalgia, *sehnsucht*, captures even more explicitly its addictive quality; literally, *sehnsucht* means "yearning addiction"—that is, not just a yearning for the past, but an *addiction* to the yearning for the past. Thus it seems the yearning state itself becomes attractive, even desirable, for some reason.

It is this kind of fixation and unending return to the depressed state in certain patients that gives melancholy the appearance of an addiction. One depressed patient spoke of a trance-like experience similar in its appeal to the mindless nirvana that drugs can provide. Another patient compared the surrender to depression to the comfort of lying down in a snowstorm. Some patients, even after years of treatment, seem continually to return to the depressed state whenever injured, or even paradoxically, in the face of a positive experience. When this is recognized in the literature on depression, however, the patient is often characterized as indulging in self-pity or as being pathetic. A certain negative judgmental attitude is betrayed by the language of such discussions, which tend to speak of a "wallowing in" or even an "orgy of" self-pity. Gourewitch (1978) recommends not to let the patient deteriorate into self-pity or cheap sentimental identification with the underdog, and Grayson (1971) writes of a depressed patient who indulged in self-pity and seemed to enjoy the wrongs inflicted upon him. While one patient thanks her analyst for not giving in to her self-pity (Valentin 1989), another is clearly unhappy about the attitude of her analyst, who writes: ". . . when I did not intervene, the frustration continued until the end of the session, and she departed red-eyed and full of pity" (Wermauer 1989, p. 283). Sullivan (1953), while grasping the inter-personal focus of depression as an "indirect exploitative attitude," was nevertheless quite sarcastic in characterizing it as a "preying" on the other's sympathy, and "an extraordinary facility at filling up time with long series of thoughts which wind up with the speaker practically in tears about how wretchedly he is treated by fate" (p. 354).

Milrod (1972), who discusses self-pity directly as a clinical phenomenon, sees in it essentially a "misdirected soothing of the self represented as victim of the other's abandonment or exploitation." It is, however, noteworthy that Milrod also thinks of self-pity at some point as the "setting up of a comforting self [for] a comforted self." But ultimately he returns to viewing it as essentially a defense against acknowledging aggressive and rageful feelings, and as a form of resistance to analysis. To illustrate his point he describes the case of a young woman whom he says entered into reproachful moods of depression, cultivating self-pity in order not to have to face her guilt feelings over the memory of having felt enraged at her mother's illness.[1] Such a view of the depressive's self-pity as defensive and manipulative is characteristic of analytic writers who are concerned about gratifying what they see as immature wishes that cannot lead to any growth in understanding and mental ability. The concern is that such a focus on actual injury by the other would not allow for the patient to come to terms with the tragic aspect of life,[2] namely that all our longing and desire sooner or later come up against the fact that complete fulfillment is not possible, as in Lacan's idea of the fundamental lack in human existence.

But not all deficit experiences are alike, and we can't always know whether the patient has the inner resources to simply drop the defense of self-pity. Working with inner-city patients whose lives show a degree of trauma that transcends the norm for the more typical middle-class patients, on which many of our analytic concepts have

1. However, surprisingly, Milrod then goes on to postulate an "unstable self-image" for many cases involving states of self-pity. However, he returns in his final discussion to viewing self-pity and self-comforting as allowing for a return to the fantasy of union covering up the reality of separateness. [*For M. it is the union with the internalised parent, the superego, that allows the fantasy of union covering up the reality of separateness.*]
2. The distinction Spero (1993) tries to make betwen the pathetic and pathos reflects such thinking.

been based, leads one to a view that addictive and depressive states often arise as a way of avoiding unbearable pain, or what one patient called "looking into the abyss." The task of confronting such experiences is no less challenging than what classical theorists emphasize as the sobering confrontation with conflicting passions. Furthermore, it is not just the content, but the container that needs to be considered here. In other words, trauma and deficit experiences often leave a poorly developed self-configuration in which the patient doesn't have the tools to manage painful emotion.

I have worked for several years with a woman who has been in analysis for most of her long life with a number of analysts. She came from a severely dysfunctional family, marked by economic hardship and frequent ferocious fights between her parents, with her alcoholic father often threatening to leave. She felt like the runt of the litter, thinking that she was ugly, that she didn't belong, and that nobody seemed to have noticed that she existed. Consequently she had a sense of herself as being a nonperson and suffered from extreme dependency, terrified of being alone. She tended to cling desperately to anyone available to her, in fear of feeling annihilated if abandoned or rejected. In her words, "I always had to hang on for dear life, this ferocious, terrible hanging on, otherwise I would fall over the cliff. I could not trust anyone not to leave me." She had become well aware that these feelings pertained to her father's having been only sporadically available to her while mostly absent, creating tantalizing expectations in her for more attention from him. She suffered innumerable bouts of depression throughout her life, often entering into a depressed mood at the slightest hint of rejection, criticism, or any of life's many frustrations.

What emerged in the course of her psychoanalytic therapy was a kind of addiction to experiencing herself as a nonperson. When depressed, she was incapable of having her own mind because she had no access to her own feelings, sensing herself instead at the mercy of the other. It was as if a Siamese twin possessed all the vital capacities she couldn't have on her own. Her first two analysts, as she recalls, interpreted this state of mind as her wish to remain attached to her father on a childlike level for fear of owning up to her more passionate sexual feelings for him. However, she was unable to use such ideas. When she went on to her third analyst, my predecessor, a remarkable change occurred. In her words: "All my life I simply got older, but I never felt that I was moving. It was not until Dr. X. spoke to me about separation that I could separate." This insight, that she could potentially think of herself as a separate person, not in splendid isolation but self-sufficient enough not to have to crave being with an other, was the equivalent of a Copernican revolution in her mental universe. Nevertheless the working through of this insight, which she steadfastly pursued with me after Dr. X. had died, still proved to be arduous and lengthy. What she is able to describe now as an impulse of addiction-like power is her wish to disappear as a person and to blend in with someone whenever she faces an unpleasant reality or the existential fact of her aloneness. "There is still this terrible pull back, which I am fighting. I had to be merged, because I could not exist; without [the other] there would not be me, I would evaporate. It is absolutely mindboggling, unbelievable, that there was no feeling, *no person there*, unless I was with someone. . . . I said that I would feel lost so many times without understanding it. I was not a person unless I was part of that other person. Everything I did was out of desperation. There was no other drive."

This patient exemplifies the paradox that depression appears to be both a passive reaction and a preconsciously chosen mood. It is a passive reaction to the experience of a collapsing sense of self, when the other, who appears to have the vital supplies, is either unavailable or may reject her. It's like a fainting or weak spell that just comes over her in response to her interpersonal situation. But the melancholy stance also has the quality of something chosen, a posture of helplessness, and an almost deliberate befogging of intellectual and emotional awareness.

The crucial aspect in many depressive states is the surrender of autonomous mindfulness and of the ability to feel feelings. This is both a defensive and a communicative mental process. Defensively, it's a complex phenomenon, when the patient feels frightened, and when her fear triggers the return of a previously dissociated memory, she will defend against the emerging perception of the painful truth with a surrender of autonomous feeling and thinking (Bose 1995). On the other hand, it is also a means of communicating, unbeknownst to her, the need to be taken home and to be loved by those who originally ignored her. And ultimately perhaps on its deepest level, it is the communication of a need for the other to help in the process of mourning.

It appears that the particular emotional pain that this patient needed to avoid centered around experiences of shame. Basically she opted for merging with the other whenever she felt frightened as a result of feeling ashamed. What propelled her into hiding was her fear of being judged. She was overcome by shame whenever she thought of herself as being noticed by others. She then felt in danger of being seen for who she thought she really was, someone to be indicted on two counts—for being a nebbish, or nonperson, and for being ugly (the latter a result of her family's overemphasis on good looks, which she erroneously thought she lacked). Thus standing visibly alone would invite certain rejection by others, she thought, a terrifying prospect that compelled her even more to flee into merger.

Her tendency to slide into a depressed state as she anticipates being abandoned by the other would be amplified by her abandoning herself because of feeling so ashamed. This is the point where one can gain some therapeutic leverage by connecting those two kinds of abandonment. If self-pity is the result of that double abandonment, perhaps the reason it seems to have so little therapeutic value may be that it does not necessarily entail self-compassion. This was expressed poignantly by another patient when he said, "I can be very self-indulgent; self-compassionate I am not."

It is quite a challenge to stand by a self that feels helpless, hopeless, inadequate, ugly, and unlovable. The patient will flee from that, hiding in shame. How is it possible for her to own the truth of both a miserable childhood and a consequently miserable adult life? Nevertheless at one time the patient reported a shift in her mood: "I woke up feeling depressed, but then I felt sorry for this kid, and I suddenly felt better. I felt sorry for this pathetic kid, she was having a rough time; it was not shame now, before I saw her as pathetic. When you said, 'May be you are incapable of understanding her', I did absorb it, even if you think I don't listen to you. It took me by surprise, that it was happening. For the first time, I felt sorry for this kid, and could see what a rough time she was having. Usually when I think about it, I feel shame, I must hide it. To see how needy I was, how pathetic. I was to be pitied. I had nowhere to go. What I have now is some feeling about myself where perhaps I am not lost, where I am not frightened. That connection that I made made me feel like I got out of prison."

I believe that while we may struggle with a negative counter-transference to a patient's many returns to the place of the injured self, the experience and the nature of that injury need to be carefully contemplated. It is often not in the patient's awareness what the nature of the actual injury was or whether there even was any injury in the beginning. The patient who enters again and again into a state of depressive self-pity only has the memory of what it feels like to have been injured—something resembling the feeling of a blind person who cannot see who or what hits her.

I would suggest that the dark addictive appeal of melancholy may come from an only dimly felt need to mourn. But the depressive does not mourn, engaging instead in repeated stubborn attempts at finding redemption, repair, rescue, or adoption. These attempts may have the quality of being pathetic (Spero 1993). They may present themselves as naive and sentimental pursuits, but they are also a reflection of a crucial deficit in the early life of the patient, a reflection of the fact that the patient suffered her trauma alone, without a witness, and so without it being fully acknowledged by herself or anyone else. But the presence of the other in the process of acknowledging as well as in the ultimate grieving over the losses and deficits is essential. Shane and Shane (1990) have emphasized that it is the availability of an other, more than the quality of psychic structure, that determines whether mourning is possible. The return to a depressive state may therefore in some cases signal a dimly felt need for the presence of an other. Ghent's (1990) innovative understanding of masochism sees it as a way of surrendering to an other in the hope of seeing "some buried part of the personality screaming to be exhumed." He discusses this as a surrender in faith, as a "deeper yearning to be reached and known in a safe and accepting environment," and not as an act of blind submission to a dominant other, as in Arieti and Bemporad's (1978) formulation.

Therefore, what the patient craves in the search for security is more than the other's passive acceptance. She needs someone to model the stance of compassion toward her. Once she comprehends that compassionate acceptance of her disowned self is possible, such a nonjudgmental attitude, shown to her by the other, can eventually be taken over in a move of self-compassion. In that sense, melancholy, the addiction-like return to a depressed state of mind, not only may be an attempt to coerce the other into providing an illusory gratification, but also may express a dimly felt need for substantial connection with the other, and for understanding without judgment. Experiencing such acceptance may then allow for the gradual transformation of depressive self-pity into genuine self-compassion and self-comfort.

REFERENCES

Arieti, S., and Bemporad, J. (1978). *Severe and Mild Depression*. New York: Basic Books.

Bose, J. (1995). Trauma, depression, and mourning. *Contemporary Psychoanalysis* 31:399–407.

Ghent, E. (1990). Masochism, submission, surrender: masochism as a perversion of surrender. *Contemporary Psychoanalysis* 26:108–136.

Gourewitch, A. (1978). Origins, the impact of parental background. *Contemporary Psychoanalysis* 14:226–245.

Grayson, R. (1971). Selected papers of E. Bergler. *Psychoanalytic Quarterly* 40:153–155.

Michaelis, D. (1998). *N. C. Wyeth.* New York: Knopf.

Milrod, D. (1972). Self-pity, self-comforting, and the superego. *Psychoanalytic Study of the Child* 27:505–528. New Haven: Yale University Press.

Shane, M., and Shane, E. (1990). Object loss and selfobject loss: a consideration of self psychology's contribution to understand mourning and the failure to mourn. *The Annual of Psychoanalysis* 19:152–194. Hillsdale, NJ: The Analytic Press.

Spero, M. (1993). Phallic patheticness. *International Journal of Psycho-Analysis* 74:519–534.

Sullivan, H. S. (1953). *The Interpersonal Theory of Psychiatry.* New York: Norton.

Valentin, J. (1989). Pre-oedipal reconstruction. *International Journal of Psycho-Analysis* 70:433–442.

Wermauer, D. (1989). James Ensor and the attachment to place. *International Review of Psycho-analysis* 16:287–295.

16

The Anxiety of Creativity

Olga Cheselka

After one and a half years of treatment, Jack, a 30-year-old accomplished and fairly successful sculptor, told me he would have to discontinue treatment because he could no longer afford it. As a result of the therapy he realized he needed to take better care of himself and move out of his run-down, rent-controlled apartment to a safer, cleaner, but more expensive place. This seemed like a good step. He had made significant progress with his initial therapy goals, which were to improve his relationships and to find a way to make money while his career as a sculptor was developing. We agreed on a termination date, and he said he would call me in the future to deal with some other issues he wanted to address.

About two years later he did contact me, and we easily reinstated the collaborative working relationship we had previously. However, I was shocked when Jack casually commented that the $800 a month he was paying for marijuana was more manageable now that he had a more lucrative day job. "Eight . . . eight hundred dollars . . . a month?" I stammered in my best analytic tone. "For pot?" I asked with increasing incredulity, trying to maintain a good therapeutic stance, while staying with the material and not letting my own memory or desire intrude. "Yes," he said, patiently, "I told you that before, the last time I was in treatment." (The amount, eight hundred dollars, was particularly significant because at that time that's what my monthly office rent was. This news from Jack was causing a bit of countertransference.)

Continuing with my detailed analytic inquiry, but abandoning analytic neutrality for interpersonal confrontation, I then said, "Oh, so that's why you decided to end treatment when you did!" "Well, no," he said, slightly perplexed but delicately addressing my poor recall, "don't you remember, I decided to move and my rent was going up, so I couldn't afford the therapy and the pot and the new rent?"

Putting aside the discussion of what had or had not been actually communicated, which we explored at a later date, I questioned Jack's use of pot. It turned out that he smoked it every day, although he would wait until the end of his day job, the detail-oriented management of a department. He felt he needed his mind to be clear. But for his artistic work, which he would do on many evenings and all weekend, he needed to get into a different mode. The changeover would begin, in a ritualistic fashion, with a cup of coffee, a cigarette, getting his supplies together, and then smoking a joint. He continued to smoke pot as he worked. He felt it was the only way he could be creative, and he didn't want to explore his use of pot as part of the therapy work. He felt he was managing his life well. Giving up pot would make it impossible for him to continue to do his sculpting, something he couldn't imagine. It wasn't until some time later, when his mother was diagnosed with lung cancer, that he decided to take another look at his addiction.

What is the relationship between creativity and addiction? There are several beliefs, commonly accepted, that support the idea that creative work is enhanced by the use of various mind- or mood-altering substances. One belief is that artistic pursuits require access to the unconscious, and this is facilitated by the use of drugs. Another belief is that the artistic personality is more sensitive, leading to a sense of vulnerability that must be eased by the use of substances. Yet another belief is that the intensity and stress that are an intrinsic part of creativity lead to considerable anxiety, and substances are necessary to diminish the anxiety. Reinforcing these beliefs is the fact that there are many examples of highly creative and accomplished people who are known to struggle with addictions, often without being able to conquer them.

However, in looking at clinical evidence, it is clear that addictions are not an inevitable part of a creative or artistic life. There are artists who manage to be creative, productive, and successful without having major problems with substance abuse. Yet, what does seem to be ubiquitous is the struggle to deal with the anxiety that is generated by efforts to be creative. This anxiety can cause much distress, sometimes even to the point of interfering with productive creative work, and is a common complaint of the artists I see in therapy. As a result, many find themselves turning to various strategies to deal with the anxiety, and these coping mechanisms often include compulsions and addictions.

I define a compulsion as a particular kind of behavior, habit, or substance that is accompanied both by an urgency or driven-ness to engage in it, and by a sense of relief from anxiety. An addiction is a further development of the compulsion, although influenced by physiological propensities and environmental inducements and opportunities. I believe that an addiction serves as a relief from anxiety, but also serves as a means of destroying unwanted or bad aspects of the self. Understanding the issue of anxiety can help patients deal with it in a way that precludes the necessity for relief through substance dependency.

In reviewing both the literature and my own clinical experience, I found two key concepts that can be helpful in working with anxiety that arises around creativity. These two concepts can be described as dialectics, or tensions, falling along a continuum of polar opposites. One is the dialectic of advance and retreat, and the other is the dialectic of self and other. They are interacting factors in the development of anxiety.

The first dialectic, advance and retreat, has to do with actions taken by a person that express a sense of agency, power, or will. There are many examples of the ways in which people naturally assert themselves in the course of development that are directed toward growth, expansiveness, progress, and mastery. For example, this includes efforts made to learn, to take risks, to accomplish or achieve, or to separate from other people. Some attempts lead to a sense of empowerment, whereas others, less successful, lead to disillusionment, discouragement, and even shame. Fortunately, human beings are resilient, so new efforts continue to be made. Commonly there is a cycle of progress that begins with movements or advances, but which includes some disappointments or reversals that lead to retreats. Then there is some kind of repair, and other attempts, and finally other advances.

There is inherent anxiety in doing something new and unfamiliar, especially because frustration or failure is often the result. This is even more true of creative endeavors, which by nature are attempts to stretch boundaries and to move into uncharted territories. Anxiety also arises from the fact that creative acts may be threatening to important others, who experience them as competitive or aggressive. In the case of creative attempts that lead to loss of self-esteem or security, the common reaction is some kind of retreat.

If the results of the creative undertakings are good, self-esteem is enhanced. There is a reward for the effort expended, and the sense of personal power is increased. In addition, the ability to communicate a message through art can be immensely gratifying and can lead to a feeling of transcending ordinary experience. Ironically, however, this can again lead to anxiety, since tension arises about being able to re-create the effect.

The second dialectic, self and other, is explicated by theories of intersubjectivity (Beebe and Lachmann 1998, Benjamin 1990, Stern 1985). These theories address the initial powerful effect on the infant of encountering the idea of self and other. Separation and differentiation begin at around two to seven months of age, according to Stern (1985). But Beebe and Lachmann (1998) report that much earlier, even within forty-two minutes after birth, babies will mimic adult expressions, which indicates how related and interactive infants are. The authors go on to say that micro-analysis of films of interactions between infants and mothers (which capture split-second reactions) show that responses in facial expressions between the two participants occur in less than a second. This demonstrates how elaborate and sophisticated attunement can be. This split-second attunement occurs not only with babies and caregivers, but also in other situations, such as lovers flirting, or monkeys playing. The authors' conclusion is that this matching of one being to another is a healthy and adaptive means to self and other regulation, so necessary for satisfaction in life.

However, the need and desire for interactivity and responsivity show us how much the idea of self is intertwined with, and dependent on, the idea of the other. Self regulation (such as soothing, comforting, or stimulating) depends on the abilities inherent in the self, but also depends on the realness of the other, since the other supplies us with much of what we need. As a result, what the other wants from us has to be carefully considered and integrated into our decisions about how much we do for ourselves, and how much we do in response to the demands of somebody else. This brings up complications and questions about the pursuit of individual goals. How much does one have to attend to the needs of others, and how much can one be free to pursue personal interests? This question is particularly relevant to creative enterprises because they typically involve intense states of self-involvement.

A different aspect of the complexity of the relationship between self and other has to do with the construction of a comfortable place between reality and fantasy, something essential in creative endeavors. Winnicott (1971) postulates that people enter a space between self and other when they are in the realm of the imaginative or symbolic. This is called "potential space," a place where they are not tied to external reality, but where they can feel powerful and safe in forming an internal reality. Taken to an extreme this results in psychotic thinking, but in moderation it leads to innovative and creative work. Winnicott says, "It is assumed here that the task of reality-acceptance is never completed, that no human being is free from the strain of relating inner and outer reality, and that relief from this strain is provided by an intermediate area of experience which is not challenged" (p. 14). He then gives the examples of the arts and religion. He goes on to say that play is another example of this unchallenged intermediate experience, and that play is crucial for the creative process to occur.

Inherent in this description is the idea that other people, who form a part of the external reality, must support illusion and play. During play there is acceptance, both by the self and other, that the space of meaning and reality will be left, and the space of hallucination, illusion, or fantasy will be entered, while holding onto the safety of the memory of the other.

However, I would add that in and around the potential space there is a movement back and forth between isolated experience and shared experience. Isolation, taken to an extreme, can lead to a fear of annihilation, and therefore can only be comfortable for a short period of time. The person then must return to an interaction that helps define the boundaries of who he or she is, and where the other person is, to regain a sense of security. The other provides a reflection of who we are and also presents an edge, or a boundary, specifying where self ends and the other begins. There can be no adequate sense of self unless there is a complementary sense of other. In sum, any creative venture carries with it many shifts between reality and illusion, and between a definition of self boundaries and a lack of that definition. This produces anxiety, and this is another explanation of why people engaging in creative endeavors are more susceptible to anxiety.

What explains the urgency or driven-ness of the compulsion or addiction that accompanies creative work? In general, anxiety is generated by entering into the sphere of the artistic work. It is here that issues of disappointment, frustration, and failure, and leaving the comfort of interpersonal boundaries of self and other, abound. To continue to work effectively, a method of dealing with the ongoing tension produced by the anxiety is needed. Most people have learned strategies for dealing with their anxiety that include some behavior that brings them comfort and that involves repetition. The repetition is important because it reinforces the idea and the feeling of having some power in a situation that is uncomfortable. In addition, it concretizes the feeling of "edged-ness," the reminder of boundary between self and other.

The experience of being empowered, even though it may be a momentary or fleeting one, immediately calls forth the desire for another dose of the anxiety-quelling behavior. At this point the behavior can turn into a compulsion. Compulsions can be annoying to the person, and can often be deleterious to working effectively, but they are not harmful or dangerous to the person. For example, one writer found that he had to engage in hours of evasive "pseudo-work" before he could actually start his writing, something that was time wasting but not dangerous to him.

Addictions, on the other hand, are harmful. They involve a destructive attempt to deal with an inner perception of a part of the self as evil. This part of the self, what Sullivan (1953) called the "not me," is the most detestable part of the self, worse than the "bad me" because it includes aspects that are so repulsive that they have to be blocked out completely. However, if someone has had some confrontation with this part of the self, it typically continues to haunt him, at least on an unconscious level. At times this sense of being evil breaks into consciousness. The person who is working in the potential space of creativity may be more susceptible to these breaks since there is a loosening of defenses and rigid boundaries that allows for the emergence of all kinds of thoughts.

Confrontation with the "not me" engenders such anxiety that sometimes there are attempts to damage the self, or that part of the self, through self-destructive behaviors. Addictions are a way in which people deal with the anxiety of their negative feelings about themselves. They gain comfort from the manifest effects of the substance or the behaviors surrounding the addiction, and at the same time they find relief in the feeling of attack on the hated "not me" part of the self. The demand for both the comfort and the relief from intolerable thoughts becomes insistently greater, until it grows disproportionately stronger than any healthy, mature wishes to move away from the addiction.

Jack is a good example of the tension between advance and retreat, and the tension between self and other. Jack was one of four children and the only boy. His father and mother had an unhappy marriage, which seemed to get worse as the years went on. Jack's father was a domineering and rigid person who saw himself as having extraordinary potential. However, as he got older, it became clear that his business attempts, although moderately successful, were never going to make him rich. He became less ambitious and more passive, and more disdainful of everyone else, especially his son.

Jack didn't want to be like his father, and had no interest in the business world. His interest and outstanding ability in art were clearly evident from a young age. His father had no regard for Jack's talent, gave him no acknowledgment, and actually became more annoyed and rejecting with every accomplishment or victory that Jack experienced, eventually becoming physically abusive. As this was happening, Jack's mother became more passive and dependent on Jack, not wanting to confront her tyrannical husband, and turning to Jack for emotional sustenance. She did not encourage any of Jack's attempts to separate from her, although she was at least supportive of his artistic ability and his aspirations to become a sculptor, but only if he involved her in his plans. Jack felt his efforts to be creative were going to be met with jealous and aggressive responses from his father, and insecurity and neediness from his mother, who often felt abandoned by his outside interests.

As he got older, the conflict between being what his parents wanted him to be and asserting himself as a separate person became stronger, and he felt anxious and depressed, especially when he did his art work. During his adolescence a friend introduced him to marijuana. This quickly became a source of comfort for him, and a way to protect himself. His anxiety was considerably diminished, and he reported that he became more addicted over the years as he realized that pot allowed him much easier access to his sensorial world, especially important when he was trying to create. It also allowed him to escape from the idea that he was a bad person, which resulted from the feeling that he had been victorious in his competition with his father and had abandoned his mother to an unhappy life while he pursued his own interests. In addition, the pot enabled him to feel like he was not going to turn out to be like his father, since he could enter this state of contentment, productivity, and optimism about the future just by smoking a joint. He was in a state of denial about his addiction, until he had to confront his mother's death from lung cancer. We continue to work on this in therapy.

In conclusion, creativity involves a search for agency, meaning, and expression that is intrinsically anxiety producing. Both the movement toward the new and unfamiliar and the constant flux in the boundaries between self and other promote anxiety that needs to be quieted. Behaviors that bring comfort are repeated, and when anxiety is strong these behaviors become compulsions. When anxiety is so strong that aspects of the dreaded "not-me" emerge, the person develops addictive behavior that is self-generating, since it reassures the person that the bad aspects of self will be managed by the controlling addictive behaviors. By addressing the underlying anxiety, which is especially prominent in creative work, the compulsive or addictive behavior can be ameliorated, and the play of creative work, rather than turning into defeat, can lead to productivity and satisfaction.

REFERENCES

Beebe, B., and Lachmann, F. M. (1998). Co-constructing inner and relational processes: self and mutual regulation in infant research and adult treatment. *Psychoanalytic Psychology* 15:480–516.

Benjamin, J. (1990). An outline of intersubjectivity: the development of recognition. *Psychoanalytic Psychology* 7:33–46.

Stern, D. (1985). *The Interpersonal World of the Infant.* New York: Basic Books.

Sullivan, H. S. (1953). *The Interpersonal Theory of Psychiatry.* New York: Norton.

Winnicott, D. W. (1971). Transitional objects and transitional phenomena. In *Playing and Reality,* pp. 1–25. New York: Basic Books.

17

Creativity, Genius, and Divine Madness

Edgar A. Levenson

According to the Whorf-Sapir hypothesis, each culture develops the vocabulary it needs. If one wishes to talk about snow, talk with an Eskimo—he has fifty words for it. If one wishes to explore the subtler tonalities of lust, love, passion, madness and ecstasy, talk with a Greek, preferably an ancient one—the Greeks had a word for it! Plato, speaking for Socrates in *The Phaedrus*, identified creativity with a "Divine Madness" (mania) (Galdstone 1968, Levenson 1968). Both the Greek word "ecstasy" and its Latin cognate, "rapture," refer to being carried out of oneself, out of one's ordinary being. Plato made abundantly clear that this Divine Madness was distinct from craziness or insanity, for which the Greeks had a sufficiency of other words. There is no real correlation between creativity and mental illness. But there is a distinct correlation between creativity and its raptures. It is not a big stretch from this connection to the consideration of creativity through chemistry—the use of psychotropic drugs to "blow one's mind." So creativity, divine madness, and drug use have a long, albeit equivocal, history of association.

Tradition requires that one round up the usual suspects—De Quincy, Goya, Bosch, Baudelaire, Rimbaud, Verlaine, and the legion of alcoholic writers, painters, and musicians. Even Sigmund Freud had a notorious connection to cocaine, and perhaps even owed some of his productivity to its use. Sherlock Holmes (and Conan Doyle) used both morphine and cocaine, depending on his moods. In the 1960s, madness and addiction became chic, virtual prerequisites for creativity. Remember Timothy Leary and R. D. Laing (1967) and his "laingeurs"—"If I could drive you out of your wretched mind, if I could tell you, I would let you know" (p. 138).

Fortunately, we are now past that romantic nonsense. The gurus went out of *their* minds—literally—and madness, we concluded, was a piteous state of disarray, not a prelude to creativity. But perhaps we've thrown out the baby with the bhang. There was, in all of that a glimmer of truth, a critical assessment of the culture, the context in which we were all immersed. We saw aberrancy as having a quality of social "outsiderness," as containing, however distorted, a certain radical awareness.

For all the long list of drug-addicted artists, the relationship between creativity and the disruption of the senses remains obscure. To be sure, there are creative people with no interest in drugs, and addicts with no talent or creativity. Moreover, while there were painters whose productivity depended on drugs, there were others who were destroyed by drugs. What about those artists who used morphine and its derivatives, which are not so much mood-altering as normalcy maintaining? Whether drug use increases or destroys creativity remains a moot question; most of the commentaries seem more homiletic than scientific. Nevertheless, there does seem to be a high incidence of drug use among artists. Why should this be so?

While I have little personal experience with the treatment of addictions, and while what I am about to say may smack of bourgeois romanticism, nevertheless I would suggest that what addicts and creative people (not just artists) have in common is a penchant for *risk-taking*, for living on the edge of possibility. In this sense, addiction and creativity may share a common characterological denominator, rather than a causal relationship.

I first ran across this idea in Bateson's (1972) theory of alcoholism. It does not seem to be an idea prevalent in the addiction literature (see the exceptions of Ehrenberg, Phillips, and Brisman in this volume). It is to be found more implicitly stated in Rank (1945), Becker (1963), Fromm (1973, 1992), May (1950), and the existential analysts, that is, those theorists with a sustained interest in the issue of social defiance, risk-taking, outsiderness—even, dare we say, a death instinct, a drive to self-destruction.

Perhaps as Freud prophesied would happen in America (which he heartily detested), his dark and existential theory has been bowdlerized into an uplift program. We Americans consider cure to be living happily in one's assigned role, loving oneself, the mate and kiddies, and possibly even the job (in that order, of course). "Have a good day!" we say to each other in the elevator on the way to our offices. Mental health is conflated with happiness.

Mavericks are socially dangerous people; they threaten the status quo. And so, as cultures are wont to do, aberrancy is dealt with by either trivializing it, making it normal and harmless (body-piercing teen-agers), or extruding it, banishing it to a disowned and discredited subculture. The culture of addiction binds the outcasts together, gives them a sense of community, and makes it much harder to break away. Alcoholics Anonymous uses the first part of this coherence very effectively. But, AA says, one never stops being an alcoholic and one never outlives the need for the therapeutic community. Alcoholism becomes another country.

In contrast, some of us would agree that socially aberrant behavior is our own dark and disowned side, and that to understand it, and certainly to treat it, we must own it. A neurosis, it must be remembered, however bad, is always better than something else. It is a compromise solution, not only in the Freudian sense of between drive and ego, but also between individual and society. To treat addicts, I believe we must ask what function—disowned in our own experience—does the addiction serve? What is left when the addiction is disavowed? Does one live happily ever after? I would like to elaborate on this idea, and suggest some of the consequences of this perspective.

It is very difficult to categorize addiction. Traditionally, the addict is defined as a person who requires a substance to feel normal. This may be true of opium and morphine users, but not always of coke and crack users. Even many long-standing coke addicts may take it for the kick, not to recapture normality. What about mood-enhancing drugs and hallucinogens? What about overeating, food addiction, anorexia? What about people addicted to risk—adrenaline junkies? What about the new category of sexual addictions (McDougall 1995)?

What, for example, is sexual addiction how is an addiction different from a compulsion? Addictions are ordinarily considered to be a variety of compulsion (Dodes 1996, McDougall 1985). But are they? If I have to step on every crack to avoid having an anxiety attack, we can agree that's not addiction—that's compulsion. If a man repeatedly has unprotected sex with prostitutes, that's sexual addiction. But if a man wishes to have sex several times a day with his wife and never goes outside the home for sex, and she reluctantly goes along with it only because he gets so upset if she doesn't—is that compulsion or addiction? If he becomes agitated if refused, is that withdrawal symptoms or pique? Might we not just consider him a glutton, a hostile user? Why?

I believe that addiction always carries with it a connotation of risk, and that risk invokes passion. Can there be passion without danger? Georges Bataille, in *Death and Sensuality*, says, "Erotic excitement resides in the risk of death—not death itself" (quoted in Benjamin 1988, p. 64). I would postulate that compulsion is a ritualistic act to *avoid* danger and anxiety, whereas addiction is a ritualized act of *courting* danger.

In Stanley Kubrick's 1999 movie, *Eyes Wide Shut*, the wife has a soliloquy about a passing stranger, a naval officer she sees in the airport. The uptight, not entirely heterosexual husband listens in horror and awe at this terrible female manifestation. Can one separate the passion from the addictive impulse? We are fascinated by the connotation of danger and destruction—the moth and the flame, the "Blue Angel" motif.

Even in those addictions that sustain feelings of normalcy, the risk is there. It is illegal to buy and to use; there are medical dangers of overdose, needle-invoked infections, the eroticism of the needle itself, and what Mark and Faude (1997) called the excitement of "the hunt for cocaine." There are the expenses that may require illegal activity. Note the recent fascinating book by the Barthelme brothers Frederick and Steven, both university professors, on their passion for casino gambling, and the resulting lust for virtual self-destruction it entailed (Barthelme and Barthelme 1999). Not only do they acknowledge losing several hundred thousand dollars, but also they were indicted (and later acquitted) on charges related to card counting and bribery. I am saying that risk in addiction is not an epiphenomenon, but a primary motive for the act.

It has been claimed that adolescents start addictive behavior because they can't believe they can become addicted. But I do not believe that is the entire truth: risk is part of it. Why, otherwise, is it so astonishingly difficult to get people to heed all the cautionary tales about addiction risk? After a blizzard of warnings, people will nevertheless smoke, try drugs, and have unprotected sex. There was only a brief period of time in our society when sex was presumed safe (wrongly it turns out), free of terrible dangers such as disease and pregnancy. But wasn't everyone becoming bored? So pleasure replaced passion, and violence replaced sex as the passionate activity. Now one sees deliberately entertained risk reentering the culture, such as in extreme sports and in outer-limit trips for executives. People seem to be enjoying frightening themselves. Inupiats, in Alaska, have returned to hunting whales from long boats instead of getting drunk. What's going on? Why are people in the best-fed, most cosseted society in history taking unwarranted risks?

Besides our difficulty in delineating a class of addictions that comfortably embraces all its members, it has never been possible to make dynamic profiling predictive. All psychodynamic predictions are post facto: we see the consequences, and then we speculate on the antecedents. One simply cannot predict the development of a particular symptom from a particular constellation of experience. Family dynamics do not specify and do not predict. Years ago, there was a joke about Jewish mothers and alcoholism. To wit, Jewish men have exactly the same family dynamics as alcoholics. So how come there are so few Jewish alcoholics? The answer is, their mothers wouldn't let them! If they wanted to be self-destructive they had to eat themselves to death. (I am "happy" to say that Jews are now totally integrated and have plenty of alcoholics.)

There must be some other predictive factor, and that something may be partly biological, a genetically inherent fault; but ultimately, regardless of endowment or dynamics, addiction is an existential decision. Consider the 95 percent heroin addiction rate among soldiers in Vietnam, which largely fell away on their return to the States. Consider the people who, safely detoxified, return six months later to their addictions.

If the antecedents of addiction are not so self-evident, neither are those of talent, genius, and creativity. There is always a marginality, a recklessness, a destructive and edgy component in any real creativity. Picasso once said of another painter that he was "merely a genius." Inherent talent is not enough, nor is skill; as an example, a genius like Salvador Dali was ultimately not a great artist. Some quality of marginality, some willingness to hang out on a limb, even to risk one's sanity is necessary. Leonard Bernstein said, "If you're going to teeter on a shaky ladder, do it from the highest rung." It is what distinguishes an illustrator from an artist, a corps de ballet dancer from a principal, an artist from a Sunday painter.

Creativity also has a strongly addictive quality. It is often not pleasurable, but must be done in order to feel normal, what Isak Dinesen called "the doom of genius—the individual's powerlessness in the face of his own powers" (quoted in Rorem 1967). Ned Rorem, the composer, wrote poignantly in his diary, "The compulsion to compose was with me, until the age of twenty-eight, as intense as the compulsion to drink—and I was helpless before both: music flowed out of my body like a sweet but slightly sick liquid" (Rorem 1967, p. 129). I do not think that it would be possible to sustain the tremendous effort and concentration required for productive, creative work without a powerful addictive element.

There is a dialectic between risk-taking and safety, dependency and isolation, separation and fusion, rootedness, belonging and aloneness—all psychoanalytic dichotomies. In this sense, addiction is a perfect analogue of the sadomasochistic relationship, with its alternation of desire and rejection, fulfillment and loss. Addiction may be the compromise solution between the dependency wish, and its opposite, the desire for freedom with all its dangers, passions, and risks. Therapy often reveals the addict sans addiction as a flat and passionless person.

Treatment of addicts requires our recognizing that their return to "normalcy" may seem more boring than they can bear. Is it possible that addiction is the desire of the addicted? Does treatment require that the need for passion and risk be taken into account, not as neurosis but as a legitimate need—not just for addicts, but for everyone? Binswanger (1958), the existential analyst, wrote in "The Case of Ellen West" that addiction is "not only a somatically conditioned need but at the same time the need for filling up the existential emptiness or craving" (p. 346).

From the story of the expulsion from the Garden of Eden to the present, there is this thread of the human fascination with risk, passion, and deliberate loss. Need therapy be a variety of "shrinking"? Should people change, get rid of what's wrong with them, grow up, "get a life"? Or might it be possible to take one's aberrancies and carry them forward, develop them, move into them in a way that permits them to become a part of oneself and a useful element?

I believe we have attenuated two great central themes in psychoanalysis that might bear on this issue: first, the social contract of psychoanalytic therapy; and second, its tragic view of life. What has become of "cultural" psychoanalysis, the great revolution of the 1950s and 1960s? Psychoanalysis has become a child of its time and reflects the loss of this theme in contemporary culture. Psychoanalysis has become safety bound, and mental health a commodity. In the headier days of Fromm, Horney, Thompson, Marcuse, Brown, analysts were supposed to stand, like artists, at least partly outside of their culture and to be critical of its compromises, not least of which is our easy, rather flaccid, sense of good and evil, of infinite possibilities. With the possible exception of Kohut, we seem to have lost the tragic view of man so prevalent in psychoanalysis' earlier years (1984).

It seems plausible to me that the neglected communality between addiction and creativity is passionate risk-taking that has been largely disowned by our culture and relegated to outsiders. We are pleased to watch and enjoy it on television. Consider our vicarious fascination with the Mafia. From *The Godfather* movies to the television series "The Sopranos," Mafia killers (on the latter show in psychoanalytic treatment—a wonderful irony) combine terrifying murderous behavior and the most banal, stupefying bourgeois aspirations. Let them take the risks; we stay home! As I've suggested, this may be changing, and risk taking qua passionate activity is beginning to enter the culture.

To treat addiction exclusively as pathology, to seek the psychodynamics that motivate and specify both addiction and creativity, is to miss its existential implications. The analyst's risk-taking—and this may mean, not bungee-jumping, but risking one's income or political career by not pandering to patients, third-party payers, or one's own colleagues—may be a vital ingredient of an authentic therapy. The William Alanson White Psychoanalytic Institute was founded on rebellion and risk. It was no small thing to walk out of the American Psychoanalytic Association, to go one's own way, and it was no small thing for my generation to follow the dissenters into the wilderness. The leaders of the White institute were audacious and defiant, pushing the limits of the cultural envelope. As the physicist Pauli put it, sometimes wrong, sometimes excessive, but never not wrong enough!

As Dostoyevskt wrote in *Notes from the Underground*

[A] man, always and everywhere, prefers to act in the way he feels like acting and not in the way his reason and interest tell him, for it is very possible for a man to feel like acting against his interests and, in some instances, I say that he positively wants to act that way—but that's my personal opinion. . . . All man actually needs is independent will, at all costs and whatever the consequences. [p. 110] . . . And what makes you so cocksure, so positive that only the normal and the positive, that is, only what promotes man's welfare, is to his advantage? Can't reason also be wrong about what's an advantage? Why can't man like things other than his well-being? Maybe he likes suffering just as much. Maybe suffering is just as much to his advantage as well-being. In fact, man adores suffering. *Passionately!* [p. 117]

REFERENCES

Barthelme, F., and Barthelme, S. (1999). *Double Down.* New York: Houghton Mifflin.

Bateson, G. (1972). *Steps to an Ecology of Mind.* New York: Ballantine Books.

Becker, H. S. (1963). *Outsiders: Studies on the Sociology of Deviance.* New York: Free Press.

Benjamin, J. (1988). *The Bonds of Love.* New York: Pantheon Books.

Binswanger, L. (1958). The case of Ellen West. In *Existence,* ed. R. May, E. Angel, and H. Ellenberger, pp. 237–362. New York: Basic Books.

Dodes, L. M. (1996). Compulsion and addiction. *Journal of the American Psychoanalytic Association* 44:815–856.

Dostoyevsky, F. (1961). *Notes from the Underground,* trans. A. MacAndrew. New York: Signet Classics, 1961.

Fromm, E. (1973). *The Anatomy of Human Destructiveness.* New York: Holt, Rinehart & Winston.

——— (1992). *The Revision of Psychoanalysis.* Boulder, CO: Westview.

Galdstone, I. (1968). Psychiatry and the maverick. In *The Dynamics of Dissent,* ed. J. Masserman, pp. 1–17. New York: Grune & Stratton.

Kohut, H., ed. A. Goldberg. (1984). *How Does Analysis Cure?* Chicago: University of Chicago Press.

Laing, R. D. (1967). *The Politics of Experience.* New York: Pantheon.

Levenson, E. (1968). Discussion of psychiatry and the maverick. In *Psychodynamics of Dissent,* ed. J. Masserman, pp. 18–20. New York: Grune & Stratton.

Mark, D., and Faude, J. (1997). *Psychotherapy of Cocaine Addiction.* New York: Jason Aronson.

May, R. (1950). *The Meaning of Anxiety*. New York: Ronald Press.

McDougall, J. (1985). *Theaters of the Mind*. New York: Basic Books.

———— (1995). *The Many Faces of Eros: A Psychoanalytic Exploration of Human Sexuality*. New York: Norton.

Rank, O. (1945). *Will Therapy and Truth and Reality*. New York: Alfred A. Knopf.

Rorem, N. (1967). *The New York Diary*. New York: George Braziller.

Shapiro, T. (1979). *Clinical Psycholinguistics*. New York: Plenum Press.

18

The Muse in the Bottle

Albert Rothenberg

Heavy use of alcohol among highly creative persons, especially writers, is surprisingly frequent. In the United States, five of the eleven writers who won the Nobel Prize in Literature suffered at some time from severe alcohol abuse, dependency, or both, and many writers throughout the world have also had this difficulty. Various lists add or subtract some notable figures depending on the information available, but there is now relative certainty about the alcohol abuse of the major writers shown in Table 18–1. Among painters, there have been the following famous alcohol abusers as well: Arshille Gorky, Willem de Kooning, Edvard Munch, and Jackson Pollock. These are striking lists but, I should immediately add, they prove nothing in themselves. If we drew up a full list of great nonalcoholic writers, extending the examples shown in Table 18–2, and placed the total number side by side with the alcoholic group, we would find that nonalcoholic writers and even abstainers far outnumber the relatively small alcoholic assemblage. But the qualitative information that so many good writers used alcohol to excess asks for explanation and understanding. Questions immediately leap to mind such as whether the alcohol drug itself actually facilitates the creative process or whether, now that genetic factors have been touted as operating in alcoholism, there is some biological propensity connecting the need to drink with creativity. Is there a muse of inspiration in a bottle of gin or vodka or other spirit? Or, reaching back to a mythical image we hold in our minds, does the storyteller always have a glass of spirits in hand while spinning the tale? These are interesting but troubling questions because there are many writers who have been sacrificed on the alter of this inability to abstain from drinking at some point in their lives.

I have carried out a study of the direct influence of alcohol on the creative process. In an assessment of available pertinent biographical and autobiographical material of each of the writers listed in Table 18–1, I found that very few did the bulk of their writing, or even their thinking about writing, while under the influence of alcohol. Their writing that was done under the influence of alcohol was seldom successful, and at various points in their lives drinking absolutely interfered with their capacity to do any creative work. For example, F. Scott Fitzgerald, denying the reports in the newspapers about his drinking, said, "As a matter of fact, I have never written a line of any kind while I was under the glow of so much as a single cocktail" (Le Vot 1983, p. 117). Ring Lardner, in the more pithy style for which he was famous, said: "No one ever wrote anything as well after even one drink as he would have done without it" (Lardner Jr. 1976, p. 165). Robert Lowell said, "Nothing was written drunk, at least nothing was perfected and finished" (Hamilton 1983, p. 389). Although some authors, such as Hemingway (Meyers 1985) and O. Henry (Davis and Morris 1931), reputedly used alcohol as a kind of stimulant to inspiration or, more accurately, a removal of inhibition, such reports must be taken with large grains of salt because of the tendency of writers to develop public images or facades, as I shall elaborate shortly. By far the overwhelming majority find drinking to be an interference.

The pattern and progression of alcohol use in all the writers I studied was the same as for the general alcohol abuser. By and large, they did not use alcohol while actually engaged in writing, but tended to drink when they were finished for the day. Early in the course of their illness, they drank regularly only after work or in the evening hours. As the volume of their alcohol consumption increased, they became increasingly uncomfortable, irritable, and anxious during periods of the day when they were not drinking, including times ordinarily set aside for work. Then, in order to sedate themselves, they began to drink during work-allotted hours. This pattern of drinking for sedation and relaxation, followed by jitteriness and anxiety when stopping, and subsequently drinking again to produce sedation for those effects, is typical for any alcoholic, ranging from the skid-row derelict to the closet drinker in the executive suite. One possible distinguishing feature for a writer—or for any artist, for that matter—is that unlike other kinds of work activity, creative pursuits are often carried out in solitude. Working alone can be a lonely affair and the solitary artist can drink without interference or detection from others. This self-enforced loneliness on the one hand and freedom on the other may enhance the proclivity to drink.

What might be considered a causative or instigating factor seems to be that in many cultures, especially the modern American one, a certain tough-guy or macho image is associated with heavy drinking and the so-called ability to hold one's liquor. It is not clear what has led to this macho image related to alcohol in this and other cultures, nor is it clear why writers and other artists might be attracted to it. Somehow, an idea of physical capacity, achievement in the face of disability, or bravery in the face of danger appears to be involved. For male writers and artists, there may be a particular need to counter widespread cultural images of effeteness or effeminacy or, in some cases, to deny actual latent homosexual tendencies. Sociologist Room (1984) has pointed out that many of the Nobel laureates who were alcohol abusers were born in the late 1880s and 1890s, and were part of a rebellious "lost-generation" literary subculture of the time.

These social explanations are only a small part of the picture, however; they do not adequately account for the individual factors in heavy alcohol use among so many highly creative people. Also they do not explain how alcohol hinders or facilitates the creative process. To address these matters specifically, I shall discuss the systematic data I have collected in structured intensive research interviews with John Cheever, the author of five novels, over three hundred stories, and winner of the National Book Award for *The Wapshot Chronicle* and the Pulitzer Prize for the collected stories. He was also a National Gold Medal winner, and one of the fifty members of the American Academy of Arts and Letters, the exclusive body of the National Institute of Arts and Letters.

Born in 1912, the son of a shoe salesman and the proprietress of a book shop in Quincy, Massachusetts, John Cheever always claimed to be a descendant of an illustrious and legendary New England schoolmaster—a claim that has recently been disputed (Donaldson 1988). That his father was an alcoholic and a work failure is fairly well known, but what isn't generally known is that his mother also drank excessively despite her more responsible work history. Expelled from the prep school, Thayer Academy, because of poor grades, Cheever never went on to college, despite his wide intellectual interests.

The course of Cheever's writing career was quite erratic. Although hailed for his stories, and supported comfortably by the income, he sought for a more substantial literary reputation by the writing of novels. His first, *The Wapshot Chronicle*, was a wide success, and the second, *The Wapshot Scandal*, was less so. The third, *Bullet Park*, was not at all well received. He began his fourth novel *Falconer* (Cheever 1977), generally considered his best and now a hallowed piece of American fiction, while he was a "Writer in Residence" at Boston University. His work on this novel was interrupted by an extended period of alcohol abuse and attendant deterioration which eventually led to his hospitalization at the Smithers unit of Roosevelt Hospital in New York City. After this hospitalization, and for the first time in his life, he began a devoted commitment to Alcoholics Anonymous, and stopped drinking completely. My research interviews with him took place during the year after *Falconer* was published, and the material we discussed was directly pertinent to both his abstinence and his creative achievement.

The novel *Falconer* takes place in the fictional Falconer State Prison and concerns a university professor drug addict named Farragut, who is incarcerated after having murdered his brother. He is subjected to brutalizing treatment by the other inmates and there is much elaboration of both loving and sadistic homosexual prison relationships. Also, deeply poignant and meaningful human strivings are enacted. After having given up his drug addiction in the prison, Farragut escapes by substituting himself in the shroud of a dead cellmate. Totally evading all pursuers, he finds himself finally at a laundromat near a bus stop, and in that banal setting he experiences a new sense of compassion and freedom. Clearly, it is a tale of resurrection and redemption.

In our discussions regarding the roots of the novel, Cheever pointed out to me that he had written more than twenty stories about brothers and that brothers or men had generally run throughout his work. He said the novel was simply another "run-through of the scene" and, he emphasized, the only one in which a fratricide takes place. In the other stories, one brother hits the other over the head, or otherwise strikes him, or tries in some way to wound him.

As he told me this, he spoke—as he had at other times in our sessions—about his older brother Fred:

> It was probably, speaking structurally, the broadest and deepest love in my life. I adored him. And then, when he went away to college, I didn't see him. He came back and left—I don't know what crossed his mind. I think he saw that I was in trouble; my parents weren't speaking to one another, and he managed to be everything for me. He went to Europe when I was eighteen and I was miserable. I was completely miserable without him. More miserable, I think, than I would have been, you know, with the removal of another person in my life. When I was about nineteen, I realized how unnatural this love was and how poignant. . . . Boston [had] very easily accommodated us as brothers, it's an eccentric society. And we were the Cheever

brothers; [staying together] would have been dreadful as far as I was concerned.

Here, John Cheever directly indicated his mixed feelings about his brother; staying together, he said, would have been "dreadful" for him. Later in our sessions, he spoke about his own psychiatric treatments:

I don't think I was ever cooperative. My principal concern, as I say, was alcohol. And they would say, "Well, alcohol is simply symptomatic." [However,] I was never able to get either Dr. X, Dr. Y., or Dr. Z [my pseudonyms] to go into my brother in depth. I would say, "Look, you know, if there was any problem I would like to discuss it would be my brother." And they would say, "Well, we'll come to that." And then I would say something polite like, "You mean six thousand dollars later we will come to my brother?"

Now to the questions about his creativity and his drinking. First, the writing: Cheever told me that never in his writings did a brother murder another brother. However, in the novel he wrote before his most serious bout with alcoholism, *Bullet Park*, a murder does take place. The character Paul Hammer murders the young son of a man to whom he is inextricably linked, Elliot Nailles. (note the relationship of the names of the characters). The lives of Hammer and Nailles are inextricably intermingled in a manner directly reminiscent of Cheever's description of his relationship with his brother.

The creative process, as I have described in detail previously, involves a gradual unearthing of unconscious processes (Rothenberg 1979, 1990, 1994). In my research with over 450 highly creative subjects, I have found that writers, as well as creative people in other fields, use both the *janusian* and *homospatial* processes for ideas, images, and other creative effects in the creative process. These processes also function in an important way as a means of attaining partial insight while creating into unconscious contents. The janusian process consists of actively conceiving multiple opposites and antitheses simultaneously (Rothenberg 1971, 1973a,b, 1983, 1996). The homospatial process consists of actively conceiving two or more discrete entities occupying the same space, a conception leading to the articulation of new identities (Rothenberg 1976, 1986, 1988; Rothenberg and Sobel 1980, 1981; Sobel and Rothenberg 1980).

Both of these processes operate as templates that reverse the disguising operations of the primary process. Because janusian and homospatial processes are conscious, and because they bear a superficial structural resemblance to the disguising mechanisms of primary process such as condensation, displacement, and equivalence of opposites (Grinstein 1983), they serve to reverse and undo the disguise progressively as they are used. They thereby bring unconscious material partially into consciousness with the production of some degree of insight. This is not an eruption of unconscious material into consciousness (nor a regression in the service of the ego as described by Ernst Kris (1952)). A burst of unconscious material does not start the creative process, but the unconscious is gradually and partially unearthed during the progression. The creative person embarks on an activity leading to discovering and knowing oneself in what might be considered the most fundamental ways. Table 18–3 summarizes the means by which this comes about. The conscious janusian and homospatial processes are in a template relation with similar primary process operations. As with all templates, the functions are reversed. Therefore, the simultaneous opposition in the janusian process reverses unconscious equivalence of opposites; the superimposition of discrete entities in the homospatial process reverses unconscious condensations and displacements, the latter reversing from a shifting to less to a shifting to more.

The gradual unearthing of unconscious processes and the progression toward insight are tenuous and may go awry. Because the progression occurs without any real support or help from another person it may fall far short of the goal. It is not a form of therapy and only partial rather than full insight ever actually occurs. Indeed, even when such a process of inner self-discovery is pursued in the collaborative circumstance of therapy, it may, as we know, all too easily be diverted or go aground.

I believe that Cheever did begin to go aground on his own in the writing of *Bullet Park*. Intermixed with love for his brother was intense antagonism, jealousy, hostility, and unconscious murderous feelings and, in the writing of that novel, he had come closer than ever before to full unearthing of these threatening affects. Rather than a murder of a brother—or a brother-like figure—however, he depicted the murder of the symbolic brother's young son. I believe, therefore, that he was coming closer at that point to recognizing unconscious murderous feelings toward his brother and could not really acknowledge them to himself.

Then, at the time of his descent into drinking, he went to live in Boston for the first time since his youth, and his brother Fred was living there at that time; he and Fred (who, I hadn't mentioned, had married the author's girlfriend) saw each other more than they had done for many, many years.

This close association with his brother brought intensification of John Cheever's guilt over his constant but unacknowledged hostile and murderous feelings. With his recovery, there was distinct evidence of a degree of insightful acknowledgment and acceptance of these feelings. I cannot here say whether Cheever achieved insight directly from improved creative functioning following complete abstinence, whether he achieved insight in some other way and both abstinence and creativity followed, or whether some other type of sequence was involved. I will insist, however, that prior to that his conflict about his feelings toward his brother had both intensified his alcoholism and blocked his creativity.

Cheever was able to return to work on his novel *Falconer* after he left the Smithers rehabilitation unit, a novel in which he directly portrayed an intellectual man who killed his brother and was, from the beginning, sentenced to prison. That this fratricide represented Cheever's own wish together with a fantasied punishment was dramatically suggested by the comments he made to me about a visit from his brother shortly after he had completed *Falconer.*

[Fred] was seventy. He hurt his hip in a motorcycle spill and went into the hospital for an operation and was discharged as having too weak a heart for the operation. He immediately came here [to see me] and said, "I think you ought to know that while I was in the hospital I had delirium tremens—this is withdrawal from two glasses of sherry." And I said, "Thank you very much for telling me." And I had completed *Falconer* and I said, "Oh, I killed you in the book." And he said, "Oh, did you? Oh, good."

Another factor is that the novel's narrative of the jail paralleled Cheever's own experience at the hospital, where he felt punished (for his hostile feelings) as well as cared for.

Cheever's creative and alcoholic course was therefore as follows: in his writings, he had returned again and again to the theme of hostility to a brother, and his struggle to unearth and deal with his own unacceptable feelings was one of the dynamics that gave power to his work. When finally hostility and murderous feelings toward his brother came close to the surface and threatened to overwhelm him, as they did with the writing of *Bullet Park*, and assumedly with other events in his life, he turned increasingly to alcohol for sedation and relief. This produced a typical alcoholic vicious cycle where the physical and psychological effects of using the drug required continuation with increasing amounts to produce desired sedation effects. Finally, he went into a treatment program that helped him to stop drinking and also to continue the threatening unearthing of his feelings toward his brother in the writing of his novel *Falconer*. The triumphant, more healthy struggle involved in the creative process at that point produced a successful work of art. Healthy processes, not alcohol, drugs, or other pathological aids, are the key factors in creativity.

The role of alcohol in this account of Cheever's struggle is, I believe, broadly representative. Most writers do not suffer from the same degree of alcohol dependency and abuse as Cheever did, but that is a separate matter that I shall come back to in a moment. What does seem to be a cardinal issue, and one that applies to several writers, is the need to use alcohol to cope with the anxiety that is generated by the creative process itself.

The successful creative process, because it involves the unearthing of unconscious contents, is fraught with a good deal of anxiety as it unfolds. Also, there is anxiety and strain connected with carrying out the especially demanding work of creative accomplishment, as well as anxiety and strain connected with the use of unusual logic-defying janusian and homospatial processes. These processes are mentally difficult to employ.

Depending on a writer's stability and proclivities, he or she may cope with such discomfort and threat in various ways. It has long been widely and reliably known that writers and other artists are highly irritable during intense periods of work or for some time afterward. Some writers become depressed, some engage in flamboyant and eccentric behavior, some engage in philandering, some use the other relaxing outlets that the rest of us do, and some drink. Drinking alcohol has a gratifying sedative effect and, given the social reasons that have made it acceptable among writers and other creative people, it may even have become the mode of choice to deal with the anxiety generated by the creative process. The muse may not be inside the bottle but, starting with Dionysus, Greek god of the theater and the vine, liquor may be the mythic way to drown her glory and threat.

This is not to say that alcohol use and dependency is the inevitable penalty for a creative life. Most creative people are like the majority of the population who use alcohol in moderation. The development of alcoholism depends in each case on personality and personal background. In Cheever's instance, I do not have a great deal of data about the development of his illness. That both parents were alcoholics and had a difficult marriage in which they involved him, as well as his intensely ambivalent relationship with his brother (and very likely his father) were surely generating components. In cases where both parents are alcoholics, identification and the need to repeat traumatic experiences of childhood, as well as simple availability and acceptance of alcohol in the house, have effects as important as any postulated genetic factors. Also, Cheever had a lifelong conflict about his bisexuality; such conflicts, incorporating problems about homosexuality, passivity, and dependency often in alcoholism, have cardinal causative effects. These are general factors, however, that may or may not relate directly to his creative work.

Factors that may connect Cheever's alcoholism with his writing do have some general applicability to alcoholism in other creative people. Living with parents who were frequently in a withdrawn, inebriated state, he felt helpless as a child and unable to communicate with them. His turning to writing served both as a way to bring order into a chaotic, disorganized experience and, in a sense, to get his parents to hear him, and it also became a means for compensating for feelings of weakness and loss.

Cheever was loved and preferred by his mother. Although his father was weak and ineffective, he nevertheless seemed to have identified with him in adopting his father's more severe alcoholism. This identification with the father very likely served as a way of being closer to his mother, a woman who was attracted both to an alcoholic person and to the alcohol drug itself. Over and over again, persons who become alcoholic adopt the patterns of someone loved by their own specially beloved parent, whether it be that parent's own alcoholic father or mother, lover, or spouse. In Cheever's case, his identification with his father may, for other reasons I will touch on briefly, also have had something to do with his motivation to write.

As I have seen in many of my research subjects and have studied in extensive biographical sources, creative persons often have a same-sex parent who has been tacitly interested in a particular creative field or, in some cases, tried that field and failed. In such instances, the offspring lives out the same-sex parent's unstated wishes and fantasies as well as his overt strivings. This is done unconsciously both to gratify and make proud *and* to beat out the parent and thereby achieve the other parent's love. For example, the son perceives that his mother has at some point valued the father's implicit wishes and fantasies, even loved him for them, and the son throughout his life competes.

This was the circumstance for Cheever and his father. While being an unsuccessful shoe salesman, the elder Cheever kept a personal diary all his life. The writing of such material clearly represented a literary bent and interest, a matter testified by the author-son himself. It was this diary, he told me, that was the inspiration and focus for his successful novel, *The Wapshot Chronicle.* With regard to connections between creativity and alcoholism, this family dynamic–induced motivation to create may sometimes coincide with an identification with an alcoholic parent, as it did in Cheever's case. It is then one of the few intrinsic links between creativity and alcoholism, and may operate, because of the importance of the creative aspect, to render the alcoholism especially difficult to ameliorate.

Defeated for much of his life by alcoholism, it is sad to consider how much more Cheever, and others suffering from such affliction, might have successfully created if freed from the grasp of alcohol.

REFERENCES

Cheever, J. (1977). *Falconer.* New York: Knopf.

Davis, R. H., and Maurice, A. B. (1931). *The Caliph of Baghdad: Being Arabian Nights Flashes of the Life, Letters, and Work of O.Henry.* New York: D. Appleton.

Donaldson, S. (1988). *John Cheever: A Biography.* New York: Random House.

Grinstein, A. (1983). *Freud's Rules of Dream Interpretation.* New York: International Universities Press.

Hamilton, I. (1983). *Robert Lowell: A Biography.* New York: Random House.

Kris, E. (1952). *Psychoanalytic Studies of Art.* New York: International Universities Press.

Lardner, R., Jr. (1976). *The Lardners: My Family Remembered.* New York: Harper and Row.

Le Vot, A. (1983). *F. Scott Fitzgerald: A Biography.* Garden City, NY: Doubleday.

Meyers, J. (1985). *Hemingway: A Biography.* New York: Harper and Row.

Room, R. (1984). "A reverence for strong drink": the lost generation and the elevation of alcohol in the American culture. *Journal of Studies on Alcohol* 45:540–546.

Rothenberg, A. (1971). The process of janusian thinking in creativity. *Archives of General Psychiatry* 24:195–205.

——— (1973a). Word association and creativity. *Psychological Reports* 33:3–12.

——— (1973b). Opposite responding as a measure of creativity. *Psychological Reports* 33:15–18.

——— (1976). Homospatial thinking in creativity. *Archives of General Psychiatry* 33:17–26.

——— (1979). *The Emerging Goddess: The Creative Process in Art, Science and Other Fields.* Chicago: University of Chicago Press.

——— (1983). Psychopathology and creative cognition. A comparison of hospitalized patients, Nobel laureates, and controls. *Archives of General Psychiatry* 40:937–942.

——— (1986). Artistic creation as stimulated by superimposed versus combined-composite visual images. *Journal of Personality and Social Psychology* 50:370–381.

——— (1988). Creativity and the homospatial process: experimental studies. *Psychiatric Clinics of North America* 11:443–459.

——— (1990). *Creativity and Madness: New Findings and Old Stereotypes.* Baltimore: Johns Hopkins University Press.

——— (1994). Studies in the creative process: an empirical investigation. In *Empirical Perspectives on Object Relations Theory*, ed. J. M. Masling and R. R. Bornstein, pp. 195–245. Washington, DC: American Psychological Association Press.

——— (1996). The janusian process in scientific creativity. *Creativity Research Journal* 9:207–232.

Rothenberg, A., and Sobel, R. S. (1980). Creation of literary metaphors as stimulated by superimposed versus separated visual images. *Journal of Mental Imagery* 4:77–91.

——— (1981). Effects of shortened exposure time on the creation of literary metaphors as stimulated by superimposed versus separated visual images. *Perceptual and Motor Skills* 53:1007–1009.

Sobel, R. S., and Rothenberg, A. (1980). Artistic creation as stimulated by superimposed versus separated images. *Journal of Personality and Social Psychology* 39:953–961.

Table 18-1. Alcoholic Writers

James Agee	Jack London
Charles Pierre Baudelaire	Robert Lowell
Louise Bogan	Malcolm Lowry
Truman Capote	John O'Hara
John Cheever	Eugene O'Neill
Stephen Crane	Edgar Allan Poe
Theodore Dreiser	Sidney Porter (O. Henry)
William Faulkner	Edwin Arlington Robinson
F. Scott Fitzgerald	John Steinbeck
Lillian Hellman	William Styron
Ernest Hemingway	Dylan Thomas
James Joyce	Tennessee Williams
Ring Lardner	Thomas Wolfe
Sinclair Lewis	

Table 18-2. Non-alcoholic Writers

Saul Bellow	James Merrill
Harold Brodsky	Herman Melville
Pearl Buck	Arthur Miller
Joseph Conrad	Joyce Carol Oates
Charles Dickens	John Dos Passos
E. L. Doctorow	Boris Pasternak
Fyodor Dostoyevski	Adrienne Rich
George Eliot	Philip Roth
Nathaniel Hawthorne	George Bernard Shaw
Thomas Hardy	Isaac Bashevis Singer
John Hersey	Stendhal (Marie Henri Boyle)
Henrik Ibsen	Wallace Stevens
Archibald MacLeish	Leo Tolstoy
Bernard Malamud	John Updike
Thomas Mann	Robert Penn Warren

Table 18–3. Template Patterns in the Creative Process

Primary Processes	Creative Processes
Condensation: combination, fusion	Homospatial process: superimposition of discrete entities
Equivalence of opposites	Janusian process: simultaneous opposites
Displacement: shift to less	Homospatial and janusian process: shift to more

VI

Desires and Addictions

19

Attending to Sexual Compulsivity in a Gay Man

Jack Drescher

Themes of hiding abound in the developmental narratives of boys who grow up to be gay. Their need to hide is reinforced by the traumatizing public humiliation that ensues from either open expressions of same-sex desire or gender-nonconforming behavior. The experience of being discovered, punished, and humiliated for showing or acting on such feelings or behaviors can lead to hiding activities that persist long after the actual trauma is forgotten. The late, gay filmmaker Derek Jarman (1992) tells of such a defining moment at his English boarding school:

> At [the age of] nine, I was caught in bed with Gavin—thrown onto the floor by the headmaster's wife, lectured publicly and whipped. Frightened by this unexpected outburst, I was to have no physical contact for thirteen years. I lived my adolescence so demoralized I became reclusive. . . . I was desperate to avoid being the sissy of my father's criticism, terrified of being the queer in the dormitory. . . . My work also suffered. I dropped behind. At puberty my reports said "more concentration needed." You see I was distracted. [pp. 36–37]

In a culture that claims to value the linkage of sex with emotional intimacy, it is difficult to foster those connections in gay teenagers in the same ways they are encouraged in heterosexual adolescents. It would be an understatement to say that adult support for adolescent gay dating is a rarity. Even fewer parents would consider sanctioning a gay teenager's search for physical or emotional intimacy with a member of the same sex. Some boys who grow up to be gay, like Jarman, refrain from sexual activity and avoid emotional intimacy during the important developmental years. Others seek and find outlets for their sexual and emotional needs in furtive encounters. For some adults, such activities can become a way of life. The gay writer John Rechy (1977) idealizes what he calls the "sexhunt" in his book, *The Sexual Outlaw:*

The promiscuous homosexual is a sexual revolutionary. Each moment of his outlaw existence he confronts repressive laws, repressive "morality." Parks, alleys, subways, tunnels, garages, streets—these are his battlefields. To the sexhunt he brings a sense of choreography, ritual, and mystery—sex cruising, with an electrified instinct that sends and receives messages of orgy at any moment, any place. . . . What creates the sexual outlaw? Rage. [p. 28].

Rechy calls cruising areas "battlefields." However, the battle is being fought as guerrilla warfare, heterosexism being too large a target to take down directly. Consider the unthinkable possibility of gay men demonstrating the degree of physical activity that is routinely displayed by heterosexual couples on a beautiful day in Central Park. Even today, there are many neighborhoods in cosmopolitan and liberal New York City where two men holding hands still raises a few eyebrows. In some parts of town, it would surely lead to the raising of arms. When open expressions of same-sex intimacy are driven underground, clandestine and forbidden sexual activities, highly tinged with interpersonal anxiety, may become a significant mode of relatedness. For gay men like Rechy, this is a triumphant act of will, and not a psychiatric problem. Others, however, experience their sexuality as a compelling "force" and feel troubled by it.

Historically, psychoanalytic practitioners like Socarides (1968) argued that compulsive sexual behavior in gay men was evidence of the neurotic "origins" of homosexuality. This formulation conflated treatment of compulsive sexuality with a so-called cure of homosexuality. However, other clinical experiences have shown that gay men who experience their sexual activities as compulsive do not necessarily experience their sexual attractions as compulsive (Drescher 1998b). Nevertheless, because of the unsavory nature of the arenas in which they feel compelled to express their sexuality, these men may feel intense shame about being gay. What follows is a clinical psychoanalytic approach for working with gay men that distinguishes the concept of sexual compulsion from that of sexual identity. It allows the sexual identities of gay men to be respected while addressing the compulsive behaviors that some of them find so troubling.

DISSOCIATION

It is important to emphasize at the outset that a person's sexual identity is not pathognomonic of any defensive style. Focusing on the way gay men dissociate should not obscure the fact that they are a heterogeneous group. Denial, intellectualization, rationalization, and other defenses are as likely to be found in gay men as they are in other patients.

That being said, however, many gay men have a history of being subjected to events, traumatic or otherwise, that exaggerated the normal tendency to screen anxiety-provoking and shameful memories. From an early age, the social stigma surrounding homosexuality led many gay people to hide knowledge about their sexuality not only from others, but from themselves as well. In other words, antihomosexual, cultural prejudices reinforce dissociative activities. This makes Harry Stack Sullivan's conceptualization of dissociative defenses useful in clinically understanding and therapeutically working with gay men in general, and with sexually compulsive gay men in particular. Parenthetically, Sullivan was himself a closeted gay man (Chatelaine 1981, Ortmeyer 1995, Perry 1982), although it is not clear how central this sexual identity was to his theory of dissociation.

Sullivan (1938, 1956, 1972) regarded dissociation as an inter-personal process, one accessible to observation. In his two-person psychoanalytic model, a therapist noted "gaps" as a patient avoiding certain subjects and topics. It was Sullivan's belief that this avoid-ance, or selective inattention, was deliberate, although the patient's motive to avoid was out of conscious awareness.

Many gay men had a sense of their same-sex feelings years before openly acknowledging them. They learned to dissociate knowledge about their sexuality and also had to prevent other people from being able to recognize the quality of their sexual feelings or desires. This state of mind is commonly captured in the experience of gay men who report they always "knew" they were gay but didn't want to admit it to themselves.

In Sullivan's view, there is no self without an other, so hiding from the self is tantamount to hiding from others.

This can sometimes be an interpersonally manageable solution, as in the case of a 40-year-old single gay man who lived with his mother. He did not want to tell her he was gay and she did not want to know. In a dissociative enactment of "Don't ask, don't tell," together they avoided a subject which would have generated anxiety in both of them. She would give him telephone numbers of friends' daughters while selectively inattending all of the ways in which she knew he was not interested in dating women. When he accepted the names, he could maintain the illusion that his mother believed he was a heterosexual bachelor, while he ignored all the nonverbal ways in which she communicated her fuller knowledge of him. A kind of homeostasis was achieved in which they mutually avoided the anxiety of seeing each other more fully.

This type of selective inattention surrounding homosexuality is rather commonplace. More severe dissociative operations are illustrated by reports of sexual encounters that take place under the guise of being asleep. Sullivan's *Clinical Studies in Psychiatry* (1956) provides a dramatic example of this behavior: "During the night Mr. A. gets out from under his cotton precaution and goes around and tenderly fondles Mr. X., and then goes back to bed under his bottom sheet" (p. 176). The following morning, Mr. A. "feels fine, and has no trace of any information about what has happened" (p. 176).

Another patient described a similar incident:

An old friend from college and I had sex several times in our senior year. The first time, on a school trip, we were in a double bed together and I pretended to be asleep. His hand started coming over toward me gradually. I knew exactly what was happening, because I had done it myself to other guys. It was very exciting to be on the receiving end. He gradually worked his hand across to my cock and took a hold of it. I kept pretending I was asleep. Somehow, I took off my shorts, but still didn't acknowledge what was going on. He put his cock between my thighs and started humping me. He was moaning his wife's name. In fact, he had recently gotten married. He came between my legs, calling her name.

The last time he came over was when I was leaving town to get married. He sat on my bed. The light was on and we talked. We talked about all sorts of things, but not sex. All the while we talked, he was running his hand up my leg and up to my cock. We kept talking without acknowledging that. I started to stroke him through his pants. He pulled out his cock and started to masturbate, and came on my blanket. As long as I had that blanket, I could always see that spot where he came. The experience left me with the feeling that I had failed in some way. We haven't seen each other or talked to each other since then.

JUMPING INTO THE POOL

The following patient is a 60-year old gay man who had been severely traumatized in childhood. As a young adolescent, feeling unloved and unwanted, he found a measure of solace in movie theaters where older men sexually desired and serviced him. The pleasures he associated with his early experiences of furtive sexual activity led to a lifetime pattern of anonymous sex in cruising areas:

> I had gone out with friends and I suddenly got that overwhelm-
> ing sex drive when I got home. Although I knew it was stupid,
> I got dressed and went to a porno theater. It was the most awful
> one I've ever been to, a stage set for sleaze, with homeless
> people and people on drugs. I asked myself, "What did you
> expect?"

The patient described both surprise and annoyance with himself after he arrived at the pornographic movie theater and then
"suddenly" remembered what he might find there. Forgetting and
remembering is characteristic of selective inattention. Sullivan's
detailed inquiry (Cooper 1995, Shawver 1989, Sullivan 1938, 1954,
1956), attempts to explore the inattended, such as the patient's
foreknowledge of what he would find in the theater when he got
there:

Therapist: Had you been to that theater before?
Patient: Months ago. Upstairs, there are two bathrooms where
                people sit in stalls waiting for guys to come by and
                blow them. Downstairs, they have an awful basement
                with corridors that felt unsafe. This was a dirty and
                sleazy set. If a set designer created it, it would be
                almost too much.
T: You experienced going there as a piece of theater?
P: Yes.
T: What role were you playing?
P: Maybe I would meet someone who would blow me or

I would blow them. But no one was interesting. I've been there several times, and nothing ever happens. I tell myself, "You know more efficient ways to get sex. I saw an ad in the *Village Voice* that said, "Blond hunk looking to meet successful older man."

T: Had you considered calling the blond hunk instead of going to the theater?

P: The movie theater is less committing. But answering the ad, that's a serious commitment. When I was younger, I loved the idea that these guys wanted to suck me. I felt like I was sort of powerful. It felt like I had a scenario or a scene, that I could fall into. That I didn't have to be concerned with what I really wanted.

When patients, regardless of their sexual identity, experience their sexuality as a compulsive force outside their conscious control, their sexual activities may take place in a reverie state, a severe dissociative phenomenon. It should be noted that a reverie state can be solely confined to one's imagination, like a daydream. It can be subjectively experienced as a private, psychological space where the inflexible circumstances of everyday life do not apply. However, in this case, the patient's reverie took place in a sexual arena where other men were actors in his fantasy while he played a role in theirs:

T: What you describe feels a little like a daydream.

P: Yeah. There was an understanding that I had some kind of power. That somebody would get on their knees and I would say, "Suck that dick, boy." I think they felt sort of lucky. I think that's what I should have now.

T: Are you saying you feel powerless and you need to feel powerful?

P: (The patient laughed anxiously, and then yelled angrily) I would say that! Yes! I'm not even happy talking to you about it now. I feel like I'm pushing myself into

making sense of how I live my everyday life. This is a
stupid way of living!

Detailed inquiries can be experienced as impingements. The
subject of the inquiry can, at times, be made anxious, irritable, or
angry by its intrusiveness. Yet anxiety, irritability, and anger, among
other things, are often exactly what a dissociating patient might not
allow himself to feel. The ultimate goal with patients, when doing a
detailed inquiry, is to take them into places where they do not wish
to go—and yet not let their anxiety reach intolerable proportions.
This patient became angry as attention was drawn to something he
did not wish to attend: feelings of powerlessness. Nor did he wish to
integrate the enacted fantasies of his reverie state into his ongoing
experience of himself. He was also angrily judgmental of his own
behaviors when he openly acknowledged them:

P: Yes, I feel powerless, no question.
T: In the past, these sexual experiences made your
            feelings of powerlessness diminish. That no longer
            seems to be the case.
P: I still hope I can meet someone who might want to
            suck my dick. (Angrily) I hate talking about this!
T: You don't want to talk about this?
P: (Again, angrily) I'll talk about it! But it's hard for me
            to say why I go back to the porno theater. There's a
            possibility that something might happen, like years
            ago, somebody sucking me.
T: How do you tell yourself that it might happen?
P: I'll throw myself in there. Part of it is that you don't
            have to think. This is blind habit.
T: I'm trying to draw your attention to how you are not
            thinking in those moments. It's almost as if you went
            there in a trance.
P: I'll admit it. There is a trance-like state.
T: You don't want to understand your trances?

P: I think the function they serve now is a desperate
attempt to recapture the person I used to be. I always
had a little trance but it used to be more satisfying. It
was somebody sucking my dick. People were interested. They were after me. Definitely trance-like. It was
like jumping into a pool and not having to think about
how to swim. There would be a certain kind of
something that would feel OK for that time. Then it is
over. You get out of the pool and you go home. Now,
when I go to the porno theater, it's like throwing
myself in the pool. It's going to be like a wave. (The
patient's tone becomes more subdued): You know, the
porno theater doesn't work. It doesn't give me what it
gave me before, and yet I go. The trance thing is a
good image, like someone in a trance. "Go!" and I'll
be in this atmosphere. Getting blowjobs anonymously
was very much a part of my life. It was really like
hiding, going into the pool.

THE THERAPIST'S AUTHORITY

Helplessness was one feeling that this patient could not tolerate and
that contributed to his feeling sexually compelled. A previous
therapist had preached the value of monogamy for many years,
while the patient continued to engage in compulsive sexual activities
without telling the therapist about them. When the patient invited
me to take a similar role, I pointed out to him that the previous
therapist's discouragement had not seemed to stop these activities.
So what purpose would it serve to do so again? The patient became
increasingly annoyed that I would not play the role of disapproving
authority figure as obligingly as the previous therapist had done. It
should be noted that frustrating the patient's attempt to get me to
play this part allowed him to more fully experience his own anger
and annoyance.

    In his ongoing frustration with my unwillingness to reprimand
him, the patient would angrily lecture me, stating it was my job to

stop him from engaging in "meaningless behavior." I told the patient that all behaviors had meanings, including those he wished to define as meaningless. In labeling his sexual behaviors as "meaningless," he was judging them to be "bad." His efforts to dismiss and judge what he was doing kept him from trying to understand what he was doing. This intervention, which was frequently repeated, usually reduced his anger and aroused his curiosity.

Once he ceased trying to make me stop him from engaging in anonymous sex, he began talking about the anxious and lonely feelings that prompted him to search for human contact in that arena. As he came to understand the sources of his anxiety, and to tolerate those feelings as well, he felt a greater sense of control. This feeling increased his own sense of authority and, over the course of his treatment, he went less frequently to the movie theaters. If he felt like going, he would tell himself why he didn't want to go, and often he did not go. On those rare occasions when he did feel compelled to go, he was able to look at his actions, and talk about them more openly with himself and then later with me.

In my declining to projectively identify with the role of moral guardian, the patient gradually came to understand that he had to deal with *his* own reservations about cruising and anonymous sex. This increased his awareness of his own internal struggle regarding his sexual behaviors. The solution he gradually arrived at, going less often, felt satisfactory to him. However, a different patient might have resolved a similar struggle by giving himself permission to go cruising. And finally, contradicting historical psychoanalytic claims that equate homosexuality with sexual compulsivity, although this patient experienced a reduction in what was previously felt to be a sexual compulsion, he did not change his sexual identity or lose his sexual attraction to men.

CONCLUSION

In the Interpersonal perspective, anxiety is thought to be triggered when knowledge of the self appears to jeopardize an individual's relationship to others. Given the stigma attached to homosexuality, effeminacy, and promiscuity, it is not just gay men who may feel anxious about the impact of homosexuality upon their relationships. Many psychotherapists are also made anxious by the subject.

Freud (1912), in urging neutrality, said, "I cannot advise my colleagues too urgently to model themselves during psycho-analytic treatment on the surgeon, who puts aside all his feelings, even his human sympathy, and concentrates his mental forces on the single aim of performing the operation as skillfully as possible" (p. 115). Admirable as this admonition may be, psychoanalytic neutrality is not possible. One has only to study the history of psychoanalysis, a field that expressed its anxiety about homosexuality by integrating cultural prejudices into its theories and praxis and by infantilizing and pathologizing gay and lesbian identities (Drescher 1998a).

A related expression of psychoanalytic anxiety about the diversity of human sexuality can be found in its countertransferential idealization of monogamy. This anxiety is commonly expressed by pejoratively labeling a patient's nonmonogamous sexual behaviors as "compulsions," "acting out," or "resistance" (Drescher 1997). Many a published case report trumpets the treatment's success by announcing that the patient got married or settled into a monogamous relationship.

Unfortunately, privileging a patient's wish for conventional, monogamous relationships over his or her other feelings and activities can interfere with a therapist's ability to empathize with the nonconforming aspects of the patient. Simply treating a sexual compulsion as a symptom can serve the purpose of psychologically distancing oneself from it. In some cases, pathologizing a behavior may reflect a countertransferential judgment of the behavior. This kind of countertransference can be a significant obstacle to empathically entering into the subjectivity of the patient. Therefore, I would recommend that when patients invite a therapist to play the part of baby-sitter or moral guardian, it is preferable to avoid being drawn into that enactment. Although it may be no easy task, therapists should make every effort to accept both a patient's desire for unconventional sexual excitement and the longing for a more conventional relationship. At the same time, therapists should also be skeptical about the patient's desire for conventional relationships and the patient's characterizing of their sexuality as compulsive. An idealized but impossible to attain neutrality will not get therapists through those inevitably tough moments when they feel counter-transferentially judgmental of their patients. Respect for difference, on the other hand, just might do the trick.

REFERENCES

Chatelaine, K. (1981). *Harry Stack Sullivan: The Formative Years.* Washington, DC: University Press of America.

Cooper, A. (1995). The detailed inquiry. In *Handbook of Interpersonal Psychoanalysis,* ed. M. Lionells, J. Fiscalini, C. Mann, and D. Stern, pp. 679–693. Hillsdale, NJ: Analytic Press.

Drescher, J. (1997). From preoedipal to postmodern: changing psychoanalytic attitudes toward homosexuality. *Gender and Psychoanalysis* 2(2): 203–216.

——— (1998a). *Psychoanalytic Therapy and The Gay Man.* Hillsdale, NJ: Analytic Press.

——— (1998b). Contemporary psychoanalytic psychotherapy with gay men: with a commentary on reparative therapy of homosexuality. *Journal of Gay and Lesbian Psychotherapy* 2(4):51–74

Freud, S. (1912), Recommendations to physicians practicing psycho-analysis. *Standard Edition* 12:109–120.

Jarman, D. (1992). *At Your Own Risk: A Saint's Testament.* Woodstock, NY: Overlook Press.

Ortmeyer, D. (1995). History of the founders of Interpersonal psychoanalysis. In *Handbook of Interpersonal Psychoanalysis,* ed. M. Lionells, J. Fiscalini, C. Mann, and D. Stern, pp. 3–27. Hillsdale, NJ: Analytic Press.

Perry, H. (1982). *Psychiatrist of America: The Life of Harry Stack Sullivan.* Cambridge, MA: Harvard Press.

Rechy, J. (1977). *The Sexual Outlaw: A Documentary.* New York: Dell.

Shawver, L. (1989). Detailed inquiry. *Corrective and Social Psychiatry* 35(4): 78–82.

Socarides, C. (1968). *The Overt Homosexual.* New York: Grune & Stratton.

Sullivan, H. S. (1938). The data of psychiatry. *Psychiatry* 1:121–134. (Reprinted in *Pioneers of Interpersonal Psychoanalysis,* ed. D. B. Stern, C. H. Mann, S. Kantor, and G. Schlesinger, pp. 7–30. Hillsdale, NJ: Analytic Press, 1995.

———— (1954). *The Psychiatric Interview.* New York: Norton.

———— (1956). *Clinical Studies in Psychiatry.* New York: Norton.

———— (1972). *Personal Psychopathology.* New York: Norton.

20

In the Grip of Passion: Love or Addiction?

On a Specific Kind of Masochistic Enthrallment

Darlene Bregman Ehrenberg

This chapter presents my work with a patient who has at various times in her life been anorexic and addicted to drugs, to compulsive shopping, to compulsive masturbating, to stealing, and to cutting herself. As a child she was school phobic. For years there were recurring nightmares of a man with a hatchet looming over her while she was in bed. She would wake in terror for her life. At the time I will focus on here, her. Her relationships had been characterized by a level of violence that at times was life threatening as she beat up her lovers or they beat her up, or as she and her lovers ignored or abused each other emotionally. One lover strangled her, and shaken as she was, and though she was not sure she would live to tell the tale, to my astonishment she stayed with him anyway. Another lover exposed her to hepatitis C and to herpes without telling her. She married him and stayed married for several violent and drug-filled years. She emphasized that the tragedy was that she really did fall madly in love with these men, and at least at the outset these relationships were indeed characterized by love and passion. The problem was that although these relationships did at first hold great promise, and these men were attentive and caring in ways that did sweep her off her feet, inevitably things would turn around completely and become worse and worse. Nevertheless, no matter how painful and destructive the relationships eventually became, she could not let go. The relationships, like the drugs, seemed to become addictive. In fact at times it seemed the more destructive they became, the more addicted she would become.

Though originally I thought of the nature of these connections as based on a kind of masochistic enthrallment, partly based on the degree of pain that she was willing to endure to sustain them, I have come to rethink this. What I have come to understand is that as bad as these relationships might have seemed from the outside, the pain was not what drew or held her. Rather, her experience within each relationship at the time was that it was somehow serving as a lifeline, and she felt she could not live without it. It seemed to help her to manage an inner agony of such proportions that, as far as she was concerned, felt worse to her than death itself. At times she thought of suicide as a way out of her pain. Because she feared she could be suicidal if she could not find relief, and because the relationships helped her to be able to simply stay alive, the actual pain of these relationships was in her eyes a small price to pay. She was not looking for pain. She was desperately seeking relief from a worse pain. In her words, "I'm always running to escape. That is what men offer me, escape from who I am." The same was true of drugs. Taking drugs was another way of trying to alleviate unbearable pain. Nevertheless, though initially the drugs were taken to ameliorate pain, once she was addicted there was an agony to deal with if she could not get more, so they ended up also enslaving her, and causing more pain than they relieved. More chilling was an insight that came much later, when she realized she would get her partners addicted to the drugs too, so they would not leave her once they came to depend on her to supply them.

Inevitably, neither the drugs nor the relationships, nor the drugs *and* relationships as they eventually became totally intertwined, solved anything internally, and the relief she found through them was short-lived. Furthermore, the drugs made her violent and contributed to her provoking her partners, which then led to having to endure their rages against her and, in some instances, as I have already noted, their physical attacks. The violence became only more extreme if they were on drugs too.

However painful this violence was, the pain of feeling ignored or neglected by a partner was even more unbearable to her. When she felt ignored or neglected she would go into a rage. This then provoked more anger and even violence. Though this seemed to effectively escalate the situation for the worse, her experience was the opposite. As far as she was concerned, the violence was less upsetting to her than feeling ignored by her lovers. However negative, it was a way of being center stage, of being reassured she existed and could have impact, and of being "recognized." The problem was, these relationships could not be sustained without a real danger of irreparable harm, even murder.

The sex too became problematic. Often it reached a point where she felt she was being "eaten alive" and she talked of feeling like she was being "captured through sex," as these men became as addicted to her as she was to them. It began to be draining and exhausting, even nauseating and more than she could bear.

Given how dreadful things became, how she was able to see the relationships as a lifeline for as long as she did was hard to imagine. That is why I use the word "enthrallment." It seemed she was blinded by her own feeling, and in the grip of a passion that lost touch with reality. She herself eventually was able to recognize how she had each one of her lovers "completely wrong." She noted, "I mistake everyone, make them into who I want them to be. I don't see them, yet all the signs are there. I ignore them." In reflecting further on this she asked: "What was the worst thing they could do to me?" Her answer was, "Ignore me." Then she asked, "What was the worst thing my mother did to me?" Her answer, "Ignore me." Nevertheless, that is also what she did to her partners. She did not see them as they were, and when she began to be able to, she would go into a rage that they were not whom she wanted them to be. She felt betrayed by them.

She linked her own suffering, and that of those she knew like herself, including siblings and cousins, saying, "We were ignored by mothers who were so caught up and tortured by their men that they could not be there for us. We are drug addicts, drinkers, near suicidal eaters, and abused."

The dilemma we were facing was that each time we made a bit of headway in our work, and her insights at certain moments were extraordinary and piercing, it would not last. Each time she could let herself begin to face the real problems in her relationships, or begin to get off drugs, or get out of one of these relationships, the pain she then experienced was so extreme that she would become so agitated that she simply could not bear it.

She was desperate, and all that mattered was relieving the pain. She tried psychiatric medications but somehow these did not really help. Furthermore, because inevitably she would end up popping her own pills and drinking alcohol along with the Prozac or whatever medication she was on, the combination became deadly. Before long she would run back to the same men she had worked so hard to leave, or become totally obsessed and preoccupied with them even after the fact. It seemed to be a vicious circle.

Her attachment to me was intense, but, because I could not be available to her twenty-four hours a day, it often felt useless to her. Sometimes phone calls between sessions seemed to get her through the worst of it. There were other times, however, when she was so strung out on drugs or with hangovers from the combination of drugs and alcohol that she simply could not get out of bed to come to her sessions. At times I felt desperate myself as to how to help her, given how extreme the situation could get. Whatever work we were able to do seemed to have no impact once she was gripped by the most extreme kinds of feelings and took off on these destructive binges.

However, in more constructive periods we were able to do very intense and meaningful work, and we both felt extremely attached to each other. Thus, going through the negative episodes was all the more upsetting and painful. Because at her best she was extremely brilliant and talented, it felt all the more tragic to see her when she was out of control and barely able to function.

In thinking about the issues in the above case, another case, recently presented to me by a colleague, comes to mind. The problem of this patient, a woman who had been abused and who left two husbands, having had affairs each time, was described in terms of her having affairs, which destroyed her marriages. In terms of the external picture, this was obviously true. Nevertheless, it seemed to me the real issue was what was going on internally, not externally. Internally these marriages seemed to last as long as they could help her to stay intact psychically. When they no longer served this function, and she felt psychically at risk, she would find another relationship that could provide what she needed. It was not frivolous in the sense of something fun. It was desperate and a matter of survival. The issue was not how to help her to stay put with any one of these partners as though that might be a measure of "cure." Rather, it was to realize that these relationships were themselves symptoms and solutions, and the real issue was how to understand the inner agony that she was always living in, and how to help her become free of it. For this patient who saw herself as having been vampirized by her sexually abusive father, and now saw herself as a kind of vampire, a werewolf who was equally dangerous, relationships involved vampirizing and being vampirized, terrorizing and being terrorized. There was no conception of anything else. It was a terrifying universe. It was no less so for my patient.

What is evident is that to simply relate to the behavior in these situations is not enough. We must be able to relate to the inner agony to be of any real help. The challenge is to help make it possible to begin to look at the agony such patients are trying to escape or to heal with the drugs, or through these addictive relationships, or through the compulsive buying or stealing, or the bingeing or starving, or cutting. Sometimes part of what is key is to be able to help the patient feel we do understand so that they are not left isolated and alone.

*   *   *

Perhaps the complexity of what is at issue here can be captured by using an example involving a very loving relationship between a mother and a child. Even in a very loving context, where the mother is trying to be there as best she can, this kind of relating is not easily achieved. What comes to mind here is a situation between a mother I treat and her child of 4½ who was diagnosed with attention deficit disorder (ADD). When he was agitated and started acting up, she would get anxious as she began to feel more and more "out of sync" with her child. Her pattern was to respond from the outside, trying to contain him, and this was particularly so when his behavior involved his hurting other children. Through the process of our work she was able to realize that she was reacting to his behavior with almost the same level of agitation as he was showing. And as she began to realize it was important for her to respond calmly, and not just react to the behavior, but try to relate to his inner agitated state, things began to feel less foreign to her. As she gradually was able to let him know that she understood that if he was agitated he must be upset about something, she was astonished by his reaction. He actually was most responsive and calmed down dramatically. His knowing that she understood, rather than that she was angry at him for getting so worked up, made all the difference, and in her words allowed him to "feel less bad and more understood." She illustrated this with the following example: One Monday morning when he was very agitated and being very difficult, as she was helping him get ready for school, instead of trying to contain him as she usually had done, she said, "Is it hard going back to school on Monday morning when we've been together all weekend?" She noted that he just stopped and looked at her. She then went on and said, "It's hard for me going to work too. I miss you when I am at work and I think about you." She said at that point his whole body visibly calmed down, all the tension just fell away, and he held her hand and walked to the bus with her.

If a child doesn't get this kind of validation, and feels "alien" and/or "bad," and can become more and more agitated in a loving context, imagine how much more problematic it would be in a context where the mother is not available, ambivalent, depressed, not even trying. It becomes something akin to feeling *trapped in isolation* within a relationship, rather than being able to feel one is in communication with the other, and that it is possible to be understandable. I believe this kind of situation can be so subtle it may not even be clear to the child or to the mother that the problem is in the interaction. With this child there had been some attempts to use medication to help calm him down. But attributing it to "biology" misses the very profound sense of isolation and pain the child is in, even if the mother is genuinely loving. Things may even seem very cushy from outside. Internally however it is quite another story. For a child who grows up without this kind of understanding and care over time, as was the case with my patient, the desperation becomes more and more extreme.

An example of an interaction with my patient that touches on this occurred in our first session after I came back from a trip of several weeks. I told her that I appreciated how hard it must have been for her for me to be away so long. She said, "It's not your fault." I said, "I know that, and I'm not suggesting it is, but I want you to know I understand how hard it must have been." I could see her body visibly let go as she began to cry in response. A stance of being poised on the defensive shifted to a sense of being able to feel recognized, understood, and even held. There was something in that moment that felt powerful to both of us. We were kind of emotionally and psychologically naked in the room, and it was clear we both understood and were sharing something that was very intimate in terms of our feelings and rare for her. Somehow knowing I understood and cared seemed to make all the difference.

In the session following this one (our second since I was back), she was clearly much calmer. I picked up on what had occurred the session before and said, "I understand what a torture it is just to get through a day for you, where someone else might have no clue, because for them it is not like that, it is another universe." She was able to talk about how she felt as a child with a depressed mother, and the torture she felt then, and how she could still feel annihilated now if she doesn't feel seen. She elaborated that if she doesn't feel seen she begins to feel that she doesn't exist. What seemed so powerful here was simply her being able to realize I did understand and wanted to know what her inner experience was and what she was feeling, and that I could see the behavior was really the least of it as far as she was concerned. Until she could solve the inner agony issue, the behavior was simply her desperate attempt to find a way to simply be able to stay alive given the unbearable pain she was so often feeling.

A much earlier moment in this treatment occurred at a time when she was unwilling to question her participating in what I considered a very dangerous relationship, and when she clearly was back on drugs, and even talking about suicide. To both of our surprise I became tearful. I said that it was very painful to me to watch her throw her life away. I also said I felt it wasn't just a negation of herself it was also a negation of our work and of my concern. She seemed shocked and touched that I had so much feeling about it. At that point my question was what was her intention? Was she really serious about this or not? If not why continue coming? How was she using me? After some hesitation she said she could not promise to stop the destructive behavior. She said she needed time to think about things and wanted to take a break. She did not come back for a few weeks. During this time she was in touch with her medicating psychiatrist and had some sessions with another therapist. Then she called and said she wanted to come back.

Now she was able to articulate that it was as though she was using me as a fix, and that when that was in place she would tell me anything she thought I wanted to hear so long as I would see her. She herself was ultimately able to make clear that when she was agitated and in the grip of feelings she could not manage, all that mattered was to get through the moment any way she could. Toward this end she described herself as "the ultimate con artist," and a "shyster" who could fool anyone including me, and as someone who would lie, cheat, and steal when in the grip of this kind of desperate feeling. She noted that she could not stop herself even if she wanted to. She warned me I was no match for her, and it was clear to me that she was right; there was no contest. The irony here, however, was that once she was able to "confess" this to me, we seemed to be already at a new and different place. At that point we could begin to monitor when she was using me as an analyst rather than as an addictive object and address it as an issue. (She elaborated later, on reading this summary, that her fear was that if she were to be honest with me she was afraid I might throw her out. She felt being the shyster was not what was horrible, it was what she was hiding that was horrible.)

As she was able to acknowledge having used me in this way, and having lied to me, she began to be able to talk to me about the impulse to take drugs rather than just take them and lie to me and say it was not an issue as she had before. We both felt that being able to talk about the impulse and not just act on it was a monumental achievement. It reflected a real shift, even if we had no clue how lasting it might be.

At this point, I had to wonder about the times I had taken her at her word when there had been no reason to do so. Was my thinking that I could help her or even be a match for her if she was out to deceive me or to "use" me badly a measure of my own grandiosity? As I talked about this with her, she was surprised that I was not immune to her and that I had my own vulnerabilities. My being clear about my own limits and vulnerability seemed to have great impact. It forced her to realize that she wasn't the only one in this relationship with feelings, and that I was not immune to her, just as she was not immune to me. I think of what occurred here as a form of opening of what I have come to think about as the *internal boundary* of the relationship. It has to do not with the external boundaries, but with how emotionally available we are willing to be within the normal external boundaries.

Now she became very invested in the work in a way that she had not been before. She described feeling for the first time a sense of a possibility that she could work something out and have a life rather than simply just trying to get through each day in this desperate way with no hope of anything changing. Where before her investment was more like it was with the drugs, to get relief from immediate pain and then it was forgotten, now she began to take our work much more seriously.

Interestingly, as I let her read early drafts of this chapter, it profoundly affected her and led to even more intense work. Just being able to look at all of this through the perspective of this chapter, seemed to help her grasp something she had never quite been able to before. She also was touched that I was devoting so much time and thought to understanding her. This led to a new phase where we were collaborating on understanding her, and she began to feel that analysis was the most important thing in her life. In one session she felt she now could let go of her current man and of the drugs, with a conviction that instead she wanted to try to work things out and see what she could do if she tried to stay with the feelings.

I believe the nature of the patient's internal agony is the critical issue. What became clear as we explored this was that it had to do with a profound ambivalence involving loving and hating the same object with such intensity that the feelings were unmanageable. For her to be close to anyone ultimately put her in touch with both feelings simultaneously, with no way to resolve them. The details of what emerged and what evolved in the course of this exploration are presented in a lengthier essay.

21

From Impulsivity to Paralysis: Thoughts on the Continuing Pursuit and Thwarting of Desire

Jill Howard

The widely accepted adage, "You can never get enough of what it is you don't really need," seems to be the motto that many of my relationship-addicted patients live by. Webster's defines desire as the "conscious impulse toward an object or experience that promotes enjoyment or satisfaction in its attainment." These patients, unfazed by Webster's, seem to continually pursue partners who bankrupt them of enjoyment and satisfaction and inevitably bring them to the brink of despair. The pursuit, itself, is filled with intense erotic excitement, but the resulting relationship seems to organize around varying degrees of agitation and rejection.

The tenacity with which this pattern continues to repeat and to remain entrenched in treatment suggests some kind of inner template that is being continually enacted. While Freud's (1920) theory of the repetition compulsion and Sullivan's (1954) ideas on anxiety reduction certainly offer insight into addictive relationships, I have found Fairbairn's (1952) theory of the exciting-rejecting object particularly useful. His theory not only helps to explain the continual pursuit and ultimate thwarting of desire seen in these patients, but also is useful in sorting through the complicated transference–countertransference enactments that occur in their treatments.

One of the things that drew me to Fairbairn was the awareness that a number of my patients were choosing the same words to describe what they found compelling in these attractions. The words *mysterious, enigmatic, aloof, superior, elusive,* and *remote* were invariably used, and I was reminded of Fairbairn's (1940) comment about one of his own patients: "He had that vaguely mysterious air which I have come to regard as pathognomonic of an underlying schizoid tendency" (p. 15). He also elaborated on the superior attitude these individuals conveyed as well as their tendency toward secrecy. Altogether, this was reminiscent of the mysterious, enigmatic, and remote characters my patients were drawn to. Additionally, the experience of pursuit was often described as feeling out of control, taken over, or possessed; all echoes of the dangers of being swamped by the aggression tied up in bad object representations.

Fairbairn's (1940) comments on the intensity of schizoid infatuations had a distinctly similar ring. He spoke of the schizoid tendency to create elaborate intellectual systems rather than emotional relationships that might threaten to unleash their underlying aggression. He noted "a tendency on their part to make libidinal objects of the systems which they have created. Being in love with love would appear to be a phenomenon of this nature" (p. 21). My patients seemed to be more in love with love than with the individuals they were so ardently pursuing. In fact, I doubted that they knew much about love. They did seem to know something about choosing a mysterious, remote figure who they felt they *had* to have and who ultimately left them feeling "emptied out," "used up," "depleted," "diminished," and fundamentally rejected. However, what my patients did not understand was that the tie was to an object that was *both exciting and rejecting at the same time,* and therefore, the excitement could never be satisfied.

Fairbairn's theory of the exciting-rejecting object is based on the idea that the infant internalizes a bad external object in an effort to get control over it. This unsatisfying, or bad, object has two aspects: it both frustrates and tempts. Mother is seen as a temptress precisely because she evokes the needs that she will never satisfy. Thus, the process of internalization results, for Fairbairn, in a state of bondage. Additionally, what was originally intolerable, the awareness that the infant's love seems to destroy, is cruelly reinforced each time the patient seeks a new love. The futility and despair that emerge at the failure of one of these love relationships is often of suicidal proportions and brings to mind the desperate state of a helplessly dependent child.

One of the difficulties with this dynamic is that the patient may be continually drawn to exciting-rejecting objects or may, at times, be in the role of exciting-rejecting object to another. More complicated still, from the point of transference–countertransference analysis, is the fact that the patient can be playing the role of the pursuer with one person while simultaneously being the temptress and rejecter to another, as the following case demonstrates.

CASE STUDY

Halle, a 39-year-old woman, was referred to me in June 1997 by the pharmacologist who had stabilized both her bulimia and depression in 1990. She presented for treatment because she was torn between remaining in a "loveless" marriage with her husband, Dan, or pursuing a life with her lover, Allan, a married man and colleague. Halle was clear that she did not love her husband and had never enjoyed having sex with him. She doubted she had ever loved him, as she married him to get away from a married man at work with whom she had been conducting a tempestuous affair. Dan presented at the right time with the right credentials (except for his alcoholism), and she married him and moved out of town. Even if she did not love Dan, she was quite "taken" with their 2-year-old son, Steven. I say "taken" as I am not clear Halle has much capacity to love. Halle, however, was reading *The Art of Loving* by Erich Fromm and told me that she loved her son but had turned away from her father and, as a result, all men since then except for Allan. "Fromm," said Halle, "believed you had to have the ability to love a man and mankind. It's easier for me to love mankind than 'a man.' I love from a distance without intimacy."

Halle, a very attractive, accomplished professional woman, described herself as a woman of many secrets. Beginning with shoplifting in seventh grade, Halle also smoked, abused drugs, and later became bulimic. Free, at least symptomatically, of the drugs and bulimia, Halle's current addiction is to shopping and to Allan. She met Allan, a married man with two daughters, at her office. They both share the same specialty and often travel together for work. They began their affair a year before, and Halle has described it as an obsession. "Allan has some kind of power over me," she said. "In his presence I feel inferior in much the same way I did with my father. They are both very intellectual and live life with a *less is more* attitude. Allan has a condescending nod, and people at work find him arrogant and aloof, but I find that very seductive. Dan is too chatty and sociable. He would do anything for me and I feel no emotion for him, no desire, no spark. I have this yearning for a family, another child, but there will always be a part of me that is turned off to Dan and he senses that too."

Allan is clearly Halle's exciting-rejecting object but she is that same figure for Dan. At one moment Halle is again the little girl with the cold, perfectionistic, critical, controlling mother who she can never please and the extremely intellectual, self-centered, Seventh Day Adventist, alcoholic father who she described as "a strange bird." She longed to connect emotionally with one or both of these figures but instead was left embittered, rageful, and alone. Although she had three brothers, she was not close with any of them when she was young. The pain and isolation she described as a little girl was monumental and was compounded by her family moving every two years, so she never had a best friend or companion until she was in college.

At other times, Halle, who identified with these bad object representations, is the one who is aloof, cold, demanding, and impossible to please. This is her most frequent stance in her marriage. She reports that both her mother and her father conducted numerous affairs when she was young, and they finally divorced when Halle was an adult.

The first eight months of a weekly treatment were characterized by Halle's swinging back and forth between Dan and Allan. When she would decide to leave Allan, she would fall into a deep, dark, depression, and be riddled with despair. When she would decide to leave Dan she would be faced with the fact that Allan had a compelling reason not to leave his wife, (who would take his daughters and move back to the country she was originally from.) Only when Halle was invited to consider making no decision until she better understood this conflict did a thrice weekly analysis, initiated by her, begin. In keeping with the transference of the moment, I was rather surprised she wanted this, as I felt she had one foot out the door at all times. I was always a bit surprised when she arrived for a session because I wasn't clear she felt much attachment to either me or the treatment. Halle, however, was already enacting her exciting-rejecting dynamic with me. The material she presented was tantalizing and enticing, and yet I always felt on the verge of rejection.

Three weeks later, Halle's ambivalence became more accessible to us. Halle was in Europe on a business trip with Allan and lost all of her medication when the airline lost her suitcase. A few days later she called me in the middle of the night and left a dream on my answering machine. Notably, she did not call my twenty-four-hour number where she could have reached me directly. She was both reaching out with material that was erotic and dangerous and simultaneously rejecting me. She reached her male pharmacologist before she reached me. The dream, presented in a breathy, terrified voice was as follows:

"I was lying on a bed in a black cotton nightgown. Someone was pulling it over my head. There were fingers at my throat. I couldn't move or fight it. I was praying. I felt Allan's presence there. I knew his fingers well. I pulled myself out of sleep but I fell back to sleep and the same dream began, but longer. Allan's fingers were on my throat, keeping me back. I never saw his face but it was Allan's fingers. I know his fingers so well."

When Halle awoke in a state of panic, she called Allan, me, and the pharmacologist. Allan did not awaken quickly enough to get the call directly. When he heard the voice mail he began calling her room repeatedly. However, he kept calling room 605 instead of 505 and it never occurred to him to just go to her room. She called me next but not at the number she had to reach me in an emergency. Finally, she reached the pharmacologist, who told her it was a panic attack from stopping all of her medication and she should not worry. He got her an emergency prescription for lorazepam, a benzodiazepine with antianxiety and sedative effects, and Prozac, and the next time I saw her she had filed the dream as "just a panic attack."

I told her that I thought her panic attack had more to do with starting the analysis and being away from me, and alone with Allan, than it had to do with her medication. Clearly she had felt intensely threatened and overwhelmed. Interestingly, when I first heard her phone message, it was so intense that I began to wonder whether she had been sexually abused by her father. Rather than keeping this thought on the back burner until she returned with more information and associations, I began to obsess about how to talk to her about this thought. I consulted a colleague who rightly questioned why I was so unnerved, if not paralyzed. When Halle returned and told me that Allan had been so panicked by her message that he didn't know what to do, I realized that both Allan and I had been caught up in some enactment with Halle. She had turned to each of us in a state of great need and both of us had let her down. She was left alone with her terror until she reached the pharmacologist who also let her down by not appreciating the seriousness of her communication. What Halle needed was to be heard and attended to. However, she had all three of the people she turned to, at least initially, giving her a lot of what she did not need.

Fortunately, by the time she returned, I had reached a better understanding of my countertransference and did not fall deeper into the enactment of rejection and betrayal. My invitation to reexamine the dream in relation to beginning the analysis brought us closer and helped her see the terror she experienced at the possibility of being close to somebody. Her associations were quite interesting, but did not convince me that my initial fantasy could be forgotten. About Allan, she said, "His hold on me is strong. It's liberating to be in love with him, but also oppressive." She continued, "I thought I was going to die, suffocate, I couldn't call out to anyone for anything, like I gagged. I've had this kind of dream before—on a bed trying to move to the right. I can't move and the headlines read, 'Woman Found Dead.'" When asked when she first had such a dream, she said at age 11 or 12. "I went to my cousin, and I had a feeling of a sexual crush on him. I felt trapped and like someone was holding my hands down. I thought it was something Satanic—like a demon or devil was holding me down."

Halle then recalled that she had had another dream, on that terrible night in Europe, which she thought preceded the one she had first reported. "I was up in the mountains in a beautiful home. A strange woman lived there. It was a beautiful Victorian. She had beautiful grass—something about horses. She had everything I wanted in that house, and she wouldn't share it. She was talking to someone about how she wouldn't share it. Everything I wanted—so close but so far away." She then recalled a childhood memory of a trip to Oregon with her father. "My mother told him he'd better spend time alone with me, and it ruined the magical aspect of the trip."

In this dream, apparently the first of the two, Halle helped me locate myself in the transference. She apparently identified me (a lover of horses) with the tempting/rejecting aspects of both her mother and her father. Like Halle's mother, I had everything she wanted, but would not share it with her. No wonder she didn't bother to call the correct phone number that night.

I asked Halle what she thought about the repetitive nature of this dream, which preceded her relationship with Allan. Instead, she offered more of what happened the night of the terrifying dream in Europe. "When Allan finally came, I was hysterical, and I pushed him out. He said that I screamed out, 'I don't want you close. I can't let you see what I'm feeling and who I am. I'm not worthy of being loved.'"

A disappointment set in about Allan and that trip, which was the subject of many sessions. A future session recalled an evening when Halle's parents were having sex and her mother kept giggling and calling Halle to come and help her. She was laughing and giggling, and Halle had no idea what to think or do. I began to understand that Allan and I were now in good company with our paralysis.

A few months later, Halle commented that when she's with her husband and son, she has that wonderful family feeling, but when he touches her, she feels repulsed and invaded upon. "But now," she said, "when Allan goes to hold me, I feel that too. There's some kind of rejection going on too. I wonder if I'm losing desire for Allan. You know, I never saw my parents hold hands!"

Three months after the European dream, Halle read *The Kiss*, by Kathyrn Harrison. She said, "It is a case study of me, but more severe; a critical mother, unavailable father." She paraphrased the introduction to the book saying, "We are all formed and shaped by those who love us . . . they don't have control of what we will be in the end." She explained: "Both the father and the daughter wanted the love of the mother, and in the end it brings the girl and the father together in an incestuous relationship. They fall into an obsession with each other. I'm not thinking about my father here, but Allan has taken his place." Later she told me that the book's title refers to a French kiss, and she remembers her father French kissing her once when he was drunk. "Her mother," she said, "wasn't quite as narcissistic as the woman in the book, but her aloofness, distance and 'hard-to-win-her-praise' style were what brought the father and daughter together. When the mother found out about their affair, she said, 'It's about me.'"

Halle referred to this book in many sessions. She said, "I am aware of the pull the father had over the girl, and Allan has that pull over me. Sometimes I think it is love, and at other times I'm afraid it's an obsession."

At this point, Halle has come to see her marriage as a fairly close replication of her parent's marriage. In her own marriage, she says, "Dan has the ability to love for a long time and be committed to me. I, though, am part my mother and part my father. I have my mother's critical nature and high standards and my father's distant stance. I just close off and shut down. I do that a lot with Dan. He's boring and obsessive." She also does this with me, I might add, by presenting tantalizing and rich material and then deciding to cut back on her treatment.

Unfortunately, I have seen her replicate this pattern with her son, Steven, as well. She lacks a basic maternal sensibility that would help her be more in tune with her little boy. For example, after going to work for an entire day, she doesn't naturally realize that her son cannot be made to wait forty-five minutes to interact with her when she comes home. His level of excitement and delight at her return is met with frustration as she washes her face, undresses, reads the mail, and then turns her attention to him. Additionally, much of the time they could spend together has been taken up not only by her affair but also by the daily hour she spends with her personal trainer, when, although she is in the living room, Steven cannot be with her—so close but so far away.

Halle has begun to get a sense of her pattern, and she chose to end her affair with Allan, when she realized that while they were both married, only she was willing to leave her marriage. She commented, "I was thinking about what you said about always having another man to fall back on when the primary one disappoints me. When I started seeing Dan, I was running from Tom. I married Dan and fell in love with Allan. But Allan isn't there in a real way for me. The thought of leaving him was unbearable, but the futility of filling this nagging insecurity with men who are fashioned into patchwork relationships is definitely not working."

Halle may have ended her affair, but she is a long way from a satisfying relationship with Dan, and I'm not sure what the future holds for them. Halle's desire to have a stable family life and her insight into her attraction to exciting-rejecting objects have won out for the moment. She is now 41 and pregnant with twins. Needless to say, this is a source of concern to me as Halle better understands her attraction to exciting-rejecting objects than her own tendency to be that figure to her son, her husband, and to me.

CONCLUSION

Halle has provided a great deal of rich material that can be heard in many different ways. The question of incest still persists and is not readily accessible for exploration at this time. While the oedipal material is extremely rich, I suspect the primary concerns at this time are more preoedipal in nature. Fairbairn is quite clear that the original traumatic situation is the mother's inability to satisfy. (This does not rule out any later traumata such as incest.) The oedipal situation may then be configured in any number of ways, including seeing one parent as exciting and the other as rejecting. However, ambivalence must ultimately persist toward both parents, as the original object who tantalizes and rejects is the mother.

Each time the stage is reset with a new lover, the unconscious fantasy to gain the love of the mother (and later the father) is reenacted. However, the ending has already been written and cannot be changed as it exists in another time and place. The only chance to change "who we will be in the end," to quote Halle, is to renounce this fantasy and create another that makes a real relationship attainable. The trick, I suspect, is to accept that what we really don't need is what may, at base, always seem most tantalizing.

REFERENCES

Fairbairn, W. R. D. (1952). *Psychoanalytic Studies of the Personality*. London: Routledge & Kegan Paul.
Fairbairn, W. R. D. (1940). Schizoid factors in the personality. In *Psychoanalytic Studies of the Personality*. London: Routledge & Kegan Paul.
Freud, S. (1920). Beyond the pleasure principle. *Standard Edition* 18:7–64.
Fromm, E. (1956). *The Art of Loving*. New York: Harper & Row.
Harrison, K. (1997). *The Kiss: A Memoir*. New York: Random House.
Sullivan, H. S. (1954). *The Psychiatric Interview*. New York: Norton.

22

A Philosophical Assessment of Happiness, Addiction and Transference

M. Guy Thompson

This chapter discusses the relationship between happiness, addiction, and transference, a topic that no doubt confronts all therapists who are treating a person who is suffering from addiction, whether or not the treatment offered is of a psychoanalytic nature, and whether or not the patient is specifically seeking treatment for the addiction itself. The literature on this topic is vast and there is no way I could do it justice in the space that I have to review the literature on this important subject matter. Instead, I shall explore the philosophical underpinnings of the nature of transference in general, and the conditions that give rise to addiction specifically, culminating with their intersection.

The perspectives on addiction presented in this book and the breadth and richness that characterizes the scope of the topics covered are so varied that it would be impossible to arrive at an overarching, undisputed definition of addiction that would satisfy everyone. Instead, I hope that the context in which I address this issue will serve, if only by inference, to convey a sense of what I take the nature of addiction to be.

Let me begin with a disclaimer: The collection of papers in this book are devoted to an appraisal of addiction from an interpersonal perspective, and while I admire this perspective enormously and feel it is suggestive of the way I employ psychoanalytic principles in my own practice, I have nevertheless been less than successful over the course of my professional career with couching my views in such a fashion as to "fit" into one psychoanalytic school or another. The distinctions currently employed between, for example, drive theory and the relational perspective, or one-person versus two-person psychology, or the nuance that is said to distinguish even further the relational perspective from the interpersonal one, or the intersubjective paradigm versus relational and/or interpersonal theories leave me admittedly bewildered.

No doubt this is due to a deficit of my own; an inability, you might say, to think numerically. Another problem, perhaps, is my reluctance to imbue theory with the significance that most psychoanalysts find indispensable. I have always read extensively, and over the years I have been impressed by and continue to find sustenance with points of view that have now fallen grievously out of fashion, including, I'm afraid, some of the views of Sigmund Freud. Hence, it is perhaps ironic that I would choose to begin my remarks on the relation between transference and addiction by invoking some of Freud's insights into the nature of addiction and the problems that inhere in its treatment. I only ask that you bear with me, and forgive my inability to understand why one paradigm should be so antithetical to another when I have learned much from proponents of any number of allegedly incompatible points of view. To this end, I shall not resort to any theoretical perspective in my remarks, nor shall I employ metapsychological considerations of any kind. I will instead stay strictly within my experience as a clinician and as a student of the human condition, rooted solely in my experience in these matters.

I shall begin with a philosophical reflection on the nature of life and the suffering that we invariably experience because of it, and then the roles that misery and the quest for happiness play in the transference relationship and its addictive nature. Some of these views are consistent with Freud's, but they are also consistent with a great many philosophers over the millennia, including the Stoics, Cynics, and Sceptics in the Hellenistic era, the views of the sixteenth-century essayist and philosopher, Michel de Montaigne, and more recently with Nietzsche, Kierkegaard, Heidegger, Sartre, and other contemporary observers of the human condition. In the main, all of these thinkers would agree that life challenges us from the moment we are born with pain, frustration, and disappointment, and that it confronts us with tasks that are extremely difficult to perform, and which leave scars that are impossible to erase. Though as children we are convinced that things will become easier as we grow older, experience tells us the opposite: that life becomes even more difficult, and that this state of affairs persists throughout our existence until finally—if we are among the fortunate few who grow old—we are faced with the inevitability of our own death.

In fact, so much of our lives is focused on one form of suffering or another that we spend most of our time pursuing relief from the burdens that our trials thrust upon us, from one day to the next, and the next, and so on, in perpetuity. Freud believed that we could cluster the devices we employ for obtaining relief from our plight into three distinct categories: (1) "deflections," which help us to make light of our misery; (2) "substitutive" satisfactions, which serve to diminish our suffering; and (3) "intoxicating" substances, which serve to render us insensitive to the pain that is otherwise unavoidable. Examples of deflections from suffering include work and intellectual activity, whereas "substitutive" satisfactions are characteristic of the pleasure we derive from art, entertainment and the like. Though Freud's formula is no doubt consistent with the basic outline of his drive theory, I find them perfectly amenable to virtually any theoretical formulation. In fact, they make perfect sense to me even without a supporting theory of any kind, and we can confirm their efficacy solely from the fruits of our personal experience, including our observations as psychoanalytic practitioners.

Yet none of the methods that Freud enumerates ever succeeds to the degree that we would like, no matter how clever, resourceful, or enlightened we are in our pursuit to gain mastery over our emotions. This raises the inevitable question: Why is life so difficult, and, allowing that we agree that this difficulty is intractable and more or less consistent with living, what purpose could the sorry nature of our existence ultimately serve?

This is a question that has been examined from the beginning of recorded history, and we have yet to find a satisfactory answer. Of course, we are all familiar with Freud's dismissal of the religious argument, which more of less suggests that suffering is a test and a means of preparation for a future life that becomes available *only* if we are willing to endure our suffering on this earth with a benign sense of acceptance. Those who do not have recourse to such a comforting solution are left to wonder what to do with their suffering and ponder its effects on their attitude about life and, if only indirectly, their death.

Naturally, the question of suffering is uppermost on the minds of anyone who turns to psychoanalytic treatment, since the relief of their suffering is the principal motivating factor that brings people to therapy in the first place. What are the effects that a life of pain and frustration have on the human soul; how do such sufferings affect us and what do they inspire us to seek from life in response to it, not merely in spite of our miserable state but because of it? For Freud, who addressed this question in perhaps his most philosophical work, *Civilization and Its Discontents* (1930), the answer was never in doubt: our suffering inevitably causes us to seek happiness, to want to become happy, and, ultimately, to remain so. Suffering and happiness, then, enjoy a complementary relationship: it is because of suffering that we seek a happy state whose purpose is to alleviate it, and when we obtain happiness we wish to preserve it as a means of insulating ourselves against the likelihood of suffering again. But this quest is not as simple as it may seem, because the nature of happiness is such that we typically experience it, not as simply relieving our suffering, but, more importantly, as a source of well-being in its own right. Indeed, we must ask if it is even possible to attain happiness if its sole purpose is to provide a utilitarian relief from our suffering at the expense of all else.

Most of us would probably agree that relief from pain and the incidence of happiness are not the same thing, though it is probably the most difficult distinction that any human being is ever asked to consider—and one, I would submit, that the vast majority of analytic patients struggle with throughout their treatment experience.

But what are the principal sources of our suffering? The first is perhaps the most obvious one—our own body, which, according to Freud (1930), "is doomed to decay and dissolution" (p. 77), and even relies on pain and anxiety as warning signals. And though we don't give it much thought until disaster strikes, we must acknowledge that *the external world* is a second source of suffering, "which [periodically] rages against us with overwhelming and merciless forces of destruction" (p. 77) in the form of hurricane, earthquake, flooding, and the like. Third, and by far the most important source of our suffering, is our relationships with other human beings, the consequence of which is far more painful to us than any other suffering we are capable of experiencing.

Freud's emphasis on the third of the three sources of suffering is worth examining. Despite his emphasis on biology and on the pervasive presence of sexuality in our symptoms, Freud believed that our interpersonal relationships constitute the most painful experiences of which we are capable. One only has to meet a new patient who is suffering the loss of a husband, wife, or a child to witness the greatest pain we are humanly capable of enduring in order to appreciate Freud's insight into what, by now, all of us have no doubt witnessed and experienced ourselves.

Not surprisingly, all human beings seek ways of avoiding such suffering once they have encountered it, and the ingenuity with which we are capable of engaging in all manner of scheming, denial, and vindictiveness is, as we all know, legion. Some people opt to avoid relationships altogether, or at least the most intimate forms of relationships, in their attempt to protect themselves from being rejected, frustrated, and disappointed by other people. Of course, this strategy is never entirely successful, because there is also no greater source of happiness than in our associations with other human beings, whether they be lovers, spouses, friends, children, or colleagues. Without them we feel unremittingly unhappy, and due to the weight of isolation, alienation, and loneliness, we are obliged to seek an alternative means of relief from our self-imposed isolation.

But why, it must be asked, do our relationships with others cause such suffering? And, if Freud is correct, why should it be the source of suffering that is unparalleled? What do other human beings promise us that is ultimately thwarted? Freud suspected that the answer to this question lay in the quest for the so-called oceanic feeling that a friend of Freud's described as the kernel of the religious experience. Consistent with certain forms of love, this feeling was described to him as something akin to eternity, a feeling, says Freud (1930), "of an indissoluble bond, of being one with the external world as a whole" (p. 65).

Freud admitted to never having experienced such a feeling himself and even questioned whether it could be described as a "feeling" at all. It seemed more likely to him that the oceanic feeling is the consequence of an idea that one finds pleasing and that, in turn, results in the feeling it elicits secondarily. In fact, Freud found the notion that one could ever feel "at one" with society so alien to his experience that he wrote *Civilization and Its Discontents* in an effort to find an alternative explanation for the source of this sensation. He concluded that the only experience any of us ever has of this feeling is during the earliest stages of infancy, when we are welcomed into the family in which we were born. As we develop and discover that the paradise we enjoy with our mother is doomed, we seek alternative sources of this feeling of "oneness" that had previously required no effort on our part whatsoever.

Based on this formulation, we reserve the word *happiness* for any experience that serves to return us to the momentary bliss that our relationships with others may promise, but ultimately subvert. Happiness is fleeting because we experience it in contrast to the drudgery and frustration that our daily existence entails. Though we are loath to admit this, we cannot be happy all of the time. If we were hypothetically capable of preserving the happiness that we occasionally enjoy, our life would become boring, and the happiness that we had previously cherished would evaporate into that familiar state of anxiety that characterizes our existence. Then, the quest for happiness would begin all over again, only to be doomed to erosion the moment that we succeed in approximating it again. This observation can best be summarized with the adage that no honeymoon can last forever, a phenomenon that all psychoanalysts have encountered when the honeymoon they initially enjoyed with a new patient begins to wane.

If periodic doses of happiness are as much as we can get, this would explain what the drug addict seeks in his quest for the "perfect" drug, and why any drug that promises to approximate this feeling is similarly doomed to disappoint. No sooner do we find our solace in an addiction than the sublime experience of it wanes and we find the gain we once enjoyed diminishing until all that we are "addicted" to is a memory of an occurrence that is impossible to repeat. This is the state that our patients are in when they undertake treatment: they are either addicted to something or someone that no longer rewards them, or they have discovered that their neurotic "abstinence" from sources of potential reward are simply too painful to bear.

Some therapists even speak of people who are "addicted" to love! This, I admit, I find ironic, because the compelling and often obsessional nature of love is the prototypical source of every addiction of which we are capable, and the model that all the other addictions imitate. If this were not so, then the transference that every patient experiences with her analyst would be impossible, or its incidence would be so erratic that this treatment paradigm would be difficult to maintain.

Moreover, I submit that all of us are born "love addicts," in one form or other, and that there is no cure for this ailment, but a myriad of schemes to appease it, including psychotherapy, which endeavors to replace one form of addiction—whatever form of attachment it may be—with another—the transference relationship, which must eventually be abandoned, no matter how serviceable it has become.

It should be obvious from what I have said so far that, following Freud, I see transference as simply another word for *love*. In fact, the suffering that every one of us experiences throughout life can be assigned to the simple observation that we can never receive as much love as we would like, and that we find it difficult to love others with consistency, for reasons that are never entirely clear to us. The so-called addiction, it would seem, serves as nothing more than a substitute for the love that we are unable to obtain, or perhaps as a sense of deadness that relieves us from our pain altogether. It makes little difference whether the addiction is a drug, food, a person we cannot manage to get over, or the symptoms to which we have become attached. What they all share in common is an inability on our part to take the hit, suffer the loss, and tolerate the feeling of emptiness and despair that we convince ourselves we are incapable of bearing alone.

All patients suffer from some form of addiction, as I define it, even if the only things they are addicted to are their symptoms. It is a matter of indifference to me what their addiction might be, whether alcohol, drugs, love, neurosis, and so on. I do, however, hold the conviction that the goal of therapy is to foster sanity, and that addictions, however we define them, compromise our capacity for it. I agree with the conventional wisdom that in order for therapy to work, a serviceable attachment must be made to the therapist, so that the treatment may become at least as consuming as the problem from which the patient seeks relief. But once an attachment has been made, what then? The biggest difficulty in therapy is not the fastening of such attachments to the treatment situation, but in bringing them to a satisfactory resolution. Our patients seek happiness in their treatment where previously they have failed. However much they come to value the treatment and however much they may gain from it, sooner or later they must come to terms with the same problem that has always plagued them before: how to cope with a life that is capable of much reward, but never as much as they believe is their due. Similarly, no sooner do our patients become "addicted" to their therapy and their therapist than they discover that the satisfaction they seek fails to meet their expectations. Thus the principal goal of therapy is to teach patients not to put all their eggs in one basket, but to satisfying their needs from as many different sources as possible.

Yet, our patients struggle valiantly against this counsel, because addicts are loath to abandon what had once served as a panacea for their suffering, whatever that panacea may have been. This is because, in its absence, their desire to be happy, and maintain it, can never be fulfilled. Yet, that doesn't mean they should abandon their efforts to approximate it, however much they are able to and by whatever means are available. In the words of Garcia Lorca, "Many roads may be taken, but none will lead to Cordoba." Ultimately, patients must decide how much happiness they can expect to obtain from the world, which is to say in their relationships with others, and how far they dare go in making themselves independent of these relationships.

If whatever means patients employ are pushed to extremes, including the attachment to one's therapist, patients will eventually be exposed to ruin. Just as a wise businessman avoids tying up all his capital in one investment, it is an equally prudent lesson for our patients that they learn not to tie up all of their aspirations in one solution, however compelling it may be.

We hold no magic key, no special technique or insight that will make the burdens of our patients less difficult to bear. Life is complicated and the available sources of happiness are perilous. It has been my experience that no analytic patient is ever prepared for the degree of sacrifice and abstinence that we ask of them. We have little solace to offer, save for this one philosophical principle: if therapy teaches us anything, it's that it is far better to settle for whatever measure of happiness we are capable of procuring, however fleeting or imperfect, than to dispense with the effort altogether.

REFERENCE

Freud, S. (1930). Civilization and its discontents. *Standard Edition* 21:59–145.

Winnicott and Masud Khan: A Study of Addiction and Self-Destruction

Masud Khan's Descent into Alcoholism

Linda B. Hopkins

For the past three years, I have been doing research for a biography of the late Masud Khan. I have found his life to be a complicated mystery that will never be totally solved. Although Khan is usually remembered these days for the scandals he created, he was also a man who was at least close to being a genius, and who was much more complex as a person than is generally known. I have interviewed seventy of Khan's friends, family members, and peers. I have had access to four collections of correspondence, which, since Khan loved to write long letters, are quite valuable.

M. Masud R. Khan (1924–1989) grew up in rural India and moved to London, where he lived for forty years and became a major player in the world of international psychoanalysis. He mixed with the most creative and accomplished people of his time and then suffered a dazzling fall from grace, after which he almost disappeared from the conscious thinking of those who knew him. The fact that no lengthy biography has been published on Khan is remarkable, because he was the principal disciple of D. W. Winnicott (1896–1971), a man who is one of the most highly regarded

and most influential analysts since Freud. Khan's life is so fascinating, his contributions so many, his brilliance so shining, and his fall
so disastrous, that one wonders why there are not multiple biogra-
phies of him. Khan's life story is of interest not only to analysts and
therapists, but also to scholars in the worlds of ballet, literature,
Hollywood, cross-cultural studies, and the intellectual life of the
1960s. However, even in his own home—in the analytic literature—
there is a denial of Khan's contributions. For example, although his
crucial role in editing and publishing works by Winnicott and many
others is known, it is not well known that he was singularly
responsible for bringing Winnicott's work to international recognition and that he actually wrote or cowrote some of Winnicott's
major papers. When reference is made to Khan, it is usually to his
paper on cumulative trauma or his work on perversions—important
work, to be sure, but his clinical papers are equally important.

In the context of this book, however, the reason for thinking
about Khan is not because he was brilliant or interesting, but
because he was severely addicted to alcohol. This chapter focuses on
Khan's addiction to alcohol—what happened and why? I review
Khan's entire life story, but focus on three critical periods in his life:
childhood, 1924 to 1946; the years of Khan's success in England,
1946 to 1971; and the period of 1975 to 1976, when Khan's alcohol
addiction became unremitting. I'll start with 1975 to 1976, and then
go back in time to consider Khan's childhood and the relentless
development of his adult addiction.

In the fall of 1976, Masud Khan's life was in a precarious
position and could probably have tilted either toward health or
downfall. On the positive side, he was beginning to recover from
what he called "the terrible year," 1971, a year in which Winnicott
died, Khan's mother died, and his wife, the ballerina Svetlana
Beriosova, moved out. After 1971, Khan had stayed professionally
active in clinical work, writing, and editing, but his personal life
included a disastrous series of affairs with several women. In 1974,
Khan faced up to his drinking problem and, with great determination, he stayed sober for an entire year. Then, in 1975, he started to
drink heavily again. In August 1976, he went to his estate in Pakistan

to "dry out" and "lie fallow," in his terminology. He had been feeling physically unwell for several months, however, and when he returned to London he coughed up several cups of blood one night. When worked up medically, he was found to have oat-cell carcinoma of the lung, an extremely aggressive and deadly form of cancer. His left lung was removed and he was given a prognosis of at most 12 months to live. Many of his best friends were physicians, and as they investigated this prognosis they found it to be optimistic: Khan's chances of a one-year survival were in fact well below 5 percent.

Khan was a man who very much wanted to live, and he struggled bravely to deal with his cancer, which did recur the next year. He ended up losing most of his vocal cords and having to speak with a hoarse voice and eventually a whisper. He fought back hard and suffered enormously.

Khan never accepted the prognosis of 12 months. He couldn't believe that God would allow him to die at the young age of 52. And indeed, in what many people call a miracle, he did live on, for thirteen more years. And when he died, amazingly, the cause of death was not cancer. Khan died in 1989 from liver failure and other factors directly related to alcoholism. Khan's very good friend, the California analyst Robert Stoller, wrote to a friend (letter to Paul Moor, June 28, 1989): "Khan died a few weeks ago. He had had cancer for 13 years and had destroyed his liver by chronic unending excessive drink. His death was a blessing to him."[1]

Stories from the end of Khan's life give a sense of the severity of his alcoholism and how it interacted with a narcissistic personality disorder. They show Khan at his worst.

The first account is from a French analyst and it occurred in the late 1980s:

Masud was a very, very nasty person at the end of his life. He had no household help because his reputation was too well

---

1. Letters from Robert Stoller quoted in this chapter come from the Robert Stoller Archives, Department of Special Collections, University of California, Los Angeles. They are reprinted with the permission of Sybil Stoller.

known—for example, he would wake up a houseboy at 3 A.M. to prepare tea. He was so penetrated with the idea that he was a prince, that to do any of these tasks for himself was just unthinkable.

So when we visited in London, we would go to a restaurant to eat. I remember one scene in particular. There were two tables connected to each other and Masud was at the end of our table, which touched the other. Two couples were seated there. I am a good observer, and I notice that Masud is behaving strangely. He is pushing our bucket of champagne with his elbow. Eventually the champagne fell to the ground. And Masud makes a scandal. "SEND ME THE BOSS!" he yells. And he tells the boss that the man at the next table had pushed the champagne off the table. The boss offers to replace the champagne, but Masud says, "No! I want the gentleman to apologize." The boss doesn't know what to do, so he says, "Sir, the gentleman at the next table wants to talk to you." Masud starts up, "I am Prince Masud Khan!" "Oh yeah? And I'm the Duke of Edinborough!" "You have thrown my bottle!" "Not on purpose. But if I did so, I regret it." So that ended it. All Masud wanted was to humiliate that man in front of the women. We all knew it. [Interview with Anonymous, November 20, 1997]

Wladimir Granoff, another French colleague, also commented on Khan's restaurant behavior:

You would go to a restaurant with Masud and try to eat quietly and in peace. But after 15 minutes, Masud would start to yell and create a scene. For example, once there was a couple in love looking at each other and Masud screamed at the waiter, "Get these people out! I can't stand the familiarity!" Or you would go to the cloakroom and if a woman was holding his coat, he would yell, "I want a MAN to hold my coat, not a woman. Get a MAN!" [Interview, November 21, 1997]

Another late story comes from G., an American therapist living in Paris:

I had seen Khan for supervision in 1971 and 1972, after Winnicott died. Then I moved to Paris and we would see each other socially, just occasionally. This is an incident from about 1986.

After Masud's cancer, people were gossiping that he had become increasingly schizoid and aggressive. Then I saw him myself and I had a very different perception.

I had gotten a phone call from Victor Smirnoff that Khan would be in Paris and he asked, would I make a gesture to see him? I said I would, of course, and Masud then called and asked me for lunch. He was staying at the Hotel Lutetia, in a dingy room on the top floor. The curtains were all drawn.

When I arrived, Masud was still in pajamas and a bathrobe, and he was so hung over he was trembling. He was there with a Pakistani woman who said very little and seemed embarrassed. He told me that he was ill and asked what I wanted to drink. I had tea, and he had a small bottle of wine.

Masud took one sip of wine, and with that first sip he started to slur words and he became almost delusional. I remember a slip of the tongue he made. He meant to say the word "circumscribed," but he said "circumcision." He couldn't keep his words straight, and he was just babbling. He talked with venom about Winnicott, saying things about his impotence. I didn't like being told that. It was unsettling because it was an attack on someone he loved.

I saw a man who was clearly hung over. I've rarely if ever seen that in Paris. And I was amazed at how little wine it took to get him totally inebriated.

It was very clear to me that this was not psychosis, as the gossipers were saying—it was alcoholism. I wondered how much people who were calling him psychotic didn't pick up on his alcoholism. Some people are so good at disguising alcoholic behavior, they pass themselves off as having a different stigmata than the one they have.

In the 1970s in London, Masud had not seemed alcoholic.

And after his surgery he was still not alcoholic. This was a major change in his behavior. [Interview, November 15, 1997]

G. is one of the only people I interviewed who stated that Khan's decline was primarily due to alcoholism. Most of Khan's friends and colleagues give him a primary diagnosis of narcissistic personality disorder—and indeed he was a haughty and grandiose person throughout his life. Khan is also diagnosed as being psychotic, psychopathic, and—not a *DSM-IV* diagnosis!—demonic. You will not hear much gossip that his downfall came from untreated alcoholism. But Khan was severely alcoholic from 1975 to the end of his life. It seems to me that most of Khan's colleagues, friends, and analysts failed to understand the severity of the consequences of alcohol for him. One wonders: Did they overlook the most important problem? And could Khan have been helped if his alcoholism had been better understood, both by himself and by others?

CHILDHOOD

What do we see in Masud's childhood story that might help to explain his addiction? Masud Khan was born in 1924 in Chakwal, province of Montgomery (now Sahiwal), in the Punjab area of India, which is now Pakistan. (Pakistan was carved from India as an independent Moslem country, distinct from predominantly Hindu India, in 1947.) His father, Fazaldad Khan (1846–1943) was a wealthy Moslem horsebreeder and landowner with military connections and he had had three other wives when he married Khan's mother. The mother, Khursheed Begum (1905–1971) was a beautiful courtesan, mother of an illegitimate son. At the time of the marriage, Khan's father was 76 years old and Khursheed was 17. The illegitimate son was sent away to be raised, and the couple had three children in rapid succession: Tahir (1923–1983), the oldest son; then Masud (1924–1989); then a daughter, Mahmooda (1926–1942). Masud also had seven surviving half-brothers, all of them much older, all pursuing careers in the military, and four half-sisters.

The Khan family was not princely, as Khan claimed, but they were wealthy and powerful and extremely attractive.

Masud was very close to his sister Mahmooda and he was deeply affected when she died in 1942 at age 16. Six months later, Masud's father died. Upon his father's death, Masud was principal heir to his father's estate, despite the fact that he was the youngest son and in defiance of Islamic law.

Masud went to Government College in Lahore and received a master's degree in English literature, with a thesis on James Joyce. He emigrated to England in 1946, planning to get a doctorate in literature at Oxford and to have a personal analysis to help him with anxiety and phobias. He got into analytic training by mistake, when John Bowlby mistook his letter requesting analysis for a letter requesting training—an interesting story in itself.

Robert Stoller, who knew Khan's life story very well, believed that his personality was shaped by a fundamentally disparaged mother and a father who contributed a fiery mix of love and humiliation (letter to V. Smirnoff, March 29, 1978). Khan idolized his father throughout his life, but he was more forthright about criticizing his mother: "My need to learn French derives from the necessity of having words that are not confused with the chattering anxious countenance of my mother from infancy. Only thus can I hope to speak from my true self. All the other languages, especially English, are my manic attempt to drown her voiceless chatter and muttering in my head" (WB,[2] January 11, 1968). A variety of sources suggest that Khan felt impinged upon by both parents, and that it was a lifelong struggle to find his own true self. Later, Winnicott also impinged on him by using him professionally, and Stoller believed that Khan repeated his pattern by hiding his self behind Winnicott.

---

2. The initials "WB" refer to Masud Khan's workbooks, his private and unpublished diary, copies of which he entrusted to Robert and Sybil Stoller over the years. Workbook entries are printed with the permission of Sybil Stoller. Khan considered the workbook entries to be the written expression of his true self: "In 1965 Wova (Granoff) gave me 23 copybooks bound by Tisne of Paris. This accidental gesture launched a weighty project, because these Workbooks are my truest idiom of daily self actualization" (Khan, WB, May 8, 1975).

In understanding Khan, it is important to know that he was born with an "elephant ear," a very large ear that was lacking in cartilage. He was teased about his ear by other children. Surgery to reduce the ear was extremely painful, and for that reason the ear was left alone until Khan came to London and Winnicott insisted he have surgery prior to beginning his analysis. The ear was never normal, although, as an adult, Khan could partially hide it with long hair and sometimes a beret or other hat.

Khan was a reserved and asocial youth in his young adulthood. He was an intellectual and a serious student, and he stayed largely apart from the major political turmoil occurring in Lahore as India and Pakistan prepared for partition. He had some major psychological problems:

Now my own subjective memories of the years 1943–1946 are of a youth confused, terrified and bewildered, inconsolable and bleak, who drew a sort of magical circle round himself and survived by isolation. I certainly felt I had been born to become special in some peculiar way, but I had really no competitive sense of being superior to anyone in my shared or shareable area of life. [Letter to B., June 5, 1965]

In Lahore, Masud had a girlfriend who was Hindu. Both families broke up that relationship, and it was years before Masud dated anyone else. At some point in college, Masud had a psychological breakdown and went into analytic therapy.

Khan's Indian legacy was an important part of his identity throughout his life in England. He returned regularly to Pakistan and found peace there as he immersed himself in the everyday life of managing his estate. Pakistan was the place where he specifically went in repeated attempts to "dry out" (Pakistan being a country where alcohol is forbidden) and control his alcoholism. The only other place where he regularly attempted sobriety was the home of Robert and Sybil Stoller in California. Pakistan was always "home" to him, and, when he was dying, he made arrangements to be buried next to his father.

I disagree with some people who have claimed that Khan felt conflict about abandoning his roots; I think he had very strong separate identities as a Western man and an Eastern man throughout his life. However, I do agree that after leaving Pakistan, Khan was in many ways a man without a country because he never felt that he totally fit in anywhere. He was always thinking about moving out of London (to France or back to Pakistan) but never did. And the India of his childhood no longer existed, having become Pakistan, a country where Khan had never lived.

We can look at cultural factors leading to Khan's feeling of separateness, but our understanding must include psychological factors that go beyond culture. When Khan vacationed on the French Riviera, he wrote, "How utterly different I am from everyone I have encountered in the West—but I was not any nearer to anyone in my country either" (WB, August 6, 1968).

EARLY YEARS IN LONDON AND MARRIAGE TO SVETLANA

Khan moved to London in 1946. He started analytic training almost immediately upon his arrival. He saw Ella Freeman Sharpe and then John Rickman for analysis, both of whom died while he was in analysis. Then he went to Winnicott, shortly after Winnicott had had his first heart attack. Khan repeatedly refers to Winnicott as a clinical and theoretical genius, "the man who was destiny for me" (WB, February 15, 1971). Khan started analysis with Winnicott in 1951 and the analysis continued until 1966.

Professionally, Khan was a star student at the Institute. He was the second youngest student ever to enroll at the British Institute of Psycho-Analysis, after his rival Joe Sandler. Khan trained both as a child and adult analyst, and he finished his qualifications in 1959, the same year as his marriage to Svetlana Beriosova. In general he was well liked. Colleagues from the 1950s recall how interesting it was to hear him speak, how intuitive he was, and how he could be kind and very funny. They also remember that he often spoke too openly and too harshly, and that he had a tendency to be moody.

Although most analysts who knew Khan late in his life agree that he had a narcissistic character disorder, he seems to have been more neurotic than character disordered in the 1950s. He was anxious, and he had the capacity for insight and change. For example, in a letter written in 1957 to a friend, he thinks about his behavioral problems and wants to get them under better control. Referring to a professional meeting where he had criticized a case presentation by another friend, Jim Harris, he writes:

And did I go for him. Coldly, acidly, point after point. I must have been really lethal, because it pulled everyone up and the discussion was sober and thoughtful. Harris was left obviously bewildered. Only in retrospect, when he left early, was it pointed out to me that I had been very severe and harsh, and I realised the hurt I must have caused him. . . .

I can see now that I suffer and have suffered from a curious delusion of sincerity. I never attack those I don't care for. And so when I am critical I do not lose my affection, but that is not how the other part experiences it. I really molest savagely.

Yet, I feel that I only seek a dialogue. I do not think what I say is absolute. If it is challenged and corrected, I am all too willing to see it. The pity is that everyone withdraws behind a quiet cold rejection and I am left holding an angry disassociated monologue.

But I am going to watch my tongue in the future. Put a restraint on my over-eloquent sincerity of criticism. I only make enemies, and no one is helped. [Letter to B, November 12, 1957]

This period of time and into the early 1960s is when Masud was in his prime. In many ways, he got to have the dialogue he wanted, because he associated with brilliant and accomplished people who could keep him in control. And he was growing intellectually and personally. In close collaboration with Winnicott, he built a very successful private practice and was sought after for analysis by intelligent, creative, and often wealthy patients. Svetlana was a famous ballerina, and she introduced her husband to a world of artists and glamour in which he thrived. Werner Muensterberger remembered Khan's comment, "What other analysts get invited to Buckingham Palace?" (interview, July 15, 1999). This glamorous life may have fed Khan's narcissism, but he was giving back as much to the world as he was taking in. Alcohol was not a problem: Masud drank heavily, but appropriately to his social situation.

The early years of marriage (1959 to 1965) were very good for both Masud and Svetlana. People who knew them remember that they were clearly in love. Masud provided a home base for Svetlana, who had never really known a home, and Svetlana gave Masud companionship in his loneliness and somebody with whom he could share his accomplishments. She also helped him to control his impulsive behavior.

Masud had two major problems, however: insomnia and depression. Many of his diary entries are written at 2:30, 3, or even 4 A.M., when he preferred to work rather than lie awake. He sometimes took naps in the daytime, but he still had major sleep deprivation. The depression was more episodic: it tended to follow periods of stress and often lasted two weeks to a month. The depressions had a quality of collapse that seem more anaclitic than conflictual:

> I am no longer oppressed by that bleak *un*psychic physical sort of pain which swamps my being and flattens me out into an insipid mechanical state. This weekend I am really better. . . . I feel I am living in time and space. I really couldn't account for the past three weeks. Apart from the clinical and professional work . . . I have vegetated in a subhuman way. . . . This is so hard to describe. . . . While I am in the dazed ferment . . . there is no acute conflict. There is no sense of tragedy. Only a bleak aloneness and bare nonexistence. While all this is happening the best one can do is suffer it fully and without distraction. [Letter to B., May 23, 1965]

In this letter, Khan seems to have been able to think about his feelings and contain them. His statement that he did not feel conflict is quite typical of his self-understanding in the years to come. He never felt that Freudian conflict theory explained him, and he viewed life more in terms of choice points than conflict. In line with this thinking, Khan came to believe his patients did not need to analyze the influence of the past to understand and resolve their conflicts, and the focus of his treatment was more to teach them how to communicate with their "hidden self" and to help them to live well in the world. He was moving far away from classical analysis, in which insight is considered critical to success: "Yes, until life-experience augments and corrects the analytic experience, a person does not grow in analysis" (WB, March 7, 1971).

It is interesting to see what Khan felt about alcoholism in the days when he was developing his theory and when alcohol was not yet a problem for him or for Svetlana. We get a sense of this from a private letter:

I have done something clinically only half an hour ago which I have never risked doing before: A patient (a new case) turned up and bemusedly, complacently, told me he had got drunk last night and is still pretty drunk. I asked him, had he tried to stop getting drunk? He changed my question into the statement: "I do not know why I got drunk." I told him that I hadn't asked him why he got drunk, but whether he had tried NOT to get drunk. He said, "No!" he had not tried. I politely but firmly told him that, in that case, there was no use going on with the session. . . . I had no use for a drunk patient: it merely wastes his time and mine. That he is an adult intelligent person and should be able to control himself and arrive sober. That I was not interested in the equation: "Poor patient, he does not know why he gets drunk. Let us help him find out." . . . He was rather taken aback by this. I gave him an appointment for Monday and showed him out. . . .

It became clear to me that this patient has learnt all the tricks of exploiting the *status* of being "neurotic, ill, helpless," and hides behind these to live exactly as he pleases. . . . If one gives in to the *myth* of the patient's total helplessness, then one becomes the victim and accomplice of his omnipotence. No adult is ever totally helpless.

To some extent, psychoanalysis has sponsored this myth of the helpless neurotic who can be helped in spite of his effort to destroy himself. . . . We believe that if only we succeed in imparting true and full knowledge, people will act nobly and responsibly and creatively. But that is not true. People or a person can have all the necessary self knowledge and yet refuse to make use of it. Here the issue takes on essentially a moral and metaphysical, uniquely human dimension, to which neither science nor psychoanalysis have so far offered any answer. [Letter to B., May 29, 1965]

This letter contains knowledge that Khan might have wished his own analysts and colleagues would have had. Khan needed to stop drinking more than he needed to understand why he was drinking, and he was not helped by compassion and tolerance when he was drinking. Khan saw that the problem drinker can have enormous self-knowledge that is of no help. With this insight, Khan was far beyond the analytic thinking of his time, which did not include the knowledge that psychoanalysis is of no help to somebody who is actively alcoholic. In refusing to see his patient until he got his drinking under control, Khan did for the patient what no analyst ever did for him.

Around 1965, Svetlana became severely alcoholic quite quickly, and Masud showed the first signs of problem drinking. Their charmed lives started to unravel. Within just a few years, the marriage was over and both had destroyed their careers. Neither one would ever find a new and satisfying life, and both would die alcoholic.

The precipitant to Masud's drinking problem was the loss of his relationship with Svetlana, which occured when she became a problem drinker. And how did this happen? Svetlana had always enjoyed alcohol, but when she was a star ballerina, on a track to become prima ballerina at the Royal Ballet, she had enormous control and her drinking was not a problem. But in the early 1960s, something quite unexpected happened: Rudolf Nureyev defected from the Bolshoi Ballet, and Margot Fonteyn came out of retirement to dance with him. It became clear that Svetlana would never get the number-one spot because, by the time Fonteyn retired, Svetlana herself would be too old. Although Fonteyn's return was glorious for her in its defiance of age, it had serious negative consequences for a whole generation of dancers, including Svetlana.

Svetlana was a quiet drinker at first. Many people remember being at social occasions where she would suddenly, without warning, pass out. Later her drinking became "obvious and catastrophic" (interview with Ted Lucie-Smith, June 3, 1999). At more than one party, she lay down and passed out in a bathtub, fully dressed, having to be taken home. She also started to miss performances, something that had never happened before.

Masud drank differently. Sometimes he had binges with outrageous behavior that he regretted the next day, but usually his style was less dramatic than Svetlana's. Lucie-Smith remembers:

> He was alcoholic in such a different way from Svetlana. He was constantly drinking well-watered whisky, so you never noticed how much he was consuming. Watering the whisky heavily was a way to conceal the quantity, not only from others, but even from himself. . . . One thing I thought was that, as long as Svetlana was around, Masud could pretend that alcohol was her problem, not his or perhaps theirs.
>
> Masud would get aggressive when he was actually drunk. You would get a warning because he would first start to talk only in French, which he spoke fluently but with an incomprehensible accent. [Interview, June 3, 1999]

Svetlana was given the best and most intensive of medical treatments for alcoholism, to no avail. In the early 1970s she was dismissed from the Royal Ballet. Shortly after that, she separated from Masud and went to live on her own in a fourth-floor walkup. She lived in that flat as a recluse for the rest of her life, never reestablishing a career or a private life, addicted to alcohol until her death from cancer in 1998.

MASUD'S ALCOHOLISM—1970s TO 1989

Why did Masud start drinking again in 1975, after his year of abstinence? The immediate problem was an exacerbation of his insomnia. Despite the use of prescription sleeping pills, he was sleeping just two or three hours a night. And he began having bad dreams during the brief period when he could sleep:

> Had retired to bed early and managed to fall asleep. But was jilted out of sleep by an ungraspable dream. [WB, July 1, 1975, 2 A.M.]

> Attempt to sleep hasn't worked. This faceless unrest in me which I do not experience either as anxiety or stress, but know only through the ego's insomniac vigilance. In itself, my life is so well arranged now, but on its fringes I sense menacing ghosts! [WB, July 4, 1975, 2 A.M.]

At the end of July 1975, the International Psychoanalytic Association Congress (IPAC) was held in London. Khan was on several panels and delivered a paper. Robert and Sybil Stoller stayed with him and Khan had "idyllic days of companionship" (WB, July 25, 1975) with them: "I always feel so safe amidst others when the Stollers are here" (WB, July 22, 1975). Khan's favorite French friends, Victor Smirnoff and J. B. Pontalis, were also there. Masud was pleased that he was able to control his drinking again and his professional contributions to the Congress went well:

> Yes, I have established myself as THE intellectual creative thinker of my generation with this Congress. Now I have to sustain that status with quiet persistence of effort. [WB, July 25, 1975]

[At the end of the Congress] Martin Azarian had asked me who I thought was the one person who had emerged from this Congress as the most creative and powerful mind in psychoanalysis. Quite unabashedly I answered him: Masud Khan! [WB, July 27, 1975]

We have to balance Khan's possible grandiosity with the reality of the situation, which was that Khan got a great deal of attention and praise at this conference and was indeed highly regarded: "Pontalis called and told me that in the summing up of the Congress, my dreaming paper was singled out by the reporter for its imaginative quality" (WB, July 25, 1975). "Colmanaris tells me that Erik Erikson had remarked to him: 'The next decade in psychoanalysis belongs to Khan!'" (WB, July 27, 1975).

After the Congress, Khan's apprehension returned. He interpreted it as a symptom of his dread of having to move from his flat at Hans Crescent, opposite Harrod's Department Store (in Knightsbridge), to a less expensive and less luxurious flat on Palace Court (on the opposite corner of Hyde Park, opposite Kensington Gardens in Bayswater.) He had already leased his new flat and would not move for another year, but the thought of the move was very unsettling, or, at least, *something* was unsettling:

A terrible gnawing madness clings to and seeps from every object here (in this flat). Even that which was once beautiful and exultant now has an anguished bite in it. [WB, August 5, 1975]

Have immobilised myself into wreckage. Cannot grasp the incessant apprehension that is haunting me at present. An uncanny acute dread at leaving this flat. I do realise that once I leave it all my links with Svetlana will perish. The space here is so essentially hers. [WB, August 26, 1975]

How many fugitive and anonymous little deaths one dies. These sudden panics that seize and paralyse me at present. All of these are a way of clinging to this space. But now there is no staying. Again, the mind knows and refuses to know. [WB, September 1, 1975]

That fall, after a year of sobriety, Khan started to drink again. He wrote, "[I] am drinking again. That can't be helped. So much confused ungraspable stress" (WB, September 15, 1975). Soon he was drinking bottles of whisky every week, despite repeated efforts to abstain. His hands started shaking, and his physician, Barrie Cooper, warned him that his blood tests showed liver damage.

For the next few months, Khan's diary was filled with reports of his awareness that alcohol was poisoning him and leading him to absurd "excesses and dangerous antics" (WB, December 15, 1975). He wrote, "Alcohol now alienates me not only from myself but from others as well" (WB, December 17, 1975). He canceled a Christmas trip to Paris, knowing he would drink too much there. He considered asking Barrie Cooper to take him into a clinic for an appendectory, as a means to drying out (WB, December 27, 1975). He created a scandal at a banquet in London, polishing his jack-knives in public and talking in a paranoid way.

When Bob and Sybil Stoller visited in February 1976, Khan was unable to relax with them. Instead, he lay in bed—but with the Stollers there, at least he was able to sleep and dream. He accepted Bob's advice and canceled plans to give a paper at a Congress on borderlines at the Menninger Clinic.

Throughout this period, Khan was constantly trying to figure out what was happening. He first concluded that he was trying to "cure" himself of ungraspable terrors that he could not consciously grasp. He believed that if he could just become conscious of the content and meaning of his terrors, he would be in touch with his true self and he wouldn't have to drink.

Woke up today with a lucid and exact comprehension of why I got dislocated into heavy boozing since my return from Paris. I was celebrated there by my colleagues and friends, and London is a void edged with envy from my colleagues. This I did not let myself register out of pride. [WB, June 6, 1976]

Suddenly I had a moment of epiphanic insight about my heavy drinking. It started when I began to feel dismay about Svetlana. Once Svetlana went out of my life, I lost the capacity to feel deeply for anyone This void of affectivity in myself I have screened with the haze of alcohol. [WB, June 19, 1976]

It is ironic that Khan tried to solve his problem drinking through insight and access to feelings, when his own theory of management of the environment would have been much more effective. He needed to apply his 1965 insight regarding his own patient: he needed to stop drinking more than he needed to acquire knowledge about his drinking.

Khan had no idea that he was seriously ill. It is very sad to think that he was probably aware of his lung cancer on a deep somatic level, which would explain his horrible nightmares and his pervasive terrors. Just when he had been sober for an entire year, in 1974, this anxiety may have caused him to start drinking again. He definitely had a wish to stop:

Once unpoisoned by alcohol, how lucid, orderly and insomniac my mind becomes. The devil of it is, I do not even enjoy alcohol. [WB, June 8, 1976, 3 A.M.]

Spent a wretched night of sweat and withdrawal reactions plus fever and toothache. Serves me right!
   Today I am already flimsily IN myself, but my hands are still inept and shakey. If I am to [do editorial work] I have to be totally dry. My mind plays wicked tricks on me when alcohol poisoned. When dry, there are few to match it. [WB, June 16, 1976]

In fall 1976, Khan's life went through a dramatic upheaval. Upon return to England from Pakistan, he had resumed his heavy drinking. Oddly, he developed a new symptom of dipsomania—the excessive drinking of fluids, not just alcohol, but any fluid, primarily orange juice. Within weeks, he was in the hospital getting ready for exploratory surgery: "I am still too close to all of this to know my responses. But I feel that the stable world I had built has suddenly come apart, and I am lost" (WB, October 14, 1976). On October 20th, exploratory surgery revealed cancer, and Khan's doctor removed his lung and also had to cut a phrenic nerve, which affected Khan's voice. Khan wrote, "Yes, after this crisis, a lot in me will change. . . . The whole task is existing alone from moment to moment, holding pain, and gradually mastering it. My past is achieved and behind me. I have no sense of a future" (WB, October 22, 1976).

A week later, after his surgeon told him that his prognosis for survival was very poor, he wrote, "In this aseptic room, life is so unreal. I am dazed by what has happened so suddenly, but not dismayed" (WB, October 29, 1976). He tried to accept his situation and to be brave: "What was to be a destiny has now changed into mere fatedness. And even that does not distress me. I am only concerned with how and what to do for those who love me and are my friends" (WB, October 31, 1976).

Bob and Sybil Stoller flew from Los Angeles to visit, and Masud wrote,

Now I am in the care of fate and physicians. [But] as long as I have friends like Bob and Sybil, who can fly from LA to surround and shore me, and the love of X [Khan's girlfriend] I need only to use myself and reactivate my mind and being. And that is precisely what I am going to do. So help me God. When death comes, it will be an end not of my concoction and instigation. I mean to live what I have in me cleanly, vigorously, and creatively. It will take mammoth effort! [WB, November 12, 1976]

But Khan's mammoth effort was not enough. He soon started drinking again, and within a year, when a new lung cancer was diagnosed, he was severely alcoholic. This time around, he gave up the fight, and started the heavy drinking that would eventually kill him. He had plenty of insight into his situation, but his insight could not help him:

> My hands have been paralyzed and full of refusal of my mind, and for a brief period of one month I have kept myself soaked in whisky 24 hours. I can see now only too clearly that I could not accept, or to put it more accurately, the omnipotence in me could not accept my situation. I wanted to find my own death through alcohol before cancer could get me. Also, I could not accept the physical handicaps that the operation in October [1976] imposed on me. So I abandoned both my body and my consciousness, and I have lived in a transitional psychic state in which I was stuporous from alcohol and where even dreaming was unfeasible. [WB, October 2, 1977]

> [Commenting on his girlfriend leaving him:] [I see that after my surgery] when I began to recover physically, I split into two persons. The sober one who loved and was grateful to X for her tender affection and care, and the alcoholic who molested her being and person with insult, and created in the end the same terror of insecurity in her that unconsciously was all the time threatened from within. Eventually she had no option left except to save herself by leaving me—and that she did.
>
> That my sickness destroyed her love shall always stay a deep sadness within me. [WB, November 23, 1978]

> [Agreeing with Robert Stoller's interpretation that he had orchestrated X's leaving:] I could not tolerate total dependence and regression, so I screened it with alcoholism. [WB, December 28, 1978]

Khan went back into analysis with Anna Freud, one of his early supervisors. She had always liked him. The analysis was, as might be expected, totally ineffective, because throughout the time he saw her he was drinking heavily. Victor Smirnoff described his friend's alcohol intake in the postsurgery period as a bottle of scotch a day plus wine, starting each morning. This amount soon increased to a bottle and a half of scotch each day (letter from V. Smirnoff to R. Stoller, June 21, 1977), and the drinking existed in the context of continued dipsomania, in which he also drank "gallons and gallons" of orange juice and tea (letter from V. Smirnoff to R. Stoller, October 14, 1978).

Eventually, Khan lost the capacity to think about his illness, and he totally stopped writing. When he died, he had spent months sitting or lying in a dark room, not even watching television, barely able to talk, and mostly unwilling to see any of his friends. A few weeks before he died, he did see a few friends, including Victor Smirnoff, to whom he wrote a short note: "What an end to my life!" (letter from V. Smirnoff to R. Stoller, May 15, 1989).

Khan died on June 8, 1989.

DISCUSSION AND CONCLUSIONS

Robert Stoller wrote about the tragedy of Khan's alcoholism:

When Masud was well, it was so exciting to sit with him as he played with ideas, needing only the mildest stimulus from the listener in order to set him off. Often his anecdotes were clinical fictions, and yet they had truths more enlightening than the more accurate descriptions with which some of us must make do. And sometimes, when—just for the hell of it—he scrambled for a new theoretical position, the flight was spectacular. Being with him when he was in those moods was like being drunk—the excitement, the exhilaration, the mania of ideas. Later, when examined in a sober light, these ideas had to be used differently, but nonetheless, they left behind a quality that still shone.

But [as time went on] there was less and less of the joy. He had to simulate it with addiction. I am not sure that he needed the cancer in order to get off the hook of his creativity. He could have been one of those artists who lives precariously on the edge of disaster, but who keeps springing back forever to astonish us with one more great performance. The unrolling of reality as the years passed certainly did press him down, as it does many others, but I think he was crazy enough to roll aside, without being totally crushed. Without the cancer . . . he might have continued to produce at his own high level, at least intermittently, but I think he might have needed more and more crutches in these next years [had he not gotten the cancer]. His problem is that he turned to the wrong crutch—alcohol—though considering his life history, that is not so surprising. [Letter to V. Smirnoff, March 29, 1978]

[After Khan's death, partly in reaction to Masud's anti-Semitism in his final book:] [Masud] burned down the house, while he was inside it. If only he had been schizophrenically psychotic, then we wouldn't have had this sense of his being willfully destructive. . . . [I had thought that I wasn't really mourning] but I realize now that my mourning is taking the form of this complex anger. For that is my mourning, one can mourn with the thoughts: "Fuck you. Why did you do it this way?" I join you in RIP [Rest in Peace for him], but I don't agree that he was a faithful friend. I think he was, in the end, faithless to himself, to the goddamn tradition he was always hooting about, and to the rest of us. [Letter to V. Smirnoff, January 16, 1990]

In blaming Khan for destroying himself, Bob Stoller was assuming that Khan could have controlled his drinking. Khan himself would agree with that idea, as he had commented in 1965 about his own patient, "No adult is ever totally helpless." But Khan and Winnicott together wrote about the role of environment, and another side of Khan's story is the story of environmental failure regarding his alcoholism.

There is certainly ample evidence that Khan wanted to stop drinking and that in certain situations he was able to control his drinking. Sybil Stoller, for example, was unforgiving about Masud's alcohol abuse and, in her presence, for days and weeks at a time, he never drank to excess. Barrie Cooper also confronted Masud, with more limited success. But Sybil and Barrie had very little help, and Khan was essentially left alone to deal with his addiction. One wonders: What if Winnicott and others had listened to Khan's plea from 1963, "I seek only a dialogue"? What would have happened if more people had confronted him about the way he was publicly destroying his life? What if they had been less frightened of him and more brave? If the drinking was a cry for help, why was there so little response? And, perhaps most significantly of all, what if Winnicott had used the power of the transference to insist that his patient stop drinking?

It is my belief that Winnicott was both naive and ineffective in helping Khan with alcohol addiction. In 1965 alcohol began to be a problem in Khan's life, and in 1966 Khan ended his analysis and entered into a professional collaboration only with Winnicott. Why would Winnicott agree to end at such a time? I have written an article on this question (Hopkins 1998) that raises some possibilities: Winnicott's psychological difficulty with accepting and detoxifying destructiveness in the actual clinical situation, the possibility that Winnicott's cardiac condition caused him and his patients to avoid rage interactions out of health concerns, and the benefits Winnicott got for himself from their extra-analytic relationship.

In the 1960s, analysis was viewed as a cure-all for just about any problem, so Masud's problem with alcoholism would have been viewed by both Winnicott and Khan as a failure of the analysis. But what was the failure? I still believe what I wrote in my article about the problems in the analysis. However, two years later, I now think that the greatest part of the failure was more simple: Winnicott did not insist that Khan stop drinking, and he did not utilize Khan's very strong transference in such a way as to motivate Khan to want to stop drinking. Winnicott was a clinical genius and, despite his limitations, he could have been a "good enough" analyst for Khan if he had done just one thing differently: focus on Khan's drinking and insist that he get it under control.

What is my evidence that Winnicott didn't focus on the drinking? It is mostly indirect. Winnicott was trained as a pediatrician and did mostly child consultations, so his experience with treating alcoholism was limited. He did not have a drinking problem himself, and he and Khan were living in an era when heavy drinking was socially acceptable and its consequences poorly understood by analysts in general. Theoretically, Winnicott considered antisocial behavior to be a cry for help, and he never wrote about alcoholism being a form of pathology for which treatment requires abstinence, not just analysis. In fact, Winnicott makes just two references to alcoholism in all of his writing. The first reference, in 1953, talks about addiction in general as an example of pathology in the transitional space. The second reference is to a patient who, based on a number of factors, is probably Khan.[3] This is the famous case (1966) of a man with a dissociated "female" side who experiences penis envy. Winnicott interprets to the patient that he drinks too much because he suffers from disintegration anxiety, that he is trying to convince himself that he can produce the feelings of disintegration under his own control—by voluntary drinking. Alcohol is not considered to be a problem in and of itself in Winnicott's interpretation. We see more a hint of a belief that understanding will be sufficient to control the symptom of drinking. And, in case the reader is still doubting Winnicott's failure to understand the problem of alcoholism, we look to Khan's (1987) report that Winnicott regularly drank whiskey (malt) with Khan at times when they were doing their collaborative work on Sundays—a socially understandable gesture that would, nevertheless, have been a very mixed message to a former patient who was destroying his life with alcohol.

Masud Khan never believed that there was a single "truth" and, as a result, he liked questions more than he liked answers: "I am all for papers that define the problem in order to arrive at a significant question. I have little use for the reassurance of answers. No one can

---

3. Some people have believed that the patient was Harry Guntrip. However, consideration of the date when the person began analysis rules out this possibility.

use answers, but we can all, in our own way, take up a question and enquire further upon it" (letter to R. Stoller, May 11, 1964).

In that spirit, I close this paper with a series of questions:

How did Svetlana's alcoholism contribute to Masud's downfall? What would have happened to Masud if Svetlana had become a prima ballerina rather than an alcoholic?

What are the psychodynamics underlying Masud Khan's alcoholism? What was the contribution of his family history and his cultural upheaval? How did alcohol interact with his narcissistic personality disorder?

Should Khan have been helped to focus more on living effectively in the world and less on understanding himself? Could he have cured himself if fate had been kinder to him? What was the role of cancer in precipitating the shift of dependence to addiction?

Why were Bob and Sybil Stoller consistently able to bring Masud back to health?

Did psychoanalysis and specifically Winnicott as analyst fail Khan in this area? Was the problem a kind of ignorance in the 1960s and 1970s? What would be done differently today?

REFERENCES

Hopkins, L. (1998). D. W. Winnicott's analysis of Masud Khan: a preliminary study of failures of object usage. *Contemporary Psychoanalysis* 34(1):5–47.

Khan, M. (1987). The long wait. In *When Spring Comes: Awakenings in Clinical Psychoanalysis.* London: Chatto and Windus.

Winnicott, D. W. (1953). Transitional objects and transitional phenomena. In *Playing and reality.* London: Tavistock Publications, 1971, pp. 1–25.

24

Winnicott's Complex Relationship to Hate and Hatefulness

Marcia Rosen

More than thirty years ago, I discovered Winnicott's work on hate in the countertransference (1947), as well as Searles's (1965) assertion that the therapist's benevolence may be a defense against his sadistic feelings toward the patient. I was impressed by Winnicott's boldness in acknowledging that we may hate our patients, just as mothers may hate their babies at times. However, it was not until I consulted Lawrence Epstein for some help with a very difficult, scornful patient that I really grasped the transformative power of Winnicott's ideas for our work.

The patient, a man in his fifties, had been relentlessly critical of me in our sessions, in very effectively scathing fashion. He was very depressed, having just lost his wife to his best friend. I found I was experiencing dread in anticipation of his sessions, and it was taking me a few hours to recover from them. At wits' end, I arranged a consultation with Dr. Epstein. The consultation enabled me to acknowledge my feelings of hate toward the patient without being overwhelmed by guilt. What followed was utterly remarkable to me. In the first session following the consultation, I found myself free of the dread and anxiety I had been experiencing with the patient. The session began with silence, soon broken by the patient's saying, "I feel much better. I can feel that you hate me." As the work proceeded, it became clear that the patient knew he was hateful and vastly relieved that it was no longer being denied or avoided, as had been the case throughout his family history. It also became clear that his hatefulness was a communication to me of his experience at the hands of an extremely hostile and sadistic mother. I became able to address his hatefulness when it occurred, and we were able to talk about it. I also realized that what had previously been my silence in the face of his hostility was sadistic and hateful on my part.

There may be a complementarity between the patient's hate and hatefulness and the therapist's. Winnicott appears generally to have omitted much direct interpretation of the patient's hate and hatefulness, and evidently expressed little of his own. Winnicott (1947) stated:

> In the ordinary analysis the analyst has no difficulty with the management of his own hate. This hate remains latent. . . . In the analysis of psychotics, however, quite a different type and degree of strain is taken by the analyst. . . . The analyst must be prepared to bear strain without expecting the patient to know anything about what he is doing, perhaps over a long period of time. . . . The analyst . . . is under strain to keep his hate latent, and he can only do this by being thoroughly aware of it. . . . In certain stages of certain analyses the analyst's hate is actually sought by the patient, and what is then needed is hate that is objective. If the patient seeks objective or justified hate he must be able to reach it, else he cannot feel he can reach objective love. [pp. 17–20]

This last comment strikes me as exceptionally cogent, particularly in the light of my experience with the patient I described above. He knew he was hateful, and was immensely relieved to have this aspect of his behavior acknowledged.

Another of Winnicott's most central contributions was the concept of use of the object, which stated that hate and destructiveness are necessary experiences enabling the child to differentiate himself from his mother, knowing that he can destroy her in fantasy and she will survive. Winnicott believed that one of the central functions of the therapist is to offer himself as an object to be used in this way. The patient and therapist need to address the former's feelings and fantasies of hate and destructiveness in the treatment relationship. I would add that the therapist's feelings of hate toward the patient may also need to be addressed in the treatment relationship, albeit judiciously.

Upon reading Dr. Hopkins' paper (1998), I was immediately struck by the paradoxical nature of Winnicott's relationship to hate and hatefulness, as may be inferred from what we surmise of his analysis of Khan, as well as from information gleaned from other analyses he conducted (Margaret Little, Harry Guntrip), and from other sources. The paradox is that the examples of hate and hatefulness we encounter in Winnicott's case reports and the reports of a select few analysands are discordant with his theoretical stance. In fact, some of his behaviors and responses strike me as peculiarly evasive and avoidant. When the boy he has taken into his home acts up, Winnicott (1949) puts him out of the house, saying only that he hates him, but not, apparently, addressing the boy's behavior. When Little smashes the vase in his office, he exits and does not return until the session's end. Subsequently, he replaces the vase and flowers with an exact replica and reportedly makes a terse comment that she had destroyed something that was important to him. I suppose this could be construed as restoration of the destroyed object, but the near-wordlessness of the exchange does not seem to be constructive for the patient. Guntrip (1975) recounts Winnicott's contrasting Guntrip favorably with the patient whose hour precedes his. It is easy to speculate that Guntrip must have coveted this position, and must have been unwilling to risk losing it by being aggressive or hateful. Hopkins notes that according to the reports of their peers and colleagues, Little, Guntrip, and Khan retained their characterological arrogance and superiority post-analysis.

Goldman (1993) commented that Winnicott "may have had some problem with his own aggression. . . . It was important for him to feel that his aggression was tolerated. . . . Although not afraid of stating his own opinions, he defused confrontation with disarming charm." The complex picture of Winnicott that emerges from Goldman's work includes true humility side by side with a certain intolerant arrogance. While he clearly needed to be loved and admired, and avoided direct confrontation, some of his behavior seems likely to have been experienced by others as hateful.

My understanding of Winnicott's analysis of Masud Khan leaves me with the impression that there was a gulf between Winnicott's profound theoretical comprehension of the importance of hate and destructiveness in development and his ability to make clinical use of this. Hopkins has described Khan, his history and relationships, including that with Winnicott. She has gathered material from myriad first- and second-hand sources, and analyzed Khan's work for the insights it offers about him. A number of questions and hypotheses emerge as I study the data.

It is clear that Winnicott's analysis of Khan ultimately failed, in large part, as evidenced by Khan's decline into alcoholism and madness. Khan's later years, as described by his colleagues and friends, were characterized by increasing inappropriateness, hostility, grandiosity, and self-destructiveness. He is consistently described as behaving in hateful fashion. How does this occur in the face of a fifteen-year analysis with an analyst who appears to have understood hate and hatefulness?

Khan began his analysis with Winnicott in 1951, after having lost his first two analysts to fatal heart attacks, both in the course of his treatment. He began his analysis with Winnicott shortly after the latter had suffered his own first heart attack. We have no knowledge, as far as I can tell, as to how Khan took in these experiences, what fantasies they generated, or what part they played in the analytic work. Khan was, from all descriptions, a rather seductive and probably charismatic character who evoked special treatment from many who encountered him (Hopkins 1998). He was, evidently, also an extremely anxious person, who may have elicited from others a particular sort of empathy and maternal solicitousness. Whether this might have been a defense against Khan's narcissistic rage, we do not know. Given certain attributes of Winnicott's character and personality (Goldman 1993), I am inclined to speculate that Winnicott may have been intimidated by Khan's arrogance, and/or drawn to take special care of him because of his extreme anxiety and narcissistic fragility, as well as his obvious intelligence and talent. This is a combination of dynamics that often occurs with certain gifted borderline and narcissistic patients. Additionally or alternatively, Winnicott may have been intimidated by what Khan had described as his own slashing aggression. Hopkins notes that during the early part of Khan's analysis with Winnicott, he writes of his recognition of his brutal hostility with remorse. It is also notable that Goldman recounts Clare Winnicott's comment that Winnicott suffered from an excess of "benignity," which must have hampered his ability to address Khan's aggression and destructiveness in any direct way.

A major issue arising within a year from the time Winnicott and Khan began their analytic work together is Winnicott's enlisting Khan as his collaborating editor. There can be no doubt that this immediately compromised Khan's analysis, curtailing his freedom to "use" Winnicott as an object. It is irresistible to speculate upon Winnicott's motivation in making this arrangement. Was he putting his needs before his analysand's? Was he encouraging a relationship of mutual dependency that aborted the analysis almost before it began? Was he encouraging Khan's grandiosity? Was Winnicott's need to be loved, accepted, and admired so great that he needed to bind Khan to him? Or was Winnicott so fearful of what he may have sensed as the virulence of Khan's aggression that he needed to disarm him? Whatever the precise explanation for this egregious act, we may never know. However, I believe that in the end, Winnicott's behavior with Khan was probably as hateful an act as any of Khan's florid demonstrations of aggression toward others and himself.

I want to make a distinction here between hate and hatefulness, as I am using these terms. Winnicott wrote about hate in the countertransference essentially as a feeling held in or near awareness that is basically an appropriate response to the patient's behavior. While he does acknowledge that there may be idiosyncratic "abnormal" components in the personality and identifications of the individual therapist, his emphasis is on what he calls the "objective countertransference." The tacit assumption appears to be that any well-analyzed therapist treating the patient is likely to experience these feelings. I think of hatefulness, by contrast, as an acting-out of hatred, relatively without awareness, on the part of either of the participants in the dyad.

Although we have no available explicit record of Winnicott's work with Khan, I make some tentative assumptions in the absence of data. First, the atypically long duration of Khan's analysis with Winnicott raises questions. Did Winnicott allow the analysis to go on out of a sense of hopelessness for its prospects? If he felt Khan was untreatable, or if he felt that he himself could not succeed with Khan, did he do Khan a disservice by not being honest about this and possibly depriving him of other potential possibilities? Was this an enactment of hatefulness on Winnicott's part?

Hopkins chronicles what she has been able to glean about Winnicott's supplying Khan with alcohol during their meetings. One must wonder about Winnicott's astonishing insensitivity to Khan's problems with alcohol, despite what may have been a fairly typical social custom of the time. Or was there collusion in denial of Khan's problems? Hopkins's description of the relationship between Khan and the Stollers stands in sharp contrast to the Khan–Winnicott interactions around alcohol. Evidently, Khan was quite responsive to the Stollers' insistence that he not drink while staying with them, a fact that demands a revisiting of Winnicott's definition of the holding environment. Perhaps the nature of safety of the holding environment may vary across individuals, and may be related to Balint's (1959, 1968) concept of ocnophilic and philobatic modes.

As the years went on, reports of Khan's outrageous behavior had to have reached Winnicott, and indeed he must himself have witnessed Khan's behavior at professional meetings. We don't know if Winnicott faced Khan on these issues, although we may speculate that given his propensity for avoiding direct confrontation, he may well have avoided addressing these matters, as well as that of Khan's health issues.

Finally, when Khan decided to terminate his analysis, at a time when his alcoholism was in full bloom, Winnicott appears to have acceded without argument. Ultimately, Khan turned on Winnicott and vilified him publicly and cruelly (Hopkins 1998, 1999). The idealization of the early years was transformed to virulent hate and scorn.

My purpose in raising these questions regarding the ultimate failure of Winnicott's work with Khan is not to discredit Winnicott, but to try to understand how such a gulf between Winnicott's theoretical understanding and his clinical use of it could have existed essentially unchanged over a span of so many years. The various developments in Winnicott's thinking and technique clearly grew out of his accumulated clinical experience, to which his work with Khan probably made a significant contribution. It is often said that one cannot separate the theory from the theorist, and I imagine that two major shifts in Winnicott's approach were probably influenced by his work with Khan. The first is the shift from interpretation to holding, the second the growing attention to the private self, a central concept that was carried forward and extensively developed by Khan in his own writing, although I believe their respective definitions may be divergent. Winnicott speaks of the private self as unknown and unknowable to the other, while Khan speaks of the private self as discovered in the intimate exchange with the other.

As I read and reread Winnicott, I am struck by the need to tolerate paradox in understanding and analyzing his work. Winnicott lets us know that he came to regard his own insistence on making interpretations as, alternatively, a way of making his presence felt, an attempt (often unsuccessful, he felt) to connect with the patient, and a way to stay awake. Experience convinced him that this could be intrusive at times, and over time he came to believe that if the patient is provided a safe environment, his own internal process would unfold. It appears that Winnicott's conception of what was safe varied a great deal, according to the patient and his or her relationship with Winnicott. In many cases (*Holding and Interpretation*, Winnicott 1986), safety seemed to consist of giving the patient room to speak or not, without intrusion. In the extreme, in his work with Margaret Little (1990) and others, he sat close to her and held her hand, enduring her silences and her rages, and actively intervening in her life outside the consulting room. His belief in the efficacy of providing holding is often strikingly validated in our clinical work, but I suspect that his turning away from interpretation may have been, in part, a rationalization of his reluctance to be direct in difficult, painful, and hateful circumstances. Ironically, as Hopkins has pointed out, Khan himself wrote compellingly of his own bold confrontation of a patient who came to a session drunk. The confrontation is reportedly quite successful. Why would Winnicott have avoided such an approach, if not for his own characterological difficulties with aggression and his need to be seen as benign? Here, paradoxically, his presumed benignity is a cover for hatefulness. It does seem hateful to watch another human being self-destruct without attempting some bold intervention. And Winnicott's optimistic belief that the patient, if left to his own resources in a safe atmosphere, will do the work he needs to do more or less by himself, is sorely tested by patients like Khan and others, who are fragile narcissists, often compulsion and addiction-driven.

Winnicott's concept of the privacy of the self also raises questions as to the possibility that one source for it is a defensive posture. It is not that the concept in its entirety must be challenged, for it speaks eloquently of the necessity of the therapist's respectful protection of the most private self, but rather that Winnicott may have been protecting his own most private self, or the parts that he somehow could not bear to expose. If he was protecting Khan's private self, the protection may have been rooted in his own needs rather than Khan's. And this too would have been hateful.

Winnicott's passionate devotion to finding what is real, for the patient and in the patient–therapist relationship, seems to have lapsed in his work with Khan, and it may be this that explains the failure of Khan's relationship with Winnicott to be successfully internalized and held past Winnicott's death.

Current work on the analytic relationship (Gabbard 1996, Ghent 1990, Maroda 1999) explores the issues of self-disclosure by the therapist of his feelings about the patient, and of the therapist's (as well as the patient's) giving up defenses and giving oneself over to the process and the relationship. It is fascinating that Khan himself (1974) wrote that malignant regression, characterized by aggressive, negative therapeutic reactions and/or excessive clinging, is a resistance to the process of surrender to benign, therapeutic levels of regression. Khan, in what may be an extremely revealing passage, states that malignant regression is an attempt to avoid and evade something else that a patient dreads and is threatened by from within, namely surrender to "resourceless dependence in the transference and analytic situation" (p. 274). Khan felt that this surrender represented to such patients an annihilation of the self.

Whatever the explanations for Winnicott's ultimate failure with Khan, I do not believe that any of us have escaped similar experiences with some of our patients, and perhaps the best tribute we can pay to Winnicott may be to try to understand his and our experiences in ways that will be useful in the future. Paradoxically, some of the very aspects of Winnicott's character and personality that might have made him the ideal analyst for Khan seem to have worked in reverse. And perhaps it is the paradoxical nature of our feelings about certain of our patients that lie at the heart of the matter—love and the wish not to abandon them in hopelessness on the one hand, and hate, in Guntrip's sense of love turned sour, perhaps by disappointment and frustration, on the other.

REFERENCES

Balint, M. (1959). *Thrills and Regressions.* Madison, CT: International Universities Press.

—— (1968). *The Basic Fault.* New York: Brunner/Mazel.

Gabbard, G. O. (1996). *Love and Hate in the Analytic Setting.* Northvale, NJ: Jason Aronson.

Ghent, E. (1990). Masochism, submission, surrender: masochism as a perversion of surrender. *Contemporary Psychoanalysis* 26:108–136.

Goldman, D. (1993a). *In One's Bones: The Clinical Genius of Winnicott.* Northvale, NJ: Jason Aronson.

—— (1993b). *In Search of the Real: The Origins and Originality of D. W. Winnicott.* Northvale, NJ: Jason Aronson.

Guntrip, H. (1975). My experience of analysis with Fairbairn and Winnicott. *International Review of Psychoanalysis* 2:145–156.

Hopkins, L. (1998). D. W. Winnicott's analysis of Masud Khan: a preliminary study of failure of object usage. *Contemporary Psychoanalysis* 4:5–47.

—— (1999). Presentation, Eating Disorders Service seminar, William Alanson White Institute, New York.

Khan, M. M. R. (1974). *The Privacy of the Self.* London: Hogarth Press.

Little, M. (1990). *Psychotic Anxieties and Containment. A Personal Record of an Analysis with Winnicott.* Northvale, NJ: Jason Aronson.

Maroda, K. J. (1999). *Seduction, Surrender and Transformation: Emotional Engagement in the Analytic Process.* Hillsdale, NJ: Analytic Press.

Searles, H. (1965). *Collected Papers on Schizophrenia and Related Subjects.* Madison, CT: International Universities Press.

Winnicott, D. W. (1947). *Hate in the Countertransference.* In *In One's Bones,* ed. D. Goldman, pp. 15–24. Northvale, NJ: Jason Aronson, 1993.

—— (1986). *Holding and Interpretation.* New York, NY: Grove Press.

25

The Outrageous Prince:
The Uncure of Masud Khan

Dodi Goldman

Since Masud Khan's removal from the British Society, most of us have appreciated his writings, without necessarily burdening ourselves with thoughts about who this man was and how he lived his life. But Linda B. Hopkins's dedication to her biographical research reminds us how seamlessly threads of inspired genius and impaired living can sometimes be woven together. Her rendering of Khan's personal story—of prolific talent both expressed and squandered; of a brilliant analyst whose personal behavior makes us cringe—naturally leads us to seek some satisfying explanation.

Invested as we are in our own work as therapists, our thoughts naturally turn to Khan's therapist. And indeed, Hopkins (Chapter 23) and Marcia Rosen (Chapter 24) raise serious questions about Winnicott's failure to confront adequately Khan's self-destructiveness. Hopkins argues that Winnicott failed to employ the power of the transference to compel Khan to stop drinking. In her words, "Winnicott would have been a good-enough analyst of Khan if he had done just one thing differently: focus on Khan's drinking and insist that he get it under control." To say I disagree with Hopkins and Rosen would be oversimplifying. It would be more accurate to state that I approach these matters quite differently. But before I elaborate, I have an important personal reservation I think it best to state up front.

Khan's anti-Semitic invective is repugnant to me. When I hear about how he would refer to someone as a "filthy Jewish tradesman," talk about a homosexual patient as having a "dirty Jewish arse," or proudly declare his yearning to "free myself of the rigid Yiddish shackles of the so-called psychoanalysis," I confess to feeling virtually no desire to engage this man. Naturally, I could choose to relate to Khan's anti-Semitism as a symptom of projection, or identification with the racial arrogance of the British ruling class of the Raj. Alternatively, I might think about his hostility as a matter of the narcissism of small differences in which particular pleasure is found in hating immediate neighbors with whom one actually shares much in common. It may also be that Khan was giving voice to the deep strains of anti-Semitism bubbling beneath the surface among British members reacting to the "invasion" of the mostly Jewish émigrés. But for me to think about Khan in any of these ways, I would have either to detach myself or be willing to register his outpourings empathically. In this case, I acknowledge a reluctance to do either.

Having said that, I already find myself in the midst of the fray. Khan has viscerally provoked me. I am repelled, disgusted, and angry. Khan has acted outrageously and I am outraged. I am incited and unforgiving, for he is intelligent, erudite, and insightful, and yet he acts hatefully and allows himself to grossly offend any sense of right or decency, forcing others to bear the brunt of his obnoxiousness. In short, he employs his considerable resources to shock, and in response I want to consign him to oblivion.

Now, what happens if I do allow myself to step outside of this destructive imaginary seesaw relationship? How then might I think about Khan's provocative self-destructiveness? How might I understand a gifted man who, after rising to such prominence, collapsed into a lonely rageful state of sickly impenetrable isolation? And can we usefully generalize from Khan's example to other patients we encounter who appear, despite our best efforts, to be heading toward a private hell of their own making?

I guess one place to begin is with outrageousness itself. There can be no doubt that Khan at times behaved with an intention to shock. The French use the word *jouissance* to express the rise or kick a person gets from a particular way of being. I think the word fits well for the kind of pleasure Khan appears to have derived from provocative behavior. How can we understand outrageousness? Is it simply a transformation of hostility?

As far as I know, Khan (1986) himself is the only analyst to ever have written explicitly about outrageousness as a distinct affective state. It is not surprising that he would engage this topic. The psychological terrain we know best, after all, is that which we know from the inside out. He was a virtual Geiger counter for the insincerity, phoniness, and half-truths concealed in outrageous behavior. Earlier, Freud had pointed out that demands felt to be outrageous were one of the precipitant causes of war neuroses. Shell shock, in other words, was a dissociative response to an outrageous current demand. Khan looks at outrageousness developmentally, linking maternal overindulgence to a restriction in spontaneity in the child. Obsessional overcare, he argues, inhibits aggressivity. In discussing such a patient, Khan remarks: "He did not succeed with me, because I had been a more outrageous person in my private life. I knew all the ruses of that affect, both in private life and professionally. I was a much-cuddled child, who grew up, very precociously. . . . So he could not get the better of me" (p. 648).

Now I would like to turn to another dimension of outrageousness, which I feel I have learned from some of my own patients. From an intersubjective point of view, a crucial element of provocative outrageousness is the opportunity it affords the individual to see himself making an impression upon another. What is psychologically vital is not so much the *making* of the impression as the profound relief in *observing the impression that one has made.* Observing the impression affords the vulnerable individual a fleeting sense of substance. Like footprints in sand, the impression momentarily reassures that desire remains alive. We can detect this in the way

Khan romped through life with the self-indulgence of a wealthy playboy. He once came to an International Congress with a Habsburg princess as his guest. They both wore riding habits and brought nearly the whole stable along with them. Glamour, which displays both vitality and decadence, is uniquely designed to generate opportunities to observe reactions. Perhaps there is something akin to a psychological law: in the absence of quiet recognition, one needs desire noisily confirmed to survive psychologically.

Khan's outrageousness, however, was also the leading edge of a far deeper self-destructiveness. But if what I said before about needing to noisily confirm desire is valid, we are, it appears, right in the heart of a paradox. How can it be that self-destructiveness preserves psychological aliveness? There is no easy answer to this question. All I can offer is the following working hypothesis: in the absence of recognition, self-destructiveness becomes a last-ditch effort to preserve a semblance of control as the illusion of the integrity of the self collapses.

Winnicott (1963) was one of the first people to introduce us to the seemingly odd link between personal agency and the destruction of the self. Even in the infant, he argued, there exists a rather fierce morality, a willingness, sometimes through life-threatening refusals to ingest food, to guard the self against threats to the elusive sense that "I AM." In his words, "The fiercest morality is that of early infancy, and this persists as a streak in human nature that can be discerned throughout an individual's life. . . . For instance, a child of any age may feel that to eat is wrong, even to the extent of dying for the principle. . . . This leads many people who seem to be doing well eventually to end their lives which have become false and unreal; unreal success is morality at its lowest ebb" (p. 102).

In a similar vein, Erik Erikson (1959) offers us the idea that some people—addicts and social cynics are two examples he cites—would "rather be nobody or somebody bad, and this totally, or indeed, *dead by free choice* than be not-quite-somebody" (p. 143). For Erikson, such vindictive choices represent "a desperate attempt at regaining some mastery in a situation in which the available positive identity elements cancel each other out" (p. 142).

Stolorow (1986), from an intersubjective perspective, has written about the utility of "rage and vengefulness in the wake of injuries . . . to serve the purpose of revitalizing a crumbling but urgently needed sense of power and impactfulness" (p. 395). Rage, even if self-destructive, can serve a restitutive function in restoring urgently required feelings of inner stability and control.

Modell (1993) has come to a similar conclusion. He notes that what we call the "efficacy of the self" refers not only to being able to act upon the world but also "to extend the hegemony of the self over intense and intrusive affects" (p. 54).

Khantzian and Mack (1983), in their work on addictions, note that self-preservation and self-soothing do not necessarily go hand in hand. While addicts clearly self-soothe in their behavior, they notoriously fail to adequately self-preserve. Put another way, the need to ensure the illusion of integrity of the self should not be confused with self-preservation. The body is sometimes an easily expendable appendage as long as we are the ones destroying our own.

Lance Dodes (1990), an analyst specializing in substance abuse, adds his voice to the chorus of clinicians recognizing the narcissistic importance of feeling in control of one's own mind. "Drug use provides a mechanism to re-establish a central area of omnipotence. By acting to take control of one's own affective state, addictive behavior may serve to restore a sense of control when there is a perception that control or power has been lost or taken away" (p. 400). According to Dodes, that is the reason most addicts feel at least some relief the moment they decide to obtain the drug, and long before any of the pharmacological effect of ingestion occurs. As a recovering substance abuser once told me, "I have only two speeds: off and broil, and I live in terror of being burned alive." He confirmed Dodes notion that deciding to obtain drugs immediately provided some relief from the utter helplessness he felt in the face of most feelings.

A lot of current research is teaching us that there is a profound difference between what Peter Fonagy and colleagues (1993) refer to as a "pre-reflective or physical self," which is the immediate experiencer of life, and a "reflective or psychological self," which is the internal observer of mental life. Most importantly, these two aspects of our experience develop differently and exist in a rather precarious relationship to each other. Mental processes, in another language, are as vulnerable to disruption as are mental representations. This is consistent with a view put forth by Spruiell (1975), who noted that among the strands of narcissism is "the pleasure in efficient mental functioning, . . . the regulation of mood, . . . and . . . a sense of inner safety and reliability" (p. 590). Feeling oneself to be in control of one's mind is apparently a vital human aspiration.

Thus, clinicians of varying orientations appear to be converging on a similar observation: whether reactive or proactive, whether out of a fierce morality or vengefulness, whether to extend hegemony over intrusive affects or to reassert control over other mental processes, the illusion of the integrity of the self is sometimes guaranteed through self-destructiveness. The problem is that self-destructiveness as guardian of integrity is analogous to blood letting; there is a race between cure and bleeding to death.

In thinking about Winnicott's treatment of Khan, I am reminded of what the English historian Philip Guedello once quipped about writing biography: "Biography, like big game hunting," he said, "is one of the recognized forms of sport; and it is as unfair as only sport can be." That captures a little of what I feel hazarding speculations about what went on in the treatment. After all, there is obviously no way we can possibly know. The best I can attempt, therefore, is to project Winnicott and Khan's experience onto the screen of my own informed imagination. Doing so, leads me to propose three distinct, yet overlapping, conclusions: Winnicott helped Khan enormously; Winnicott failed to "cure" him; Masud Khan could not be helped. I will address these one at a time.

WINNICOTT HELPED

Masud Khan, despite his tragic end, led a highly productive life. He was a prolific contributor to the psychoanalytic literature and a brilliant cartographer of the territory of archaic mental states. We have no way of knowing if Khan could have sustained these achievements without Winnicott's help.

Here is an excerpt from Khan's diary, written four months after Winnicott's death. It feels to me that Khan is being fairly honest with himself here:

> What a difficult thing psycho-analysis is to report about to others. No, even to myself. . . . 25 years of analysis with four analysts is a long odyssey and each of them helped me, without my being able to talk to any of them significantly about myself ever. . . . D.W. [Winnicott] alone was aware of it and allowed for it. . . . It is for this reason that . . . I did succeed at three occasions to sink into my Self, be silent . . . and related to him. All these three occasions were physical. . . . He was in his chair seated and I had got off the couch and buried my head into the side of his coat. I can still hear his heart and watch beating. All else was still . . . and I was at peace. And D.W. never interpreted those three occasions. He had enabled me to reach to that point [May 1971].

Now, three occasions in fifteen years may not seem like a lot when viewed from the outside. But it appears to me that moments like these both tethered Khan as a person and gave him a sense of what it means to care as a clinician. This is not an insignificant gift. Here is another excerpt, written, as far as I can tell, about two weeks after Winnicott's death: "One of the most valuable contributions of D.W.W. has been, that he has changed a catastrophic threat of loss of object into separation anxiety. He is the first significant person in my life who had facilitated me to cope with losing him . . . without it becoming the total loss" (February 6, 1971).

This, too, is no small achievement. In fact, I believe that it made life relatively bearable and productive for Khan. Winnicott appears to have offered Khan a sufficient sense of recognition so that his worst tendencies, evident long before Winnicott's death, were held more or less in check for decades.

By saying Winnicott held these tendencies in check, I am suggesting it is unrealistic to expect psychotherapy to successfully inoculate a person against all future strains. A careful look at the chronology of Khan's deterioration indicates it began some four years after Winnicott's death and nine years after the termination of treatment. In 1971 Winnicott died. Five months later Khan's mother died, and the love of his life, Svetlana, moved out. Beginning in 1975, he has a cancerous lung removed, is given a prognosis of months to live, undergoes eye surgery, and has his larynx and later his trachea removed. It is in the context of the multiple loss of significant people and the total deterioration of his body that he engages in a vengeful, raging, last-ditch effort to regain control over a diminishing sense of continuity through self-destructive drinking and attacks upon the world. If he couldn't conquer death, it seems, he vowed to defeat life.

WINNICOTT FAILED

Winnicott made his fair share of blunders. He even told Marion Milner that his analysis of Khan had not been properly completed. Khan wouldn't have been surprised to hear that. In response to a condolence letter following Winnicott's death, he wrote: "[Winnicott's] genius was in his capacity to fail each of us according to our need to refuse him. If Freud had the Judaic courage to refuse cure, Dr. Winnicott had the Christian humility to take responsibility for the *uncure*. And I, as a Mohammedan, praise them both—since I am the beneficiary of each!" (February 9, 1971). And in a private diary entry a few days earlier, Khan elaborated on the link between Winnicott's willingness to go on treating those, like himself, who stubbornly refuse what is offered and aspects of Winnicott's character. "It was most typical of his type of omnipotence," writes Khan, "that he could never refuse those he knew would compel him to fail. . . . I know all this on my own pulse. . . . Yes, I have known all his failings and he never even tried to hide them. . . . He knew and allowed for the margin of weakness and error in every human individual and worked with the 3 per cent that was creative and vital" (February 4, 1971).

As I imagine Winnicott and Khan together, I have one thought about what might have gone wrong. In Winnicott's unpublished autobiographical fragments, he laments never having had a son of his own. Envisioning his own death, he writes about his difficulty dying without a son both to kill imaginatively and to survive him, that is, "to provide the only continuity that men know" (p. 4). Baljeet Mehra, a British psychoanalyst, observed that Winnicott regarded Khan as a son (Cooper 1993). She is probably right, and as we know, it is as disastrous to treat our patients as children as it is to treat our children as patients.

On the other hand, Winnicott was certainly not the only childless therapist to form complicated relationships with patients. Were we to study such relationships in depth, we might even be surprised to discover he was hardly exceptional. I know Freud and Lacan suggest therapists "purify their desire." But what does that mean? "Purifying desire" strikes me as a rather odd proposition— more religious than psychoanalytic.

In reading Khan's personal diary, I was struck by the relative absence of grief in the entries following Winnicott's death. It reminded me of a remark the British author Iris Murdoch once made: "Love is the extremely difficult realization that something other than oneself is real." But at the same time, Khan was apparently devastated that Winnicott hadn't appointed him literary executor of his estate. To the extent that Khan might not have felt particularly lovable, he needed desperately to make himself extremely valuable. Winnicott, for his part, had cultivated the illusion of Khan as natural heir. For the narcissist, the truth always comes in blows. So, in response to feeling suddenly disinherited, Khan lashed out to destroy Winnicott. If he couldn't do this in the flesh, he would do the next best thing: destroy the father's reputation. He did this both directly—by repeatedly gossiping about Winnicott's impotence, as if to say, "He's not a man, and if I'm not his son let it be known that there could never be a son!"—and indirectly—by his outrageous behavior, which would, of course, announce to the world that Winnicott had failed.

What we might be seeing, therefore, is Winnicott's failure to help Khan tolerate disillusionment, particularly in relation to his father, and thereby find his place among others. Instead, Khan lived in perpetual dread of the ordinary, as if to say, "If I am like *everybody*, then I must be *nobody*." It is precisely around these issues that Khan and Winnicott might simply have had too much in common. Today there is a new breed of historians engaging in a sport of their own known as "virtual" or "counterfactual" history. Basically, they ask the question generally forbidden to historians: "What if?" Well, I do wonder what if Winnicott had had a son of his own? Might this, perhaps, have enabled Winnicott to better integrate some of his own dissociated feelings in relation to father? Khan knew Winnicott failed him on this point. It is no coincidence, therefore, that the clinical exploration of affective states involving rage and anxiety over disillusionment became central themes in Khan's writings.

KHAN COULDN'T BE HELPED

I imagine Winnicott knew Khan was engaged, as Robert Stoller put it, in "a prolonged fuck with death," which might be simply another language for describing Khan's hypomanic temperament. It is fruitless to try to tease apart what part of this was constitutional and what part environmental. We are now, for example, discovering that attachment to people and chemical dependency are even mediated by the same neuroendrocrine system. Khan obviously suffered enormously from a profound sense of powerlessness vis-à-vis his own mind. And it is this sense of helplessness that constitutes the essence of the cumulative psychic trauma that seemed to plague him. Hyperreactive to the presence of others, he was also easily dislocated by their absence. Put differently, he was vulnerable to shock. To protect himself, he became hatefully indifferent. And he must have known that his indifference, like that of most alcoholics, ripped through the affections of all those who cared the most about him.

Khan had a precocious mind. But a precocious mind is no substitute for the smooth intermingling of the psyche-soma. Insights of the reflective self never adequately compensate for impaired relationships involving the prereflective self. Khan knew this about himself. Winnicott had told him as much. As he wrote in a private diary entry: "I have never been able to share my Self with others through language spoken. And yet language has enabled me to know others—and often beyond my own insight into them. D. W. W. often used to say: 'You speak wiser than you know.' And that is true" (May 5, 1971).

Despite the tragic dimension to Khan's wasted potential, I imagine Winnicott approached the work with a certain acceptance that there was really little he could do. Perhaps, he figured, if he can't cure Khan, he'll at least be good to him. From the outside, one is tempted to shout "collusion." We want to believe that destructiveness, like evil, is eradicable. Blaming Winnicott keeps hope alive that things could have been better. We are tempted to fault Winnicott for not holding, forty years ago, current American notions of boundary violations or possessing contemporary conceptual tools such as mutual enactments. But it's not even that we want so much to blame as that we prefer events to be rational and people knowable. We can no more abandon the idea that someone must be held accountable than we can resign ourselves to the notion that everything is an accident of fate.

Unlike in Europe, however, there is a very powerful and distinct current in American culture to believe that almost anything is possible. Generally, this takes the narrative form of "If only . . . , then . . ." Freud had no problem being pessimistic about psychoanalysis as a treatment, particularly given his unwavering conviction in the scientific truth of his theory. We, on the other hand, have become quite shaky—and rightfully so—about the absolute truth-value of our theories. Unfortunately, however, this is sometimes accompanied by certain zealousness in our beliefs about therapeutic efficacy. Too often we are caught up in believing that clinically, "If only . . . , then . . ."

Winnicott, too, began his clinical career with no small measure of naiveté. But as he matured, he fashioned a clinical sensibility quite distinct from instrumental notions of cure. He came to believe people differ in their capacity to profit from nurturance and he stopped believing everyone could be helped. He thought it a mistake to explain a person's life solely in terms of analytic results or to reduce a complicated personality to its failings. Winnicott's focus was not on morality, or adaptation to reality, or interpersonal competence. He did not seem to care about the ego replacing the id or the finding of adaptive substitutions. In his quiet nondoctrinaire way, Winnicott saw these as a colossal piece of ideology that instates the therapist as master of reality and knowledge. What was blasphemous about him—and even as a child his older sisters frequently referred to him as blasphemous—was that he did not see himself as serving any normalizing function. As a result, he was sometimes excessively reticent about telling others what to do. He had an enormous tolerance for patients' symptoms, which is part of both why he was willing to take many cases dismissed by colleagues as hopeless and why quite a number of patients committed suicide during the course of treatment with him. A bit of an eccentric himself, he cared, for better or for worse, less about the good and more about the unique.

In 1968, three years before his death, Winnicott spoke before a closed meeting on "The Transmission of Technique." According to the notes of one of the participants, Winnicott remarked: "It is not a very great thing to fail in an analysis. The awful thing is to go on with an analysis after it has failed." Winnicott must have known that awful feeling since he went on with his analysis of Khan long after, I think, he knew it could never succeed. I believe he did this because of his dedication to the "three percent that was creative and vital" and because he never imagined curing *himself* from taking responsibility for Khan's uncure.

REFERENCES

Cooper, J. (1993). *Speak of Me as I Am: The Life and Work of Masud Khan.* London: Karnac.

Dodes, L. (1990). Addiction, helplessness, and narcissistic rage. *Psychoanalytic Quarterly* 59:398–419.

Erikson, E. (1959). *Identity and the Life Cycle. Psychological Issues*, monograph 1. New York: International Universities Press.

Fonagy, P., Moran, G., and Target, M. (1993). Aggression and the psychological self. *International Journal of Psycho-Analysis* 74:471–485.

Khan, M. (1986). Outrageousness, compliance, and authenticity. *Contemporary Psychoanalysis* 22:629–650.

Khantzian, E. J., and Mack, J. E. (1983). Self-preservation and the care of the self. *Psychoanalytic Study of the Child* 38:209–232. New Haven, CT: International Universities Press.

Modell, A. (1993). *The Private Self.* Cambridge, MA: Harvard University Press.

Spruiell, V. (1975). Three strands of narcissism. *Psychoanalytic Quarterly* 44:577–595.

Stolorow, R. D. (1986). Critical reflections on the theory of self psychology: an inside view. *Psychoanalytic Inquiry* 6:387–402.

Winnicott, D. W. (1963). Morals and education. In *The Maturational Processes and the Facilitating Environment, pp. 93–105. London: Hogarth.*

26

Further Thoughts on the Winnicott–Khan Analysis

Lawrence Epstein

Prior to reading Linda B. Hopkins's (1998) excellent paper on D. W. Winnicott's analysis of Masud Khan, I had only scant knowledge of the tragic rise and fall of Khan. Her chapter in this book provides more fascinating material.

Dodi Goldman (Chapter 25), having expressed his strong feelings of anger and repugnance evoked by Khan's anti-Semitism and the reports of his obnoxious, provocative behavior, resists his urges to join virtually the rest of the psychoanalytic world in consigning Khan to oblivion, and brings his keen analytic intelligence to bear on Khan's particular complex of self-destructiveness. He suggests that Khan's outrageousness and self-destructiveness, paradoxically, might have provided his chronically unstable self with an urgently needed sense of agency at those moments that he felt intimations of an impending catastrophic loss of self. Goldman also offers the hypothesis that Kahn's self-destructiveness was, in part, a vengeful attack on Winnicott's reputation because Winnicott failed to appoint him the executor of his literary estate. I cannot help thinking that to the extent that Khan's self-destructiveness might have been an attack on Winnicott, it was also very likely motivated by intense split-off destructive envy.

Concerning the failure of Winnicott's fifteen-year treatment of Khan to immunize him against the self-devastation that followed its termination, Goldman points out that Khan's worst tendencies were, after all, held in check during this period. Goldman, unlike Marcia Rosen, is accepting rather than critical of Winnicott's willingness to treat Khan, as well as other patients, even though he knew he was failing them. Goldman suspects that Winnicott thought that Khan was unanalyzable, and believing that he couldn't cure him, decided to be good to him.

Rosen is less forgiving of Winnicott than is Goldman. She does not flinch from holding Winnicott to current standards of clinical practice. She cites Winnicott's failure to maintain a viable treatment frame as preventing Khan from using Winnicott as the object of his destructive transference predispositions. This is unarguable. Theirs was a relationship that was rooted in a massive shared resistance to the intensely negative transference–countertransference matrix that would have inevitably arisen, had they agreed to engage in an authentic psychoanalytic endeavor.

Notwithstanding Goldman's objections to blaming Winnicott for not having our current understanding of boundary violations, I believe that even according to the shared standards of analytic practice of the 1950s and 1960s, it would be fair to conclude that the Winnicott–Khan treatment process, probably from its beginning to its end, was never an authentic analytic process. As Rosen pointed out, Winnicott made many extra-analytic accommodations that effectively barred the entry of hate, hatefulness, and other terrible feelings into their therapeutic dyad.

At one time it was thought that the main function of analysis was to enable the patient to gain insight into himself. If anyone ever exemplified the ineffectiveness of insight alone, as an agent of change, it is Khan. His personal correspondence, as quoted by Hopkins, is rife with newly gained soul-searching insights. I think Goldman puts it exceptionally well when he says, "Insights of the reflective self never adequately compensate for impaired relationships involving the prereflective self."

For Khan's analysis to have had any possibility of success in immunizing him against the malignant emotional illness that later caused him so much mental torment and drove him to destroy himself with alcohol, to ruin himself professionally, and caused him to die in virtual isolation, the analysis would have had to have been an analysis centered in the transference.

I once heard Hopkins say that people do not want to hear positive things about Khan and do not want to hear negative things about Winnicott. Actually, I am glad to hear positive things about Khan, perhaps because I have been influenced by Hopkins to see him as sick rather than bad. It is true, however, that I like to think well of Winnicott. His clinical wisdom has, for many years, profoundly influenced my psychoanalytic understanding. Therefore, regarding the question of why this fifteen-year treatment ended when it did, because I like to think well of Winnicott, I had the fantasy that it might have ended when it did because Winnicott said something like the following to Khan:

> Look Masud, you are acting-out self-destructively and your drinking is getting out of hand. By serving as your good breast and reassuring you that you are special, both in and out of sessions, I have gone far beyond Rickman in allaying your intense abandonment anxieties and in protecting you from your worst feelings about yourself. In doing so, I have deprived you of a true analysis. I have deprived you of the experience of regression to dependency and I have prevented you from using me as the object of your intense negative transference needs. *We both know that the good breast that does not survive destruction can never be internalized.* I strongly suspect that I have been sparing myself, as well, the terrible feelings that would become unleashed in me in bearing the brunt of all your negativity. With the understanding that you are becoming more ill in this treatment, I cannot, in good conscience, go on with this pseudo-analysis unless we both agree, at the very least, to give

up our mutually gratifying and very productive literary collaboration and confine our meetings to the sessions. And, in
addition, we will have to pay serious attention to what else I
have been doing or not doing that might be contributing to the
failure of this treatment.

My fantasy ends with both amicably agreeing to discontinue the
analysis due to Khan's refusal to revise the treatment contract. They
opt to continue their literary collaboration.

Hopkins asks, "What might we do differently today in treating a
patient like Khan?" For me this translates into the question, What
might we, as analysts, have to experience were we to be successful in
engaging a patient like Khan in analysis? This brings me back to
Winnicott and Khan. What might Winnicott have had to experience?

I am mindful of Goldman's caution about becoming caught up
in believing "If only. . . , then . . ." I have no reason to believe that
Kahn would have entered into a viable analytic contract with
Winnicott (or anyone else), or that he would have been emotionally
capable of tolerating the frustrations that are the normal consequence of analytic abstinence. I also strongly suspect that it would
have been too dangerous for Winnicott to attempt to serve as a
viable analytic object for Khan.

Having said that, based on my own experience in conducting analyses with patients for whom destructiveness and self-
destructiveness was, for many years, the dominant issue, and based
on what we know, both regarding Khan's negative feelings vis-à-vis
Winnicott and his hostile, denigrating attitude toward his mother,
I offer my speculations regarding the probable transference–
countertransference matrix that would have developed had Winnicott and Khan agreed to attempt to work within what we would
currently understand to be an analytically viable treatment frame.

I understand the main therapeutic function of the treatment
frame to be the establishment of those conditions that optimize the
patient's capability both to address his experience and, with a
decreasing sense of accompanying risk, put it into words. This would

require each participant to practice sufficient abstinence and tolerate a level of frustration that would favor the processing of thoughts, feelings, and impulses over action. One of the main functions of the therapist's abstinence is to reassure the patient that he is unambivalent about his commitment to serve as an analytic object, meaning that that he wants to hear anything and everything that might be on the patient's mind, especially regarding his experiences of negative impact vis-à-vis the therapist.

Given a viable treatment frame, I would imagine something like the following transference–countertransference matrix to have developed between them sooner or later. The contemptuous and denigrating comments Kahn made about Winnicott in the years following the termination of the analysis probably constitute only a benign expression of the negative thoughts and feelings he would have experienced and addressed to Winnicott in the analysis. In the absence of the mutually gratifying relationship that excluded such negative affect from the dyad, the shadows of both Kahn's contemptible mother and his hated defective, deformed, humiliated, elephant-eared child-self would have fallen on Winnicott. His actual perception of Winnicott as being deficient in masculine power and strength would have served to draw this out. On the other hand, Winnicott's creativity would have been the object of unbearable envy.

Khan's major resistance both to clearly registering his negative thoughts, feelings, and perceptions in consciousness and to telling them to Winnicott would have issued from his terror of either suffering the catastrophic loss of Winnicott's love or, perhaps, of killing him. The danger to Winnicott in serving as the object of Khan's negative transference predispositions might have been real, and not merely a matter of fantasy.

But should Winnicott have been able to survive Kahn's destructive aggression by sustaining an optimum balance of containment and the employment of limit-setting, counterbalancing aggression, and to give evidence, thereby, over many years, of surviving all of this in good health, the shadow of Kahn's denigrated internal objects might have lifted off Winnicott, and Winnicott might have become transformed into a good-enough object for Khan to internalize, an object strong enough and resilient enough to offset and stand up to Kahn's persecutory demons, and reliable and caring enough to serve as the soothing maternal presence that had never been established in Kahn. In Khan's internal self-and-object world, there was only his unwanted, contemptible mother; hence, his addiction to alcohol. Unable to be soothed from within, he needed to be numbed.

As to Hopkins's conclusion that Winnicott failed Kahn mainly by not insisting on his abstinence from alcohol, I agree that sooner or later in the treatment of any patient who persists in being chemically dependent, it will be the therapist's responsibility to make abstinence the necessary condition for continuing the treatment. I think, however that such an injunction on Winnicott's part would have come too late and would have been too little. I do not think that Kahn's positive transference to Winnicott would have been sufficiently holding to enable him to sustain abstinence. For such an injunction to have been effective, I think it would have required the holding properties of an analytic relationship such as that which I have just speculated about, that is, a relationship that has repeatedly survived destruction. However, I believe there are few therapists who would have been capable at that time, or who might be capable now, of surviving the horrendous negative emotional experience that such a relationship would require them to endure for so long.

Were any analyst to enable Kahn to place him in the position that Winnicott (1968) termed "the object unprotected," and were Kahn to reach what Winnicott (1968) termed "maximum destructiveness," I think the analyst, in response to being relentlessly and contemptuously faulted, would have had to suffer excruciating feelings of badness-and-no-goodness, what I have elsewhere termed "bad-analyst-feelings" (Epstein 1987, 1999). I think that Kahn's contempt and hate might have been so lethal to Winnicott, over the long term, as to have actually killed him.

When Winnicott presented his paper on the "use of an object" at a meeting of the New York Psychoanalytic Institute in November

1968, he had the unfortunate experience of being criticized by all three discussants. Later that evening he suffered a near-fatal heart attack. Winnicott's health had been fragile for many years (Goldman 1998). Think of the emotional consequences to Khan had the analysis ended with Winnicott's blood on his hands.[1]

Rosen, as does Hopkins (1998), cites data suggesting that Winnicott had a special problem with hate and hatefulness and that this is why he failed to engage Khan in an authentic analysis. She goes further, arguing that Winnicott's failure is actually an expression of hatefulness toward Khan. What I am suggesting is that, had Khan agreed to a viable analytic contract with any other analyst, there is no reason to assume that that analyst would have been capable of surviving the terrible feelings that would have been unleashed in him in the course of serving as the object of the full force of Khan's negative transference needs. "Surviving," in Winnicott's sense, means "not retaliating."

Over the years, I have been consulted by several patients who, having reached the point of feeling safe enough to fault their analysts, were met with retaliatory, countertransference-driven interpretations. In some cases, they were summarily discharged. In no case did any of these patients approach what I think would have been the destructiveness of Khan. From an objective standpoint, it seems justified to judge Winnicott to have been clinically and professionally irresponsible. Yet, if, as Goldman suggests, Winnicott truly believed Khan to be unanalyzable, and the best he could do for Khan was to be good to him, might this mitigate his culpability?

Prior to presenting his paper at the New York Psychoanalytic Institute in November 1968, Winnicott spoke at the William Alanson White Institute. He discussed his squiggle technique. What stands out in my memory was the very last thing he said to end the meeting. Seemingly apropos of nothing in the discussion that preceded it, he said something like the following: "The last thing I want to say is that

---

1. See Hopkins (1998, pp. 34–37) for a discussion of Khan's protective stance vis-à-vis Winnicott's cardiac condition.

we should not forget that in analysis we take away our patients' defenses, and this causes them a great deal of pain."

REFERENCES

Epstein, L. (1987). The bad analyst feeling. *Modern Psychoanalysis* 12:35–45.
——— (1999). The analyst's "bad-analyst feelings": a counterpart to the process of resolving implosive defenses. *Contemporary Psychoanalysis* 35:311–325.
Goldman, D. (1998). Surviving as scientist and dreamer: Winnicott and "the use of an object." *Contemporary Psychoanalysis* 34:359–367.
Hopkins, L. (1998). D. W. Winnicott's analysis of Masud Khan: a preliminary study of failures of object usage. *Contemporary Psychoanalysis* 34:5–47.
Winnicott, D. W. (1968). The use of an object and relating through identifications. In *Playing and Reality*, pp. 86–94. London: Tavistock, 1971.

Index

Action, eating disorders, threat and
  dare, 55–64
Addiction. *See also* Alcoholism
  adolescence, 22–24
  alcoholism, Khan, M., 322–326
  creativity and, 223–232, 235–243,
    247–261
  defined, 5–7
  desire, pursuit and thwarting of,
    295–304
  happiness and, philosophy of
    transference and, 307–315
  melancholy and, 211–220
  psychic economy of, 5–26 (*See
    also* Psychic economy)
  sexual compulsivity, 284–285
Adolescence
  addiction, 22–24
  gay men, 268
Affects
  obesity and, 177

psychic economy, 8
  storytelling and, 140
Alcoholics Anonymous (AA), 237
Alcoholism. *See also* Addiction
  creativity and, 247–261
  Khan, M., 322–326 (*See also*
    Khan, M.)
Anderson, F. S., xxi–xxii, 137, 141
Anesthetization, eating as, 174–175
Annihilation fears, obesity as pro-
  tection against, 173–174
Anorexia. *See* Eating disorders
Anti-Semitism, Khan, 362, 377
Anxiety
  creativity and, 226
  interpersonal perspective,
    276–277
  separation/individuation and,
    229–230
Arieti, S., 219

Aron, L., xxii, 44–45, 101, 138, 140, 142, 144, 165

Aronson, J. K., 200

Attention deficit disorder (ADD), 288

Authority, of therapist, gay men, 275–276

Azarian, M., 336

Bad object, desire, pursuit and thwarting of, 296–297

Balint, M., 354

Barth, F. D., xix, 56

Barthelme, F., 239

Barthelme, S., 239

Bassin, D., 29

Bataille, G., 238

Bateson, G., 236–237

Becker, H. S., 237

Beebe, B., 226

Begum, K., 326

Bemporad, J., 219

Benjamin, J., 49, 51, 153, 226, 227, 238

Beriosova, S., 322, 329, 330–331, 333–335, 338, 345, 368

Bernstein, L., 240

Binswanger, L., 241

Bion, W. R., 178

Body image, eating disorders and, 163–170

Bollas, C., 49, 176

Boris, H. N., 73–74, 76

Bose, J., xxiv–xxv, 211, 217

Bowlby, J., 197, 198

Brisman, J., xix, 31, 47, 55, 57, 109–110, 122, 237

Bromberg, P. M., xix–xx, 45, 47, 48, 51, 55, 57, 58, 75, 76, 173

Bruner, J., 139

Bulimia, psychic economy, 8–10. See also Eating disorders

Bushra, A., 138

Chatelaine, K., 270

Cheever, J., xxv–xxvi, 250–252, 254–258

Cheselka, O., xxv

Chodorow, N., 140

Competition, dissociation and, 45, 46–47, 51

Compulsion, sexual compulsivity in gay men, 267–279

Conflict theory, 331–332

Contracts, eating disorders, threat and dare, 57–58

Cooking, expression of, 154

Cooper, A., 272

Cooper, B., 337, 343

Cooper, J., 369

Countertransference
  addictions, 31–32
  eating disorders, 127–134
    comment on, 141
  gay men, 277
  hate and hatefulness, 349–358
  love and, 143
  stalled enactments, 122
  storytelling and, 140–141

Crastnopol, M., xxii–xxiii, 200

Creativity
  addiction and, 223–232, 235–243
  alcoholism and, 247–261

Dali, S., 240

Dare, threat and, eating disorders, 55–64

Davies, J. M., 45, 47, 50, 55

Davis, R. H., 248
Davis, W., 56
Defiance, eating disorders, 83–94
de Kooning, W., 247
Dependency, psychic economy,
    25–26
Depression, psychodynamics of,
    211–212. See also Melancholy
Desire, pursuit and thwarting of,
    295–304
Developmental factors
    body image, 165
    food and, 152–153
    gay men, 268
    intersubjectivity, 72–73
    outrageousness, 363
    psychic economy, 7–16
Devlin, M. J., 188
Dimen, M., 163
Dinesen, I., 240
Dissociation
    defiance and, eating disorders,
        83–94
    gay men, 269–271
    self-regulation, 101
    shame and, eating disorders,
        67–80
    stalled enactments, 115–123
        comment on, 141
    of therapist, eating disorders,
        43–52, 77
Dodes, L. M., 238, 365
Donaldson, S., 250
Dostoyevsky, F., 242–243
Doyle, C., 236
Dreher, H., 202
Drescher, J., xxvi, 269, 277

Eating, male experience of,
    149–160
Eating disorders
    body image in, 163–170
    countertransference, 127–134
        comment on, 141
    defiance, 83–94
    obesity
        male experience, 156–160
        stalled enactments, 115–123
        symbolic significance of,
            173–182
    outcome research in treatment
        of, 185–206 (See also
        Outcome research)
    self-regulation, 99–111
    shame and dissociation, 67–80
    stalled enactments, 115–123
        comment on, 141
    therapist's dissociation, 43–52
    threat and dare, 55–64
    trauma, 100–101
Ehrenberg, D. B., xxvi, 34, 140, 237
Eigen, M., 175, 178
Elise, D., 152
Enactments, stalled, eating
    disorders, 115–123
    comment on, 141
Epstein, L., xxviii, 349, 382
Erikson, E. H., 336, 364
Exacerbation, eating disorders,
    threat and dare, 56–57

Fairbairn, W. R. D., xxvii, 295, 296,
    304
Faude, J., 239
Ferenczi, S., 128, 130, 133
Feynman, R., 176, 181
Fingarette, H., 48

Fink, B., 151
Fitzgerald, F. S., 248
Fonagy, P., 140, 190, 196, 198, 365
Fonteyn, M., 334
Food, male experience of, 149–160
Freeman, L., 193
Freud, A., 340–341
Freud, S., 87, 88, 127, 128, 130, 133,
    173–174, 200, 236, 237, 277,
    295, 309, 310, 311, 312, 314,
    363, 371
Fromm, E., 237, 297–298

Gabbard, G. O., 357
Garcia Lorca, F., 315
Garfinkel, P. E., 189
Garner, D. M., 189
Gay men, sexual compulsivity in,
    267–279
Ghent, E., 154n3, 219, 357
Gladstone, I., 235
Gleick, J., 176
Glennon, S. S., xxiii
Goldman, D., xxviii, 132, 133, 352,
    353, 377, 378, 380, 383
Gorky, A., 247
Gourewitch, A., 213
Granoff, W., 324
Grayson, R., 213
Greece (ancient), 235
Greed, relatedness and, 73–74
Green, A., 178
Greenberg, J., 131, 132
Grinstein, A., 253
Guedello, P., 366
Guntrip, H., 344n3, 351, 357
Gupta, first name, 165
Gutwill, S., 35

Halmi, K., 187
Hamilton, I., 248
Happiness, addiction and,
    philosophy of transference
    and, 307–315
Harris, A., 45, 46, 47
Harris, J., 330
Harrison, K., 302
Hate, Winnicott on, 349–358
Heidegger, M., 309
Helmreich, R. L., 154
Hemingway, E., 248
Hermans, H. J. M., 139
Herzog, D. B., 188, 191
Hofer, J., 212–213
Hoffman, I. Z., 44, 57, 63, 139
Holding environment, 355–356
Homosexual men, sexual com-
    pulsivity in, 267–279
Hopenwasser, K., 37
Hopkins, L. B., xxvii–xxviii, 351,
    352, 354, 355, 361, 377, 378,
    379, 380, 383
Howard, J., xxvii
Hudson, M., 68n1

Internalized bad object, desire,
    pursuit and thwarting of,
    296–297
Interpersonal approach
    anxiety, 276–277
    psychoanalytic technique,
        139–140, 143
Intersubjectivity
    developmental factors, 72–73
    outrageousness, 363–365

Jager, B., 191
Jarman, D., 267, 268

Jarman, M., 188
Joseph, B., 102
Joyce, J., 327
Jung, C. G., 127

Kearney-Cooke, A., xxiii, 163, 194–195
Khan, F., 326
Khan, M., xxiv, xxvii–xxviii, 351
   alcoholism of, 322–326, 335–345
   biographical overview, 321–323
   career of, 329–335
   childhood of, 326–329
   death of, 323
   outrageousness, 361–366
   Winnicott analysis, 329, 343–344, 352–355, 366–372, 377–384
Khantzian, E. J., 365
Kierkegaard, S., 309
Klein, G., 48
Klein, M., xviii
Kohut, H., 199, 242
Kris, E., 253
Krystal, H., 14
Kubrick, S., 238
Kuriloff, E., xxii, 137, 141

Lacan, J., 214, 369
Lachmann, F. M., 226, 227
Laing, R. D., 236
Lang, J., 46
Language
   centrality of, 138–139
   eating disorders, threat and dare, 55–64
Lardner, R., 248
Laughter, shame and, 70–71
Leary, T., 236

Levenson, E. A., xxv, 34, 36, 57, 121, 138, 177, 235
Lewis, C. S., 68
Lewis, M., 70
Little, M., 351, 356
Looker, T., 122
Love, countertransference and, 143
Lowell, R., 248
Lucie-Smith, T., 334

MacDonald, C. S., 68
Mack, J. E., 365
Male experience, of food, 149–160
Mark, D., 239
Maroda, K. J., 121, 140, 357
Masochistic enthrallment, sexual compulsivity, 283–292
Maternal imago, psychic economy, 7–16
May, R., 237
McDougall, J., xvii–xviii, xxvi, 9, 24, 29–38, 194, 238
McGuire, W., 127
Mehra, B., 369
Melancholy, addiction and, 211–220
Melville, H., xx, 83, 85, 86
Menninger, K. A., 186, 188, 193
Meyers, J., 248
Michaelis, D., 213
Miller, A., 176
Miller, P. M., 192, 193
Milner, M., 368
Milrod, D., 214
Mitchell, J. E., 188, 191
Mitchell, S. A., 34, 55, 56, 140
Modell, A., 365
Montaigne, M. de, 309
Moor, P., 323

Moral development, storytelling, 139
Morris, A. B., 248
Moulton, R., 46
Muensterberger, W., 331
Mullahy, P., 186
Muller, J. P., 76
Munch, E., 247

Narratives. *See* Storytelling
Nasio, J., 93
Neoneeds concept, psychic economy, 24–25
Neutrality, Freud on, 277
Nietzsche, F., 309
Nourishment, sexuality and, 88–89
Nureyev, R., 334

Obesity. *See also* Eating disorders
  male experience, 156–160
  stalled enactments, 115–123
  symbolic significance of, 173–182
Ogden, T., 48, 177
Ortmeyer, D., 270
Outcome research, 185–206
  lessons of, 187–190
  patient education and, 193–195
  patient self-knowledge, 196–199
  psychoanalytic method and, 190–193
  self construction, 199–203
Outrageousness, Khan, 361–366

Pain, sources of, 311
Patient education, therapeutic alliance and, outcome research, 193–195
Patient self-knowledge, outcome research, 196–199

Patient-therapist boundaries, self-regulation, 99–111
Penetration, obesity as protection against, 173–174
Perry, H., 270
Petrucelli, J., xxi, xxii, 89, 138, 141, 200
Phillips, A., xx, 45, 49, 50, 237
Philosophy, of transference, happiness and addiction, 307–315
Pike, K. M., 191
Plato, 235
Plaut, W. G., 149, 150
Pollock, J., 247
Pontalis, J. B., 335, 336
Privacy, of self, 356
Projective identification, bulimia, 12
Promiscuity, gay men, 267–279
Psychic economy, 5–26
  adolescence, 22–24
  case vignette, 16–22
  childhood sources, 7–16
  comment on, 29–38
  dependency, 25–26
  neoneeds concept, 24–25
  terminology, 5–7
Psychoanalytic technique
  interpersonal approach, 139–140, 143
  outcome research and, 190–193
Psychosomatic reaction, psychic economy, 8, 9

Rank, O., 237
Rat Man case (Freud), 200
Rechy, J., 268

Relatedness, developmental factors, 72–73

Reparation, intersubjectivity, 73

Repetition compulsion, 295

Rickman, J., 329

Rodin, G. M., 187

Rorem, N., 240

Rosen, M., xxviii, 361, 362, 378, 383

Rothenberg, A., xxv–xxvi, 252, 253

Safety, eating disorders, threat and dare, 55–64

Sandler, J., 329

Sands, S. H., 73

Sartre, J.-P., 309

Schafer, R., 47, 138, 192

Schizoid tendency, desire, pursuit and thwarting of, 296

Schlesinger, H. J., 202

Schmidt, U., 187

Searles, H., 349

Selective inattention, gay men, 270–271, 272

Self construction, outcome research, 199–203

Self-disclosure, by therapist, 357

Self-regulation, eating disorders, 99–111
comment on, 141

Separation/individuation
anxiety and, 229–230
creativity and, 226–227
food and, 151

Sex role, food and, 150, 153–154, 159

Sexual addiction
category of, 238
desire, pursuit and thwarting of, 295–304

Sexual compulsivity
gay men, 267–279
masochistic enthrallment, 283–292

Sexuality, nourishment and, 88–89

Sexualization, trauma and, 94

Shakespeare, W., xxiv, 212

Shame, dissociation and, eating disorders, 67–80

Shane, E., 219

Shane, M., 219

Sharpe, E. F., 329

Shawver, L., 272

Slade, P. D., 163

Slavin, O., 55

Smirnoff, V., 325, 327, 335, 341, 342

Sobel, R. S., 253

Socarides, C., 269

Spence, J. T., 138, 154

Spero, M., 214n2

Spezzano, first name, 140

Spruiell, V., 366

Stalled enactments, eating disorders, 115–123
comment on, 141

Stechler, G., 78–79

Stern, D., 45, 47, 48, 102, 140, 177, 226, 227

Stoller, R., 323, 327, 328, 335, 337, 339, 340, 341–342, 345, 354, 370

Stolorow, R. D., 365

Storytelling
affects and, 140
importance of, 138
moral development, 139

Striegel-Moore, R., 163

Stuart, C., xvii–xviii·

Suffering, sources of, 311

Sullivan, H. S., 35, 132, 186, 212, 213, 229, 269, 270, 271, 272, 295
Sullivan, P. F., 191
Symbol, obesity, 173–182
Szymborska, W., 67–68

Target, M., 190
Theander, S., 187, 191
Therapeutic alliance
    patient education and, outcome research, 193–195
    patient self-knowledge, outcome research, 196–199
Therapist self-disclosure, 357
Thompson, M. G., xxvii
Threat, dare and, eating disorders, 55–64
Torre, J. I., 202, 203
Toxicomanie, defined, 5–7
Transference, philosophy of, happiness and addiction, 307–315
Trauma
    eating disorders, 100–101
    gay men, 267, 269, 272
    obesity and, 177
    sexualization and, 94

Treasure, J., 187
Tronick, E. Z., 72–73

Valentin, J., 213
Violence, masochistic enthrallment, 283–292
Vitz, P. C., 139

Walsh, B. T., 188
Weinberg, M. K., 72–73
Wermauer, D., 213
Wheelis, A., 31
White, M. J., 132
Whorf-Sapir hypothesis, 235
Wiesel, E., 138
Wilson, G. T., 191
Winnicott, C., 353
Winnicott, D. W., xviii, xxiv, xxvii–xxviii, 12, 85, 177, 227–228, 364
    hate and hatefulness, 349–358
    Khan analysis, 329, 343–344, 352–355, 366–372, 377–384
    Khan and, 321, 322
Wolstein, B., 143
Women, competition, 45, 46–47

Zerbe, K. J., xxiii–xxiv, 76, 189

22919293R00247

Printed in Great Britain
by Amazon